Bion and Meltzer's Expeditions into Unmapped Mental Life

Drawing on the influential contributions of Wilfred Bion and Donald Meltzer to psychoanalysis, *Bion and Meltzer's Expeditions into Unmapped Mental Life* explores and addresses the clinical implications of their work, both through revisiting several of their conceptions and illustrating them with detailed clinical material from the analyses of children, adolescents, and adults.

Psychoanalysis strives towards truth; this is its essence. However, emotional truth is often unknowable and not amenable to verbal communication. This ineffable mental realm is at the heart of both Bion and Meltzer's psychoanalytic endeavours.

Bion's writings reflect a developmental stage in the evolution of psychoanalysis, extending clinical work to mental realms that were seemingly unreachable. Donald Meltzer further infuses Bion's thinking with his own original notions of beauty and aesthetics, imbuing Bion's profound thinking with a poetic and lyrical tenor.

Writing in a clear and lucid manner, Avner Bergstein integrates Bion's sometimes highly theoretical thinking with everyday clinical practice, facilitating his dense and condensed formulations and making them clinically accessible and useful. *Bion and Meltzer's Expeditions into Unmapped Mental Life* is written for psychoanalysts and psychoanalytically oriented psychotherapists who are attracted to Bion and Meltzer's radical thinking.

Avner Bergstein is a training and supervising psychoanalyst and faculty member of the Israel Psychoanalytic Society.

Psychoanalytic Field Theory Book Series
Series editors: S. Montana Katz and Giuseppe Civitarese

The Routledge Psychoanalytic Field Theory Book Series was initiated in 2015 as a new subseries of the Psychoanalytic Inquiry Book Series. The series publishes books on subjects relevant to the continuing development of psychoanalytic field theory. The emphasis of this series is on contemporary work that includes a vision of the future for psychoanalytic field theory.

Since the middle of the twentieth century, forms of psychoanalytic field theory emerged in different geographic parts of the world with different objectives, heuristic principles, and clinical techniques. Taken together they form a family of psychoanalytic perspectives that employs a concept of a bi-personal psychoanalytic field. The Psychoanalytic Field Theory Book Series seeks to represent this pluralism in its publications. Books on field theory in all its diverse forms are of interest in this series. Both theoretical works and discussions of clinical technique will be published in this series.

The series editors are especially interested in selecting manuscripts which actively promote the understanding and further expansion of psychoanalytic field theory. Part of the mission of the series is to foster communication amongst psychoanalysts working in different models, in different languages, and in different parts of the world.

A full list of titles in this series is available at: https://www.routledge.com/Psychoanalytic-Field-Theory-Book-Series/book-series/FIELDTHEORY

Bion and Meltzer's Expeditions into Unmapped Mental Life

Beyond the Spectrum in Psychoanalysis

Avner Bergstein

LONDON AND NEW YORK

First published 2019
by Routledge
2 Park Square, Milton Park, Abingdon, Oxon OX14 4RN

and by Routledge
711 Third Avenue, New York, NY 10017

Routledge is an imprint of the Taylor & Francis Group, an informa business

© 2019 Avner Bergstein

The right of Avner Bergstein to be identified as author of this work has been asserted by him in accordance with sections 77 and 78 of the Copyright, Designs and Patents Act 1988.

All rights reserved. No part of this book may be reprinted or reproduced or utilised in any form or by any electronic, mechanical, or other means, now known or hereafter invented, including photocopying and recording, or in any information storage or retrieval system, without permission in writing from the publishers.

Trademark notice: Product or corporate names may be trademarks or registered trademarks, and are used only for identification and explanation without intent to infringe.

British Library Cataloguing-in-Publication Data
A catalogue record for this book is available from the British Library

Library of Congress Cataloging-in-Publication Data
Names: Bergstein, Avner, 1960– author.
Title: Bion and Meltzer's expeditions into unmapped mental life: beyond the spectrum in psychoanalysis / Avner Bergstein.
Description: Abingdon, Oxon; New York, NY: Routledge, 2019. | Series: Psychoanalytic field theory book series; 5 | Includes bibliographical references and index.
Identifiers: LCCN 2018014368 (print) | LCCN 2018035940 (ebook) | ISBN 9781351180276 (Master) | ISBN 9781351180269 (Web PDF) | ISBN 9781351180252 (ePub) | ISBN 9781351180245 (Mobipocket/Kindle) | ISBN 9780815385776 | ISBN 9780815385776q (hardback: qalk. paper) | ISBN 9780815385783q (paperback: qalk. paper) | ISBN 9781351180276q (ebk)
Subjects: LCSH: Psychoanalysis—Philosophy. | Bion, Wilfred R. (Wilfred Ruprecht), 1897–1979. | Meltzer, Donald.
Classification: LCC BF175 (ebook) | LCC BF175 .B452 2019 (print) | DDC 150.19/50922—dc23
LC record available at https://lccn.loc.gov/2018014368

ISBN: 978-0-8153-8577-6 (hbk)
ISBN: 978-0-8153-8578-3 (pbk)
ISBN: 978-1-351-18027-6 (ebk)

Typeset in Times New Roman
by codeMantra

For Alona and Yael

Contents

List of figures viii
Acknowledgements ix
Preface xi

1 The psychotic part of the personality: Bion's expeditions into unmapped mental life 1

2 Transcending the caesura: Reverie, dreaming, and counterdreaming 28

3 Beyond the spectrum: Fear of breakdown, catastrophic change, and the unrepressed unconscious 55

4 On boredom: A close encounter with encapsulated parts of the psyche 76

5 Attacks on linking or a drive to communicate? Tolerating the paradox 98

6 The painful vicissitudes of the patient's love: Transference-love and the aesthetic conflict 118

7 Obsessionality: Modulating the encounter with emotional truth and the aesthetic object 137

8 The ineffable 159

References 185
Index 195

Figures

1	Rigid motion transformation	6
2	Projective transformation	7
3	Transformation in hallucinosis	10

Acknowledgements

Many people, friends and colleagues, have helped me over the years to express, articulate, and clarify my thoughts. Their contribution to this book, each in his or her own way, has been invaluable, and I am profoundly thankful to them. I would especially like to express my gratitude to Hagit Aharoni and Hugo Goldiuk, both of whom inspire me to always think again. I would further like to express my appreciation and thanks to Afsaneh Alisobhani, Avi Becker, Moshe Bergstein, Giuseppe Civitarese, Mairav Cohen-Bergstein, Liora Goder, Ruth Kaniel Kara-Ivanov, David Ohad, Hamutal Raz-Shiloach, and Hana Wakstein.

I am deeply grateful and indebted to Mairav for her unending support and encouragement throughout the years.

I would like to extend my heartfelt thanks and appreciation to Zvi Segal.

Last but not least, I deeply thank the participants of my reading groups who have provided and shared with me the space where my thinking could evolve and find words.

Permissions

Chapter 1 is based on "The psychotic part of the personality: Bion's expeditions into unmapped mental life" published in *Journal of the American Psychoanalytic Association*, 66(2), 2018: 193–220. Reprinted by permission of SAGE Publications.

Chapter 2 is based on "Transcending the caesura: Reverie, dreaming and counter-dreaming" published in *The International Journal of Psychoanalysis*, 94(4), 2013: 621–644. Reprinted by permission of the Institute of Psychoanalysis and Taylor & Francis, LLC.

Chapter 3 is based on "Beyond the spectrum: Fear of breakdown, catastrophic change and the unrepressed unconscious" which was published in *Rivista di Psicoanalisi*, 60, 2014: 847–868. Reprinted by permission of the journal.

Excerpt from "The Kite Runner" by Khaled Hosseini. Copyright © 2003 by Khaled Hosseini. Reprinted by permission of Penguin Random House LLC.

"A Tree Within" By Octavio Paz, translated by Eliot Weinberger, from The Collected Poems 1957–1987. Copyright © 1984 by Octavio Paz and Eliot Weinberger. Reprinted by permission of New Directions Publishing Corp.

Chapter 4 is based on "On Boredom: A close encounter with encapsulated parts of the psyche" published in *The International Journal of Psychoanalysis*, 90(3), 2009: 613–631. Reprinted by permission of the Institute of Psychoanalysis and Taylor & Francis, LLC.

Excerpt from "East Coker" from FOUR QUARTETS by T.S. Eliot. Copyright 1940 by T.S. Eliot. Copyright © renewed 1968 by Esme Valerie Eliot. Reprinted by permission of Houghton Mifflin Harcourt Publishing Company and Faber & Faber Ltd. All rights reserved.

Chapter 5 is based on "Attacks on Linking or a Drive to Communicate? Tolerating the Paradox" which was published in *The Psychoanalytic Quarterly*, 84, 2015: 921–942. Reprinted by permission of John Wiley & Sons, Inc.

Chapter 6 is based on "The Painful Vicissitudes of the Patient's Love: Transference Love and the Aesthetic Conflict" which was published in *Contemporary Psychoanalysis* 47(2), 2011: 224–244. Reprinted by permission of The William Alanson White Institute of Psychiatry, Psychoanalysis & Psychology and the William Alanson White Psychoanalytic Society, http://www.wawhite.org. Reprinted by permission of Taylor & Francis, LLC.

Chapter 7 is based on "Obsessionality: Modulating the encounter with emotional truth and the aesthetic object" published in *Journal of the American Psychoanalytic Association*, 64(5), 2016: 959–982 © 2016 American Psychoanalytic Association reprinted by permission of SAGE Publications.

Chapter 8 is based on "The Ineffable" published in G. Civitarese (Editor) *Bion and Contemporary Psychoanalysis: Reading a Memoir of the Future*, Routledge, 2018. Reprinted by permission of Taylor & Francis, LLC.

Preface

"All journeys have secret destinations of which the traveller is unaware", says Martin Buber (1955, p. 23). At the same time, Bion, in his introduction to *Learning from Experience*, writes about "the impossibility of writing without pre-supposing familiarity with some aspect of the problem that is only worked on later" (1962, unnumbered). Still, unlike Bion, *we do* have the advantage of possessing some familiarity with Bion's complete oeuvre which he himself had not as long as he was still thinking and writing. From this privileged vantage point, this book follows, in retrospect, Bion's journey in thinking about an ineffable psychic reality, starting with his depiction of a psychotic part of the personality up until his conceptualization of an ultimate reality which he denotes as O. It is a path leading from the notion of a part of the personality that lacks the capacity to be in contact with emotional reality and truth, up to an apprehension of an ineffable, unthinkable psychic reality which is beyond the reach of human capacity.

Our language, as Meltzer (2000) writes, is very rich in words for describing objects and functions, but very poor in words for describing emotions. This echoes Bion (1962) who wrote that the inability of even the most advanced human beings to make use of their thoughts, since the capacity to think is rudimentary in all of us, means that our ability to be in contact with reality is limited to that which is inanimate. Our capacity is deficient when we strive to be in contact with the psychic reality of that which is animate. Although a salient characteristic of the psychotic personality, this deficiency is not only due to psychotic functioning but is, in fact, part of being human. Confronted with the complexities of the human mind and psychic reality, our proximity to psychotic thinking is much larger than a superficial scrutiny would admit.

The attempt to think the unthinkable is a constant reminder of our limitations and ultimate aloneness, amounting to a sense of loss (Cartwright, 2010). But in bearing this essential loss, we are as near as we can be to our patients and at one with the ultimate reality of being human.

When writing about unthinkable, or unverbalizable, psychic reality, the collapse to binary thinking is unavoidable. It is our human tendency to think in binary terms, so characteristic of psychotic thinking which cannot tolerate the multidimensional complexity of life. Moreover, binary oppositions are inseparable from implicit or explicit hierarchies (Flax, 1990). It is perhaps a unique capacity we must entrust to the poets who succeed in capturing the infinite emotional experience with the aid of words. I implore the reader not to be deluded by my inescapable collapse to binary or hierarchical thinking which is for the sake of my exposition alone, hence inevitably missing a truthful elucidation of the ineffable emotional reality I attempt to approach.

Throughout the book, I have tried to avoid the pitfall of the prevalent split between the so-called 'early Bion' and that which is called 'late Bion'. To my mind, this division does not do justice to Bion's complex thinking and creates an incision where there is, in fact, a *caesura* (i.e. a break *with a continuity*). To paraphrase Freud (1926), "there is much more continuity between Bion's early writings and his later ones than the impressive caesura of his radical elaborations allow us to believe". Although many of Bion's subversive ideas only gained momentum and crystallized in his later years, many elements have been there since the beginning of his writing. This is actually Bion's definition of catastrophic change, entailing a *caesura* between the pre- and post-catastrophic states. Reading his work, his ideas seem to be in constant evolution, transformation, and elaboration, and yet it is important not to lose contact with the *invariant* aspects of his thinking. In *Transformations*, Bion develops the notion of *invariance* referring to the truthful qualities that characterize the innermost nature of whatever it is, independent of the position of the observer. Detecting an invariance is a step towards the apprehension of reality (Sandler, 2005).

In this vein, I suggest that Bion's later writings are an elaboration, at times refining and at other times obscuring his early writings, but the essence, the deep despair from which Bion writes, remains. This is the desperate struggle to articulate and to communicate that which is unmentalized, and perhaps even 'unmentalizable', irrepresentable, and ineffable. Getting in touch with emotional truth, and the constant search for a way to communicate that truth, have been a strong driving force throughout his life. Bion is always trying to find words to describe the indescribable and integrate the psychotic parts of the personality in human experience.

The instances illustrating the continuity between Bion's early writings and his later ones are many. It might suffice to reiterate Bion's plea at the end of his *Caesura* paper with the frequently cited words: "... Investigate the caesura, not the analyst; not the analysand; not the unconscious; not the conscious; not sanity; not insanity. But the caesura, the link, the synapse..." (1977, p. 56). Yet, the notion of caesura, being one of the most prevailing characteristic concepts of the so-called 'late Bion', is already clearly evident in *Attacks on Linking*, one of his *earliest* papers. It is there that he writes,

> I employ the term "link" because I wish to discuss the patient's relationship with a function rather than with the object that subserves a function; my concern is not with the breast, or penis, or verbal thought, but with their function of providing *the link between the two objects*.
>
> (1959, p. 102, italics added)

Bion's emphasis on the link, the synapse, and the attempt to transcend caesuras is a thread running throughout his work and is but one significant illustration of the cohesion and continuity in his writings.

Bion's continual attempt to approach an unmapped mental life is another instance, as I try to illustrate throughout. I suggest this unmapped mental life is the realm of the unrepressed unconscious, which has one foot in the psychotic part of the personality as depicted by Bion and another in what he denotes as O, an ineffable, ultimate reality. As put by Bléandonu (1990),

> [the] model of the psychotic dream and the invisible-visual hallucination [in the period of understanding psychosis] becomes [in the epistemological period of his psychoanalytic work] the basis

> of Bion's conceptualization of the psychoanalytic 'intuition' as a non-sensuous phenomenon, of the 'invisible-visual' nature of intuition.
>
> (p. 131)

Thus, as Grotstein (2007) writes, the psychotic uses hallucinosis as a default technique of survival and of communication with the analyst, and the analyst – as a way of initiating intuition. (This is epitomized in Meltzer's conception of dream life, where the reality of the internal world is presented on the analytic stage and 'viewed', almost concretely, by the analyst's "inner eye".) It is again evident that between the early writings on the psychotic hallucination and the later writings on psychoanalytic intuition, there is a break *and continuity*. Bléandonu adds that the psychotic began to become the shadow of those people whose genius is expressed in art, mathematics, and mysticism.

Both the psychotic part of the personality and ultimate reality were described by Bion as embracing the thing-in-itself: beta-elements on the one hand, and O on the other. This is not to idealize or romanticize the psychotic. The schizophrenic, as Bion (1967a) writes, is the debris, a place where the mystic was, until an explosion took place and his personality disintegrated because he could not tolerate the emotional experiences which were available to him. However, both the psychotic part of the personality and ultimate reality denote, from different vertices, an irrepresentable, unknowable psychic reality that can only be approached through intuition. Their ineffability is the invariant element of Bion's quest from his early writings to his later ones and is the beacon guiding my understanding of his episteme.

On a more personal note...

> The need to diminish feelings of persecution contributes to the drive to abstraction in the formulation of scientific communications.
>
> (Bion, 1967b, p. 118)

An important milestone in my psychoanalytic journey was an encounter with a child on the autistic spectrum when I was in high school. One of our teachers had asked for volunteers to spend some time with her son with autism, in a treatment process that required many hours of exercise with the child, under the guidance of Dr Carl Delacato. I had worked with this boy for two years, during which time I was drawn to him without as yet knowing anything about psychotherapy or psychoanalysis.

In time, after finishing my university degrees in clinical psychology and my training as a psychotherapist, I had again found my way to a kindergarten with children on the autistic spectrum, this time as a psychotherapist. I was again drawn to getting in touch with these children's encapsulated, seemingly unreachable mental life. I was then reading a lot of theory about autism, and it was at that time that I encountered the prolific writings of Meltzer. His psychoanalytic intuition and profound faith in the workings of the unconscious were captivating.

It was only some years later, during my analytic training, that I had met with Bion's writings. I was captured by his struggle to communicate the incommunicable, and his attempt at delving into the so-called 'psychotic part of the personality', which I now realize is a more primitive mental state, perhaps akin to that which was later referred to as an autistic part of the personality.

Struggling to comprehend his thinking was almost life-giving. Over the years, reading Bion has been a source of comfort as well as of emotional turbulence. Articulating my emotional experience and my understanding of his writings has reflected my perpetual attempt to make myself understood to myself and to others. Bion's writings had reverberated a deep and unthinkable feeling I had lived with throughout my life and which I had been making every effort to communicate during the years of my own analysis.

The need to write stems from this need to communicate the incommunicable. Writing is another way of working through one's undreamable nightmares. Practically everything I write, including all the clinical material which I bring forth in this book, are, in fact, a plea to an imaginary reader to help me dream that which has remained undreamt.

Striving to communicate, I think, is what connects me to Bion. Meltzer's writings, profoundly moving in their own right, have been indispensable in experiencing the depth of emotionality in Bion's writings.

This book is the outcome of both these authors' unending inspiration for me in my clinical work and theoretical thinking, and I dare say in my adult life in general. I hope I have succeeded in conveying this throughout the book. In this, I join many authors before me, to whom I am greatly indebted, who have tried, each in their own way, to elucidate some aspect of Bion's "many faceted diamond" (Bion, 1975, p. 234).

Chapter 1

The psychotic part of the personality

Bion's expeditions into unmapped mental life

> The eternal silence of these infinite spaces terrifies me.
> (Blaise Pascal, 1669, p. 73)

A patient comes to see us complaining of distress and suffering. We decide to begin treatment. Over time, the patient brings his associations, we listen, we interpret; there might even be a surprising symptomatic improvement. But sooner or later, we find ourselves at an impasse. The patient repeats his complaints or accounts over and over again. We've run out of interpretations that provide symbolic meaning to the patient's associations, or else these interpretations don't seem to matter. The patient's symptoms persist, perhaps even become worse; we are at a loss, we become persecuted, irritated, bored, helpless, numb, or sleepy. We may feel guilty, impotent, ashamed, professionally insecure. We seek supervision. It helps for a while, but the nightmare continues and we can't wake up from it. This situation can persist for weeks, months, even years. In the best case, we have a hunch, a gut feeling we can't put to words. We may sense something at the tip of our tongue but find no way of putting our finger on it, and we just let it evade us. We are in despair, dumbfounded. The patient may become openly aggressive, even violent, and threaten to break off therapy; we think it might even be for the best.

This is if all goes well.

Alternatively, the patient brings associations, the analyst makes interpretations, and these lead to a growing array of associations and interpretations. The patient becomes increasingly aware of himself, his history, his family life, his conflicts and inhibitions. The patient may seem to be improving in the sense that he becomes better-adjusted socially and professionally. Of course, there may be periods of despair or anger, but these can be worked through over time. However, this brings to mind Bion's (1976a) description of a patient who was quite articulate. In fact, articulate enough to make the analyst think that he was analysing him rather well. Indeed, the analysis did go extremely well, but Bion was beginning to think that nothing was happening. Then, after a session, the patient went home, sealed up all the crevices throughout his room, turned on the gas, and died. Bion says he had no way of finding out what went wrong, and yet something undoubtedly had. Analyst and patient were meeting on a non-psychotic level, missing the psychotic part of the personality, present but hardly noticeable.

Bion is always trying to help us become aware of the psychotic part of the personality, lying concealed in each of us to a lesser or greater extent, and which we are so often unable, or unwilling to get in touch with. And yet,

> we are investigating the unknown which may not oblige us by conforming to behaviour within…our feeble capacities for rational thought. We may be dealing with things which are so slight as to be virtually imperceptible, but which are so real that they could destroy us almost without our being aware of it.
>
> (Ibid, pp. 319–320)

perhaps like a virus hidden in our body that can kill us before we've become aware of its existence.

That, Bion suggests, is the area into which we have to penetrate.

Introduction

Bion is one of the most innovative thinkers in psychoanalysis. Yet, any radical thinker must also be linked to his forebears in an ongoing, everlasting evolution of ideas. Indeed, it might be said that the invariant navel of Bion's thinking lies in his notion of *caesura*, a concept denoting both a break *and* continuity. Bion is no doubt nourished and nestled in the thinking of both Freud and Klein. Notably, he seems to draw on Freud's *Formulations on the Two Principles of Mental Functioning* (1911) and Klein's *Notes on Some Schizoid Mechanisms* (1946), thereby putting the concepts of thinking on the one hand, and psychotic mechanisms on the other, at the forefront of his thinking. Even though this has facilitated the incorporation of his radical ideas within classical psychoanalysis, it also seems to have created much misunderstanding of his own original contributions, leaving his ideas liable to being appropriated and swallowed up by existing, established theoretical schools of thought. Bion elaborates seemingly familiar terms and concepts but imbues them with fresh, different, and unsaturated meaning. I would therefore like to revisit his thinking about the psychotic part of the personality, highlighting the uncharted realm he seems to explore.

Much like Melanie Klein's investigations into the minds of young children, delving into the psychotic mind has led Bion to hone the psychoanalytical tools required for the apprehension of psychic reality. It has made possible the exploration of a non-sensuous psychic realm and provided the scaffolding for the analyst's state of mind in approaching both the psychotic and the non-psychotic parts of the mind. In my view, this has far-reaching clinical implications which I will illustrate with a number of clinical vignettes highlighting various aspects of our capacity to approach this non-sensuous realm as it appears in the psychoanalytic encounter.

Furthermore, I would like to draw attention to the impasses often encountered when we analyse the so-called difficult patient who cannot profit from classical transference and countertransference interpretations or from interpretations deriving from theories of defence, splitting, projective identification, resistance, and so on. Since Bion is referring to phenomena related to Klein's theories of projective identification, it may seem that he is concerned primarily with psychotic personalities, but as he testifies, this is not so (Bion, 1965). With his distinct understanding of the psychotic part of the personality, Bion is making a qualitative leap in our comprehension of the workings of the human mind.

Bion stressed that the human mind does not operate through predictable relations, such as that of cause and effect, but through non-linear processes of growing complexity[1] (Chuster, 2014). He is thus moving from a causal/explanatory attitude, to an attitude that seeks to understand and accept the uncertainty that is inherent in the infinite complexity of human development and personal relations (Meltzer, 1986). This is the move from knowing to intuiting, from a finite two- or three-dimensional space to an infinite, complex, multi-dimensional space, which the personality, in whom psychotic mechanisms are paramount, often reduces to a one-dimensional point.

Moreover, emotional truth is not static but always transient and in transit. It changes from one moment to the next because the objects involved are ever-changing; one constantly changing personality talks to another constantly changing personality (Bion, 1977a). In the attempt to grasp *transient truth*, in passage from one moment to another, Bion tries to lean on the method by which mathematics tries to measure a changing situation, a changing shape, a variable movement. "Certain problems", he writes, "can be handled by mathematics, others by economics, others by religion. It should be possible to transfer a problem, that fails to yield to the discipline to which it appears to belong, to a discipline that *can* handle it" (1970, p. 91, italics added). Yet, as Meltzer (1978) points out, Bion is now using a mathematizing format more for analogic illustration than as an experimental method. Bion himself stressed that he makes use of mathematics "for evocation of thought and for evocations intended to initiate a train of thoughts" (Bion and Bion, 1981, p. 634).

This qualitative move in the understanding of the human mind is illustrated by Bion mathematically by the move from Euclidean and projective geometries to algebraic geometry and algebraic calculus. Nowadays, he might have talked about complexity theories in mathematics.

Euclidean geometry deals mainly with the mathematics and measurement of static shapes, whereas algebraic calculus deals with the mathematics of *change, approximation, and transformation* of infinite processes. For example, Euclidean geometry can help us measure the slope of a straight line or the area of a regular shape such as a circle or square. But when we have to find a formula for measuring the slope of a curve, where every point on the curve has a different value, or to calculate the area of an irregular shape, a blob, we need the formulas afforded by calculus, and even that will yield only an approximation.

Emotional life is neither linear nor regular. The patient does not present us with a nicely shaped square or circle, but with an undecipherable blob. Are there any rules to the transformations of the emotional experience? And the complement of this question being – is there a method to the chaos presented by madness? Is there some psychoanalytic counterpart to the algebraic calculus that can be used to comprehend this method? In other words, what is the *invariance* inherent in the transformation which can help us *approach* the emotional experience that is irrepresentable, ineffable, and unknowable?

The use of geometric and algebraic conceptualizations, though often deterring to us as psychoanalysts, seems to give the analyst tools for thinking about psychic transformations in disturbances of differing degrees. It facilitates our awareness of what it is that is unknowable in psychic life.

Bion (1977b) refers to Paul Valéry, the 20th-century French poet and philosopher, who said it is assumed that the poet is a person who is undisciplined, disordered, goes into a rhapsodic state, and then emerges, waking up with a poem complete in his mind as the outcome of an undisciplined, intoxicated – literally and metaphorically – state of mind. Yet Valéry adds that he believes that, on the contrary, the poet is much nearer to an algebraic mathematician than to an intoxicated individual. It will thus come as no surprise that Lewis Carroll (originally Charles Dodgson), author of *Alice's Adventures in Wonderland*, and its sequel, *Through the Looking-Glass*, was in fact also a mathematician who studied abstract and associative algebra. His well-known books are examples of literary nonsense, which has the effect of subverting language conventions or logical reasoning. The effect of nonsense is often caused by an excess of meaning. Appreciating the transience and movement of meaning requires the release of our grip on a two- and three-dimensional reality and surrendering to intuitive perception and imagination, allowing for the apprehension of a multi-dimensional reality.

Bion is trying to describe the intensity, violence, and fortitude of the transformation of the emotional experience generated by psychotic functioning, as opposed to that arising from non-psychotic functioning. He agrees with Klein that the degree of fragmentation and the distance to which the fragments are projected can be seen as a determining factor in the degree of mental disturbance the patient displays in contact with reality (Bion, 1970). Additionally, recognizing the psychoanalyst as an integral part of the psychoanalytic process, Bion has

6 The psychotic part of the personality

put the emphasis of his work on the *analyst's* state of mind and on what is required *of him or her* in order to move towards an apprehension of the patient's transformation of the emotional experience. He uses mathematical concepts in attempting to describe the tools necessary for the analyst who would endeavour to tread on psychotic territories of the personality. He goes so far as to say that "mathematics... [is] an important element in the mental processes of the individual which makes it possible for him to be a psycho-analyst" (Bion, 1992, pp. 86–87).

Non-psychotic transformations, which Bion calls *rigid motion transformations*, require the least effort from the analyst to surmise the original emotional experience. The mathematical counterpart of these relatively simple transformations is analogous to moving a shape in a *two-dimensional* space, rotating it or mirroring it on a plane. The shape stays relatively the same, and the original shape can be determined if the angle of rotation or the coordinates of the image from the mirror line are given (see Figure 1). *For the sake of simplicity*, we might say that this amounts to the original definition of transference as described by Freud, where past feelings and ideas are transferred from significant figures in the patient's life *onto* the analyst, or vice versa. In order to observe and reveal these relations,

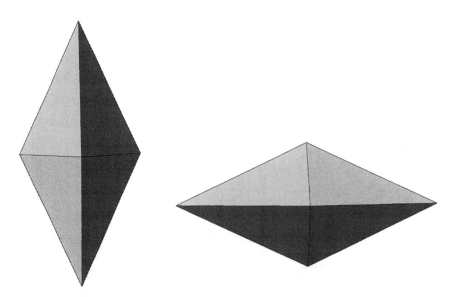

Figure 1 Rigid motion transformation

the analyst's insights are informed by the Euclidean geometric dimension of his or her mind.[2] However, this yields a rather restricted sense of reality.

Psychotic functioning, *as described by Klein*, transforms the emotional experience in a manner that requires a bigger effort by the analyst. These Bion calls *projective transformations*. The degree of fragmentation and the distance to which the fragments are projected are much greater. The analyst must now be able to comprehend, metaphorically, the essence of projective geometry, whereby the shape of a figure (square, circle, etc.) is transformed by projecting it onto a space from a point of reference. As a result, a square can change its shape to a diamond or trapezoid, a rectangle to a parallelogram, a circle to an ellipse, and so on. The shape will be distorted and will not look much like the original shape, but it does follow a formula. If there is information about the point of reference (distance, angle), the original shape and dimensions of the projected image can be calculated (see Figure 2).

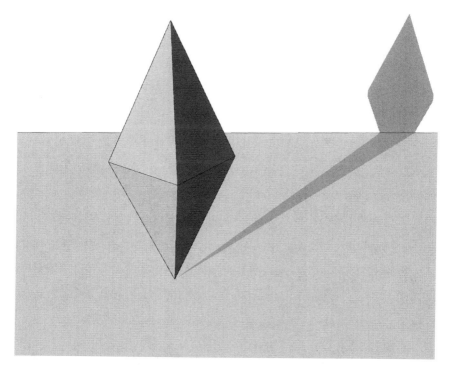

Figure 2 Projective transformation

The analyst needs flexibility of mind in order to hear and decipher the unconscious phantasy in its transformed and distorted shape. Moreover, it is not simply transferred *onto* the person of the analyst but *into* him, entailing much confusion between patient and analyst. The patient's transformation of the emotional experience now takes up the whole analytic space so that the transference now occupies the total situation (Klein, 1952; Joseph, 1985). This depiction of the psychotic part of the personality presupposes a *three-dimensional* space into which parts of the personality are projected. The analyst must be receptive to the patient's projective identifications, which is the method open to the patient for communicating or evacuating parts of his personality. However, this allows limited contact with parts of the personality that are less structured.

Meltzer (1974) observes that Kleinian analysts "began to notice that interpretations along the lines of projective identification did not seem to carry any weight in certain situations" (p. 342). And when he says "certain situations", he is referring not to openly psychotic patients, but rather to ones who, on the whole, do not seem terribly ill, people who come because of problems like poor job performance, unsatisfactory social lives, or vague pathological complaints; psychotherapists, people who are somehow on the periphery of the analytic community and want to have an analysis and cannot quite say exactly why.

In clinical work, we too often begin to sense *something* we cannot put into words. Though it does not necessarily appear in analysis verbally, it is often communicated in a way that makes the analyst feel stirred to the depths by something which seems so insignificant that it is hardly noticeable (Bion, 1977b). Its invariant essence can be grasped only if the analyst releases his attention, suspends rational thinking, eschews his grip on sensuous reality, and surrenders himself to *free floating* attention, hence "catch[ing] the drift of the patient's unconscious with his own unconscious" (Freud, 1923a, p. 239).

Thus, by referring to a *multi-dimensional* mental realm apprehensible through intuition and tolerance of approximations, transience and the notion of infinity, Bion exposes us to what to my mind is *his* depiction of a psychotic part of the personality.

I would like to approach this mental realm from different theoretical and clinical perspectives in the hope that the movement between these vertices will allow us to get into closer contact with the psychotic part of the personality as depicted by Bion.

Since the predominantly psychotic individual lacks almost any conception of containers into which the projection could take place (either because he has not internalized the containing function or due to his intolerance of the restrictive nature of the container), he is lost in the immensity of mental space. The patient's emotional experience remains as sense impressions which are then evacuated as hallucinosis, yielding pleasure or pain, but not meaning (Bion, 1965). His projections do not seem to hit against an object and do not bounce back. They get lost in space. "Fear becomes nameless dread. Rage becomes boundless or coagulates into relentless, unforgiving hatred. Pleasure becomes ancillary to ecstasy" (Eigen, 1999, p. 79). The analyst dealing with psychotic transformations, which Bion refers to as *transformations in hallucinosis*, is obliged to deal with relationships of a domain that has no finite limitations (Bion, 1965, p. 45) and is in a constant state of expansion. We are therefore dealing with phenomena that are beyond symbolization or are intolerant of the restrictive nature of symbolization. They are thus ineffable. Yet it is precisely this ineffability that the psychotic cannot deal with, and which the analyst must be able to tolerate. The essentially psychotic personality lives and communicates in a way that he himself cannot tolerate to be the recipient of!

The patient's transformation of the emotional experience is now so mutilated that if there ever was an unconscious phantasy, it is now unknowable. It is utterly dispersed in space, chaotic in a way that cannot be grasped in terms of time and space. Its original shape is almost completely lost (see Figure 3). As described by Civitarese (2015), the individual now projects not *onto* an object as in 'Freudian' transformations, or *into* the object as in 'Kleinian' transformations, but *into the void*. The patient increasingly and violently projects his experience into infinite space (or into the body), and the experience loses any meaning it might have had. One might say that the individual now projects *beyond* psychosis.

Furthermore, the personality in whom psychotic functioning predominates lacks the means to deal with the emotional experience of approximations and irregularities. The individual needs precision and can tolerate only experience which is saturated. He invariably attempts to straighten the curved line, and when he realizes he can't, he hallucinates that the curve is, in fact, straight. He tries to render a dynamic situation static as a way to avoid the pain inherent in the experience of change, transience, uncertainty, doubt, and complexity. Algebraic thinking thus seems to be the non-psychotic counterpart, or complement, of the psychotic transformations in hallucinosis. It is "an attempt to deal with internal psychic incoherence" (Bion, 1992, p. 130) and with phenomena that may have *no meaning*.

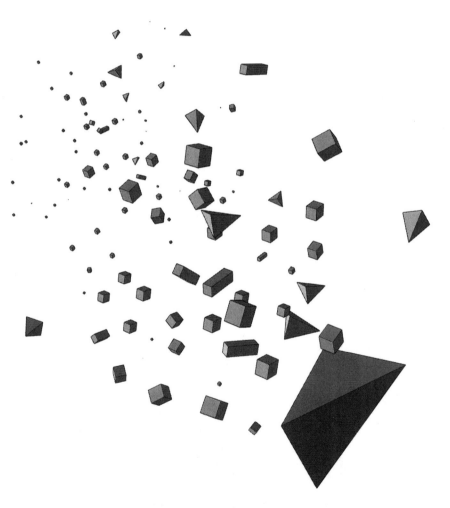

Figure 3 Transformation in hallucinosis

An inaccessible part of the personality

Bion (1977c) describes an unconscious mental state that has never been anything else, has never been conscious. He suggests that in addition to unconscious and conscious states of mind, there may be another state of mind, one that might provisionally be called an *inaccessible* state of mind. Bion tries to address this inaccessible part that has remained as a meaningless frenzy in the psyche. He thus tries to approach "a mental life unmapped by theories elaborated for the understanding of neurosis" (Bion, 1962a, p. 37).

I suggest that this unmapped mental life is to a large extent congruent with an *unrepressed* unconscious. It is this unmapped mental life that Bion seems to refer to when describing the psychotic part of the personality, especially from 1962 onwards. Yet again, I would like to stress that he is referring to the psychotic *part* of the personality which exists in every individual, and that without it, the person would be "a total character *minus*… almost a caricature of robust commonsense and sanity…because he believes a psychotic is 'mad' or 'insane'…" (Bion, 1977a, pp. 52–53). Bion distinguishes between being *psychotic* and being *insane*. The psychotic part of the personality is part of being human. About himself, he is said to have claimed that he may be psychotic, but not insane… (Mason, 2000).

I am thus referring to the psychotic part which is present in every analysis, in every session, *by definition*, and is at the focus of the analyst's endeavour.

This is a mental realm unrestricted by three-dimensional space. It cannot be grasped by our senses which are limited to a finite perception of external reality. The individual, in whom psychotic mechanisms are dominant, cannot bear restrictions that compel him to meet the limitations of reality and so creates a reality with allegedly no limits, and yet, paradoxically, he cannot bear the immensity of infinite mental life in which he gets lost. Tolerating this unrestricted, infinite psychic realm, which is often experienced as meaningless, is painful, but for the psychotic mind – it is unbearable. The individual might then be compelled to become mentally non-existent or else to hallucinate order where no order exists so as to survive the experience of this terrifying "void and formless infinite" (Bion, 1970, after Milton's *Paradise Lost*).

The differentiating factor that Bion introduces is "not between conscious and unconscious, but between finite and infinite" (1965, p. 46). A major differentiating factor between the psychotic and non-psychotic parts of the personality is thus *the capacity to tolerate this infinite complexity*. For this, an intuitive, aesthetic, imaginative, 'dreaming' mind is crucial.

A deficient part of the personality

Alongside describing destructive attacks *on the patient's own ego*, Bion seems to be markedly concerned with individuals in whom the capacity for thoughts, phantasies, symbol formation, and play is deficient. I suggest that from early on, Bion is addressing what would probably be conceived of today as a primitive mental state akin to an autistic part of the personality, as was, in fact, delineated by clinicians inspired by him, especially Donald Meltzer and Frances Tustin. The question of attacks or defects has been taken up by Alvarez (2002), who stressed that the two positions need not be viewed as mutually contradictory. Nonetheless, it is my impression that the destructive attacks are closely connected to Klein's conception of the psychotic personality, whereas the deficit in the patient's alpha-function, as described by Bion, pertains to a larger extent to a more primitive state of mind.

It is true that Bion begins with a conceptualization leaning heavily on Kleinian thought. Thus, in his *Differentiation of the Psychotic from the Non-Psychotic Personalities* (1957), he enumerates the features characterizing the psychotic part of the personality:

> There is the environment, which I shall not discuss at this time, and the personality, which must display four essential features...: a preponderance of destructive impulses so great that even the impulse to love is suffused by them and turned to sadism; a hatred of reality, internal and external, which is extended to all that makes for awareness of it; a dread of imminent annihilation and, finally, a premature and precipitate formation of object relations, foremost amongst which is the transference, whose thinness is in marked contrast with the tenacity with which they are maintained. The prematurity, thinness and tenacity are pathognomonic and

have an important derivation, in the conflict, never decided in the schizophrenic, between the life and death instincts.

(Ibid, p. 44)

It seems to me that the phenomenology described in his later writings may be similar, but its understanding has evolved. Bion is increasingly concerned with a deficient capacity which inhibits the mind's ability to tolerate the growth in complexity, sophistication, and level of abstraction. At any rate, *causality is unknowable and hence is rendered irrelevant.*

Already in *Language and the Schizophrenic* (1955), Bion hints at the notion of a deficient development when he writes that in his view, "what Freud describes as the institution of the reality principle is an event that *has never been satisfactorily achieved* by the psychotic" (p. 221, italics added). It is also evident in Bion's interpretation to the patient who says he can't properly remember what Bion has just said to him. Although one might have expected an interpretation of the patient's attack on the analyst's words, Bion, in fact, says, "since you feel you lack words, you also feel you *lack the means* to store ideas in your mind..." (p. 236, italics added).

The psychotic part of the personality is, then, a very primitive area of the mind, undeveloped and lacking crucial mental capacities. It is an area of the mind that is not embedded in language and so cannot be approached with our usual psychoanalytic tools. It is a part of the personality where thought is severely disturbed and the aptitude for mental transformation is deficient; hence, experience remains non-mental, as an overwhelming frenzy of stimuli inside the mind and body. And yet, when an emotional experience is encountered that is more than the mind can tolerate, the experience, as well as the very capacity to experience, is 'attacked' as a way of survival. The personality thus seems to be trapped between a deficient capacity to tolerate pain or frustration on the one hand, and intolerable pain or frustration on the other.

Consequently, the patient who cannot mentally elaborate, think, and imbue his pain with meaning is trapped in a nightmare where he can only repeat his distress over and over again. Just like the description in *Alice in Wonderland* of the Mad Hatter's tea-party, it is always four o'clock (Bion, 1962b).

Unfolding his theory of functions, Bion describes an alpha-function, or 'dreaming', as unconscious emotional thinking required to transform the primordial emotional experience, perceived as sense impressions from within and without, into something that can be thought, known, felt, suffered, and ultimately – repressed. Thus, *the capacity to repress seems to be a psychological accomplishment*, extricating the mind from psychotic franticness and eventually autistic encapsulation. Bion is referring to patients whose alpha-function is so damaged they cannot dream or think. They are thus trapped in anxiety of a psychotic intensity, overwhelmed by undigested and indigestible sense impressions he calls beta-elements, which carry almost no symbolic meaning. Alpha-function, or 'dreaming', is thus equivalent to the mind's ability to deal with the emotional experience and to bear its turbulent impact on the personality. Inasmuch as beta-elements cannot be mentally elaborated and transformed into alpha-elements and dream thoughts, they cannot in effect be repressed. It is not possible to repress something that has not yet been represented through some mental process. These beta-elements are then either evacuated or go to make up that part of the unconscious that is *not repressed* – experience which in effect *has not* been experienced, thoughts without a thinker (Bion, 1970), "un-mantled" rather than "dis-mantled" (Alvarez, 2002).

Beta-elements, when accreted, press for evacuation. An inability to dream the emotional experience thus places the personality in an intolerable emotional storm that has to be acted out and evacuated through projective identification, somatic disorders, addictions, perversions, and the like. Hence, what is often referred to as an attack on the mind's linking function is, to my mind, the consequence of the mind's attempt to survive when threatened by an overwhelming emotional experience the individual cannot "dream". Bion (1955) describes the psychotic who makes destructive attacks on all those aspects of his personality that are concerned with establishing contact with external and internal reality. It is my understanding that these attacks on the awareness of reality are aimed at *avoiding the encounter with the overwhelming pain accompanying excessive emotionality*. Thus, paradoxically, the individual attacks the very function that might make it possible for him to bear the emotional experience.

Moreover, the person cannot tolerate the live, unpredictable, and uncontrollable aspects of emotional life. As a model, Bion (1962a) suggests that when the emotions aroused by the loved object are too strong and intolerable for the infant and thus cannot be worked upon mentally, it may withdraw from the nourishing breast so as to avoid the complications intrinsic to the awareness of life and of animate objects. However, hunger and fear of death through starvation force the infant to resume feeding. The infant is thus compelled to split the material milk from the psychical breast, allowing the resumption of feeding without acknowledging the emotions aroused by the animate feeding object. The need for love, understanding, and mental development is now deflected into the search for material satisfaction. This is a state originating in a need to be rid of the emotional complications inherent in life and to deaden emotion, or one that serves as a survival mechanism protecting the personality from being overwhelmed by excessive, unbearable mental pain. Splitting the material milk from the psychical breast facilitates the individual to live in an omniscient world of allegedly predictable, emotionless, inanimate objects, much like an autistic child making use of autistic objects. This implies living in a delusional world dominated by causal thinking unsuited for an animate, often capricious, emotional world of people, where almost nothing is predictable.

Bion is describing a splitting that is enforced upon the individual who is overwhelmed by emotions too great for him to bear and whose capacity for dreaming and thinking is deficient. It is a protective survival mechanism designed to avoid the pain of a premature awareness of an intolerable emotional reality. The individual thus cannot appreciate the possibility that his pain is due to the existence, or lack, of something psychic, but rather relates it to something tangible in external reality, or its embodiment in an allegedly physical illness.

Adam

Adam, 40 years old, is known to all his acquaintances as a very successful person in all areas of his life. He sought therapy following an anxiety-laden crisis and somatic complaints with no medically explicable source. "It drives me up the wall", he says. "I can't find any reason for this filthy feeling, this disgusting shit, as if all systems are kicking and beating me up from the inside and nothing makes any sense. Suddenly everything just blows up. Every day I have to go through these unending battles whether to go and see a doctor, or not. The physical symptoms are just unbearable, I'm just squirming in pain, headaches, loss of stability, I'm afraid to walk around, afraid to get dizzy and fall down".

And then at another moment, he might say: "The truth of the matter is that in all this time I've never really gotten dizzy; it's just the *fear* of getting dizzy. With me it's always on this irritating, impossible, thin line. The dizziness is not precisely dizziness because it's not like I see the whole world going around, and the instability is not precisely instability because I never actually fall down, and the headaches are not exactly migraines…".

Adam is experiencing violence all around him. He says: "When I'm on the road I feel people's behaviour is on the verge of an assault. What people do *is* downright offensive. At home too, I feel Nina is violent with the kids. She grabs one of them by the arm or screams at the other one. I can't even watch. It drives me crazy. You'd never see *me* behaving like that!"

Adam feels attacked from within and without. However, it seems that he's describing the turmoil of unbound stimuli raging *inside him*. In clinical psychoanalytic work, one often encounters psychic material that is devoid of form or shape. This kind of material is often manifested as concrete somatic sensations at the border of body and mind (Grimalt, 2017). The patient may feel them as real bodily pain or as violence coming from without. The concrete pain thus gives an illusory boundedness to the formless and meaningless experience. Painful as it may be, the patient seems to embrace an allegedly meaning-ful hallucination rather than truthfully confront an opaque and for him as yet meaningless emotional experience.

One cannot approach the irrepresentable psychic experience with conventional psychoanalytic tools such as dream interpretation, slips of the tongue, free associations, and so on. Instead, these are experiences that the analyst must live in the here-and-now of the analysis with the patient; it is only then that the analyst begins to make contact with them.

I spent countless hours with Adam, immersed in a thick, heavy cloud of meaninglessness, listening to him recount over and over again his bodily pains showing no capacity to move to another train of thought. Both of us indeed experienced the pains, but not the suffering. The pains persevered, as things-in-themselves, with neither of us able to provide any significant meaning. It seemed we could go on like this forever. He didn't protest, and I was grateful for the peace of mind he granted me in his silent accord.

Evidently, I can articulate this only in retrospect. While immersed in the experience, I was engrossed and absorbed in it but had no capacity to think or feel. I was blind and trapped in a nightmare without being able to transform it into a dream and eventually wake up. It was only *after* the sessions that I became aware of the stupor they induced; my state after the sessions was like emerging from a troubled sleep.

When psychotic functioning predominates, the personality's inability to dream creates a state of mind that is one-dimensional and "substantially mindless, consisting of events not available for memory and thought" (Meltzer, 1975, p. 225). It is a world furnished with inanimate objects and a frenzy of beta-elements. It is a primitive area of the mind of things-in-themselves, which are beyond our capacity to know or to verbalize except through their phenomenological derivatives.

In one of our sessions, Adam says: "It drives me crazy. I sense every tiny little thing. It reaches a state where I walk barefoot and then, when I put on my shoes, I can feel the change in the sole of my foot. I walk over the rubber surface they put in the playground so that the kids won't get hurt, and I feel the elasticity under my feet and it drives me insane. And I don't know if I believe myself anymore, but I do sense it! I have to persuade myself not to go to the doctor's. I'm looking for someone who will finally tell me that it *is* worrisome and that I should see a doctor. But no-one takes me seriously anymore".

I think it's not with his bodily pains and sensations that Adam is left alone but with his sensitivity to nuances of emotional experience beyond his capacity to make sense of. Adam seems to have always been oversensitive to the emotional undercurrents in his surroundings and in his objects but to have lacked the ability to metabolize them. It seems he has, as Bion (1967a) put it, a hypersensitive contact with reality, which makes reality intolerable. One has to consider the sharpness of the psychotic patient's observation which is so great that it is intolerable. Adam is tortured by the acuity of his perception and its intensity. He cannot, however, attribute any adequate meaning to it. Obviously, this is not good contact with reality because reality is always both sensuous *and* psychic, whereas Adam can relate only to the sensuous aspects. Lacking the capacity to find psychic meaning, he hallucinates explanations and pseudo-meanings which give him some peace of mind but do not rid him of his anguish and dis-ease. All these unmetabolized and meaningless sensations go to make up the psychotic part of his personality, encapsulated inside him without being able to be dreamt or thought about. It is these sensations that drive him mad.

An oversensitive infant may perceive too much stimuli in his surroundings but lacks the mental apparatus to deal with all his perceptions. In fact, not only an oversensitive infant's, but any infant's receptiveness, as Bion (Ibid) notes, is really adequate only to a limited range of experience, the kind one would suppose could be contacted between a baby and a loving, affectionate mother. If it falls out of that, if the mother is disturbed or upset for example, then the baby is made aware of experiences for which he is not fitted. He needs a facilitating environment to help him modulate this overstimulation. In its absence, the baby, flooded by psychophysical needs and stimuli, may resort to evacuative actions to resolve his emotional turbulence, as well as an intensified use of concrete sensoriality (Chuster, 2014). He might encapsulate himself in auto-sensuous autistic protections (Tustin, 1992), as Adam may have done when he wrapped himself, in his first year of life, in a skin rash with no medical explanation.

Later in life, we see a person who is outwardly controlled, but it's quite obvious he's not really controlled as evidenced by the continual leaks of feeling of one sort or another, in transformed ways (Bion, 1967a). As indeed Adam says, "I already know how it works. Inside it's a block of deadness. I don't feel a thing. Nothing. But I'm no sucker, and so it comes later, at night, in nightmares!"

Moreover, wrapped in his hard, shell-type protections (Tustin, 1992), we find that this oversensitive infant has grown into a person who is hostile to any new development. He feels he knows best and nothing can nourish him. Anything that comes from the external world is felt to be inimical. He becomes closed up in his views and often maintains a sense of moral superiority.

Before the cracking up of his defences and his psychic world, Adam felt as if heir to a noble family, intoxicated by his competencies achieved only by few. He looked down on most of those around him who were "dummies". He moved in a quasi-hallucinatory world where people had no chance of getting along without him. And yet, there was always an opaque anxiety lurking behind his confident façade. This was kept at bay with the aid of obsessional thoughts and secret compulsive acts.

When the reality of his life fractured his world, the grandiose defences collapsed and exposed him to intolerable dread. This dread was incarnated in insufferable physical pain that disrupted his life.

We will come back to Adam later on.

*

The incapacity to bear the frenzy of unmentalized stimuli drives the personality to hallucinate coherence. Thus, even though these beta-elements – felt as agitation by foreign objects and sensations – carry hardly any mental meaning, they do often accumulate and come together in a seemingly ordered, *ostensibly* meaningful visual image. Hence, they acquire hallucinatory meaning that may *appear* indistinguishable from a dream or a dreamable narrative. This accumulation of beta-elements, referred to by Bion as a beta-screen, may be illustrated pictorially if one imagines a mass of flies that, from afar, seem like a black curtain, but with the wave of one's hand they are scattered, leaving no trace. This differs from a dream made up of alpha-elements that connect to each other through a network of associations, forming a "curtain of illusion" (Bion, 1965, p. 147; Grotstein, 2009), a narrative that can be stored in the mind, communicated, and made use of as a transitional object. The beta-screen may thus be disguised as a dream, deluding the analyst who is determined to seek order where disorder reigns. The analyst may then be in danger of missing the fact that the patient cannot 'dream' and is functioning in a more primitive dimension of the mind.

The concept of a beta-screen thus tries to capture the experience of an agglomeration of unbound, unconstrained, diffused stimuli, dispersed in space, unable to be integrated. In the face of this unmentalized and unmentalizable experience, one might feel sleepy, tired, out of wavelength, as if lost in space, immersed in a dense and thick sort of mist (Chuster, 2014). Tolerating this sensation of fragmentation requires a different attentiveness by the analyst, one driven less by rational thinking and more by his intuitive vigilance to his own self. "The analyst who essays…the treatment of such patients must be prepared to discover that for a considerable proportion of analytic time the only evidence on which an interpretation can be based is that which is afforded by the counter-transference" (Bion, 1955, p. 224).

Johnny

After a session with her five-year-old patient with autism, an analyst said in supervision: "I'm in a crisis. I cannot understand a thing! I sit with this kid who looks as if he's driving a car back and forth; no thought comes to my mind. I can't articulate anything. I usually try to find some word that might help me gather the material somehow, so I can write it up after the session, but I can't put it together in any way! Nothing! I can't focus. I try to pull myself together, to pay attention, but I just can't. And then I feel guilty for dropping him, for not being able to keep him in my mind".

However, as Bion (1962a) writes, "thanks to the beta-screen the psychotic patient has a capacity for evoking emotions in the analyst" (p. 24), and these emotions can be used to get in touch with the emotional experience where there is a predominance of the psychotic part of the personality.

Listening to this account of the analyst, lost in the child's beta-screen, one might conjecture that her feeling of being lost might also be the emotional experience of the child, if he could ever articulate it as his analyst could. This is not necessarily an attack on the analyst's mind, or even an attack on the child's mind, but rather an illustration of an immature mind in which crucial functions have not been internalized or developed. It may be an expression of a deficient mind overwhelmed by an accretion of stimuli searching for a thinker to think them or a container into which to evacuate them. Since the child cannot think, he can only live and act out his experience.

Johnny's analyst goes on to describe moments, when after *seemingly* being cut off from the child, she suddenly realizes that the boy is no longer moving the car to and fro but is driving it along the floor like a real toy car, even making the sounds of a car. She is at once awakened and resumes her capacity for thinking and feeling.

I suggest that the analyst was *not* cut off from the child but was very much immersed in the beta-screen emitted by him, lost in the immensity of fragmented and dispersed non-mental particles. Through suffering/dreaming the current emotional experience, she had actually set his halted play back in motion. I believe it is important for this to be interpreted to the child so that the experience will not disperse and that a process of *learning from experience* can be attained. Yet, even if an interpretation does not come to the analyst's mind, just being in touch with this process is to my mind, nonetheless, of utmost significance. A premature interpretation, of any kind, would have flooded the child with even more unmentalized particles and would have led him to entrench himself in his protective encapsulation of nothingness.

*

An adult patient may seem to be talking and free associating, but this may have a similar effect as the child's moving the toy car aimlessly back and forth. When unable to dream, the patient's words do not cohere and do not evoke an integrated emotional response other than perhaps feelings of confusion, irritation, impotence, or boredom. This in its turn may evoke a further emotional response from the analyst who may become critical, or even laudatory, thereby colluding with, or perhaps one should say *reflecting*, the psychotic part of the personality assuming moral superiority and omniscience. The patient evacuates masses of words with which the analyst may try futilely to connect and find meaning to, thereby missing the fact that the patient can hardly think or dream. Rather, the patient is verbally discharging an excess of tension or distress that has been harboured within him as a result of not being able to do anything mental with them. This requires *the analyst* to 'observe' and 'dream', through the exercise of analytic intuition, an emotional experience unobservable or undreamable by the patient. This often amounts to suffering long periods of painful distress, helplessness, despair, or persecution, of not knowing where we are headed or what we are actually doing. It seems to me that this is a vital part of what is meant by the notion of 'dreaming the patient'. Being immersed in this state is different from the analyst's musings or a state of reverie. The emotional experience cannot find shelter in any nicely formed words, visual imagery, or even sounds. It remains an experience that cannot be articulated, because it is so dispersed in the immensity of infinite space.

Maria

Maria, a 55-year-old high school teacher, has been in analysis with me for some three years now, following three previous analyses. She was referred to me by her last analyst who felt she couldn't help her. Maria said she was unhappy and wanted to come for a few months just "to get a little happier". I soon offered her an analysis which she accepted.

Clearly, everything I will recount is articulated only in hindsight.

Maria's analysis began with a strong idealization of me and a feeling that she had finally come to the right place. She was overjoyed with our work and often said she had the urge to hug me in gratitude. However, I often found her speech very flat, unreal, false, melodramatic, even grovelling. She misuses, or abuses, psychoanalytic jargon, and it was very hard for me to connect to her emotionally. I began to feel alienated from her. In sessions, I was bored and often very sleepy; I couldn't think and often felt unable to say anything. Everything I could think of felt forced and clichéd.

At the end of sessions, Maria habitually needs to make some extra comment as she sits up on the couch before getting up. Somehow, this infuriates me, and I find myself keeping silent, stifling the rage I feel. Although Maria is outwardly appeasing, I feel she never really accepts the setting, or the fact that she's the patient and that I'm the analyst, the one who ends the session. She often refers to me as a brilliant analyst, and yet I have a constant feeling of being subtly belittled and placated.

As time goes by, our sessions become intolerable for me. I am literally unable to keep my eyes open. At the same time, I am very tense since many times she turns back to look at me and see what I'm doing when I'm silent, and I feel very persecuted.

At times, we seem to be doing some work which, to me, feels very artificial. We might, for example, talk about the rivalry between us or the struggle over control which seems evident in many areas of her life. With the help of two- and three-dimensional formulations of transference and projective identification, it is possible to talk about her violent behaviour towards authority figures – her father, her mother, and me. But this seems to address experience-remote, theoretical violence. There's no emotionality to what we discuss. Everything feels stale, or else at some point, I realize she's been listening to everything in a masochistic, victimized way and that I have erroneously taken for granted I was talking to a person able to comprehend my words. She seems to want more and more interpretations from me but then takes them as concrete advice, as criticism or praise. I am partially aware of my aggression, rage, and detachment, but nothing seems to help me extricate myself from these feelings or work through them.

As she enters the room for a session, I watch her going over to the couch and think, as I often do, how ridiculous and pathetic she looks with her teenage clothes, so inappropriate for her age. Surprisingly, however, this time, I am struck by how aggressive and cruel *I* am to her. *I* now appear as the one belittling *her*. I am astonished and shaken. I can't comprehend this sadomasochistic dance we've been drawn into. We both seem to be locked in despair and a lot of denied anger. I realize it is not only she who is unreal and artificial; I too am withdrawn and in denial of my feelings. She seems to be dealing with her violent emotions through intellectualizing, as a way to downgrade her aggression, whereas I am entrenched in pseudo-analytic silence. We have become imprisoned in powerful defences against a potential explosion. Perhaps the nightmare has become so unbearable that it has finally awakened me. This is a crucial moment in an analysis. It is a moment when we realize we too have fallen prey to the psychotic part of our personality, finding shelter in the tendency to avoid a painful encounter with the emotional truth of the session. On waking, the analyst transforms into dream the nightmare in which he has lived for a time with the patient. He may thereby free himself from the state of excessive hallucinosis by the very fact of living through an experience of emotional at-one-ment and communicating to the patient the understanding he has acquired (Civitarese, 2015).

This is a moment when the analytic field suddenly expands and our mind breaks free from the restricted two- or three-dimensional space. It is always a moment charged with uncanny surprise when we realize that the patient is unconsciously addressing the unconscious aspects of *our* mind. We then realize we've been hiding behind two- or three-dimensional, one-person psychology interpretations, without being aware of our unconscious participation in the nightmare in which we are trapped with the patient. It is a moment when we acknowledge in ourselves not what distinguishes us from the patient, but what resembles him or her (Press, 2016).

Following this, the sessions go on much like before. However, as long as the analytic encounter was fogged in a dense haze of beta-elements, nothing could be seen or heard. It could only be *lived* by the analytic couple. Perhaps it is now possible to attend to the non-psychotic part of the personality, which speaks in a more comprehensible, symbolic language. The non-psychotic part of the personality always coexists alongside the psychotic part. This can be detected in the patient's associations as well as in the analyst's dreaming, which is invariably also an unconscious elaboration of the patient's nightmare. Nonetheless, listening to the *contents* of the patient's associations alone, or even that of the analyst's dreaming, is not enough when we strive to go beyond non-psychotic phenomena and hear the echoes of unrepressed unconscious experiences. In order to avoid experience-remote interpretations that do not promote psychic transformation, the analyst must go through an emotional experience, or rather an emotional crisis, before formulating it in an interpretation. For that, the analyst must renounce linear, two- or even three-dimensional thinking.

*

In one of the sessions, Maria says: "I wonder what I am looking for. I always have to be someone I'm not and then I act against my own beliefs. So should I stop being who I am and become what the world wants me to be?"

She recounts a movie about "a woman who is looking for some guy who's hiding and mustn't be found. But in fact she's having a relationship with the same guy she's looking for without knowing it's him because he has had facial plastic surgery. These changing identities are the theme of the movie" she says. "How do I stop trying so hard to be who I think people want me to be?"

Having been awakened from the nightmare we were both immersed in, I am struck by hearing her talk about *our* encounter in the here-and-now of the analysis – two individuals hiding behind plastic surgery, each looking for the other to no avail. We are both trying to reach some idealized object that cannot be reached. I want her to be someone she's not, perhaps a more mature baby and not a biting, little one. She needs me as someone able to endure her.

However, it is the plastic surgery metaphor to which I react most strongly. It is the fakeness that is a predominant invariant element accompanying us throughout the analysis; it is the nightmare she must be trapped in throughout her life, albeit its defensive function of preserving her psychic equilibrium. Both of us, analyst and patient, have been struggling against, and yet paradoxically towards, facing a truthful emotional experience; a struggle that had to be lived in the here-and-now of the transference relationship. I seem to have been forced to experience this fakeness, and it was forced into me because all other channels were closed due to my lack of intuition or understanding (Bion, 1967a). It was only after living through something that could not be thought, that we could now address it more openly with conventional interpretive work. It was only now, after months and months of suffering, that I could articulate in words what had been happening to us.

The fakeness and inauthenticity have been present throughout the analysis. I could think about *her* fakeness and falseness and even interpret it, but I had not yet felt it in my flesh. I had not yet been through an emotional crisis myself. No doubt it was immensely hard to be with her, but this was contained in a one-person psychoanalytic field which could be understood without "com[ing] out of [the philosopher's] chair and sit[ting] on the floor with the patient" (Winnicott, 1969, p. 90). The real emotional crisis descended on me only when I realized how fake *I* had become, which subverted *my* professional identity. Only then could something that could not have been said, because it had not yet been experienced, penetrate into the realm of language. It is the realization of the impasse that is so hard to accomplish, requiring us to move from linear thinking to a non-linear, frightening, infinite mental space where we lose our conventional anchors. The sudden realization is as if a higher form of meaning suddenly breaks free from the constraints of two- or three-dimensional space. The unconscious always bursts out unexpectedly. It is then that the ineffable psychotic part of the personality becomes visible. One might say that the patient's *irrepresentable*, essential experience is thus captured by the analyst's mind and eventually dreamed; it is *transferred* from one mind to another, *contingent on the latter's receptiveness*. This does not merely imply, as would be the case with projective transformations and projective identification, an *unbearable* emotional experience that is projected by the patient and ultimately introjected by the analyst's mind. Rather, by allowing himself to stumble upon the *irrepresentable, unknowable* emotional experience and through his readiness to let it resonate within him, the analyst unconsciously *becomes* that emotional experience.

Viewed from this vertex, transference is the path by which the unrepressed unconscious can evolve and express itself, and hence be registered in the analyst's mind. It is the function through which the individual can live through for the first time aspects of his mental life that have never been experienced, an infinite space where the new and unknown may emerge (Chuster, 2013).

Undoubtedly, on emerging, this 'selected fact' immediately finds refuge in another three-dimensional formulation. As Matte-Blanco (1981) writes, we try to cross the boundary between the infinite and the finite by translating the experience of the ineffable into relatable thoughts. But even though this attempt is essential to thinking, it is an absurd activity of trying to think the unthinkable by treating it (unsuccessfully) as though it were thinkable. Instead of thinking the unthinkable, we only succeed in thinking what is thinkable, because when we are contemplating the undifferentiated unconscious, we are in a differentiated, conscious state of mind. And yet, I would like to stress that the very *experience* of encountering something truthful does leave its stamp on our psyche.

Often, the analyst may be tempted to work at a more symbolic, insight-giving level, assuming higher psychic and mental integration in the patient. However, interpretations focusing on conflicting desires, or linking repressed and displaced parts of the personality with the defences against them, or interpretations adding alternative symbolic meanings, do not reach patients in whom alpha-function is predominantly disturbed, certainly not in a way that facilitates psychic change (Alvarez, 2010). Analysis may then go on indefinitely with the patient knowing more *about* himself but with very little psychic transformation towards *becoming* who he is.

Back to Adam

Some weeks ago Adam recounted a dream: "I arrive at some clinic to have eye surgery. This doctor comes over and says to me, 'I'm going to take off a part of your eye and your field of vision will be reduced, but it'll be much more cosmetic, much nicer' [Adam laughs]. As she begins to operate I get all stressed out and scream, 'No! Stop! What the hell?! I don't want you to do it! Don't touch!'"

This may illustrate the rehabilitation of his dreaming capacity. He may be telling me he's not interested in another cosmetic cover-up or an illusory guise of perfection; he prefers a wider field of vision, with a capacity to bear what confronts him: a capacity to bear his truth.

And yet, at the same time, I'm struck by the realization that he may be unconsciously addressing *me*: in our distant past, Adam had been coming to see me twice a week. Nowadays, at his request, he comes only once. Contrary to my habitual conduct, I accept this and do not suggest that he come more often. From time to time, the thought crosses my mind, but it soon dissipates. But now, his dream disconcerts me and awakens me to the possibility that I too have renounced a deeper encounter with his psychic world. I too have sunk into a numb serenity where I'd rather let sleeping dogs lie. This time it is *he* who is alarmed and alerts *me*. It seems I have become a deadening object, reducing our field of vision with my scalpel so as to maintain an outward calm, and leave the emotional turbulence inside of him.

However, he is no longer psychically dead. He is alive and suffers the pain.

This is an intense and painful emotional encounter, yet one that is full of life.

Notes

1 A complex system is characterized by its interdependencies. Complexity theory describes the behaviour of a system whose components interact in countless ways culminating in a higher order of emergence greater than the sum of its parts. The emergence is the phenomenon whereby larger entities arise through interactions among smaller or simpler entities such that the larger entities exhibit properties the smaller/simpler entities do not exhibit.
2 Bion used rigid motion transformations as a model, even though the purely geometric model does not take any distortion into account and mainly emphasizes displacement.

Chapter 2

Transcending the caesura

Reverie, dreaming, and counterdreaming

A very bright and isolated 11-year-old boy in analysis spoke of the various monsters in the playroom, those from "Here", those from "There", and the ones that came from "Somewhere". These creatures from "Somewhere", he said, could not hear the ones from "Here" or from "There"...

I would like to consider the way one might move within the space, or the gap, between two minds, and meet the psyche of an other. How can we get in touch with a patient's mind, at times so 'psychotic', or 'autistic', that the gap between us seems impressive, inaccessible, and impenetrable; and, ultimately, how is one to traverse the gap and penetrate the fear, which exists between oneself and oneself?

Caesuras

Freud (1926) writes, "There is much more continuity between intra-uterine life and earliest infancy than the impressive caesura of the act of birth allows us to believe" (p. 138). In a footnote to Freud's paper, Strachey notes that the word 'caesura' is a term derived from classical prosody and means a particular kind of break in a line or verse, after which the verse continues. In music, it is a pause or breathing at a point of rhythmic division in a melody. So, 'caesura' seems to bear the meaning of a break *and* continuity. Freud's notion of the caesura between prenatal and postnatal life, probably the most acute and dramatic separation experienced by Man, serves as a *model* for transcending every gap, space, or break. It portrays the continuity between states and events that seem to be so disparate, and yet are closely linked: sanity/insanity, past/present, memory/desire, sleep/wakefulness, emotional experience/interpretation (abstraction), etc., and ultimately the caesura between one state of mind and another, between one person and another (transference/countertransference), and between Self and Self (conscious/unconscious, psyche/soma). Thus, the patient may drift from one association to another in the analytic hour, with no evident link among them. However, the associations are not separated by incisions, but by caesuras, by gaps *with continuity*. How can we move between them, transcend them, without finding shelter in any one only because it appears clearer, out of a hunger for certainty (Yeret, 2004) or because it awards the illusion that we 'understand' and so is convenient to grip onto.

Reading his paper *Caesura*, one feels that throughout his entire life, Bion tried to articulate that which he came closest to doing in this paper, published in 1977 and based on a paper read to the Los Angeles Psychoanalytic Society in June 1975.

Although relating to Freud's reference to the caesura between pre- and postnatal experiences, it seems that it is not discovering what actually occurred in utero that is of major significance to Bion, but rather creating a model for thinking that which seems unthinkable, and for linking states of mind which seem unbridgeable and even unreachable. Getting in touch with primal mental states and with the origin of the self is strived for, not so much for discovering historical truth or recovering unconscious content, as for generating motion between different parts of the psyche, for transforming *barriers* within the mind into *caesuras* (i.e. breaks after which there is continuity), and for incorporating and integrating different parts of the Self, even those seemingly inaccessible ones.

Nevertheless, Bion does begin with a description of the caesura of birth.

Although there seems to be an impressive rift between prenatal and postnatal life, Bion dares to conjecture that what we encounter in postnatal life is a continuation of intrauterine events and experiences. He assumes that with the aid of speculative imagination and imaginative conjecture, one might suppose a link between mature emotions or thinking and intrauterine life. This is a possibility Piontelli (1992) will try to illustrate empirically with the aid of ultrasound observational studies. Again, it is not so much gaining knowledge of actual intrauterine events that is significant, but rather the inspiration to think creatively, to let our minds roam freely, never resting at any convenient, theoretically familiar stop on the way.

Bion (1976b,c) describes a baby, quite satisfactorily born, crying and yelling at birth without being able to be quieted. The more the mother soothed the child, the more it yelled. Bion suggests this to be a late event in a story began in utero, hidden only by the 'impressive caesura of birth'. We cannot understand a symptom, he claims, if we assume it only developed *after* the child was born. Similarly, one might think of the analysand who refuses to lie on the couch. Although one might interpret this refusal in familiar terms as envy, love, hostility, etc., Bion asks, "Is it possible that lying on the couch subjects [the patient] to physical pressures of a kind which are beyond [his] capacity to tolerate, or to verbalize, or to 'understand'?" (1977a, p. 44). Could these pressures be linked to primal experiences from his life as a foetus? Bion (1976c) speculates a situation in which, due to variations in pressure of the amniotic fluid, the foetus could see light which might be intolerably bright, or hear sounds which might be intolerably loud. Could these be experiences the personality remembers? And when is that personality born? In the same way that we can detect the remains of vestigial bodily organs, could we speculate the survival in the human mind of prenatal functions including 'embryological intuition'? (Bion, 1977a).

Intuition is an unmediated knowledge or understanding of truth, not supported by any information derived from a familiar sensual source. Since it cannot be communicated to an other and cannot be corroborated by a rational method of scientific knowledge, it is often seen as close to mystical revelation (de Bianchedi, 1991). Could we speculate that in the absence of rational thought and mentalization, this same intuition is that by which the foetus perceives the intrauterine world and that remnants of this capability continue in postnatal life?

The existence of these archaic states of mind seems to be one of the fundamental discoveries of psychoanalysis. These may be prenatal parts of the personality evacuated in the caesura of birth, rendering them mentally irrepresentable (Bion, 1977c). Again, Bion imaginatively conjectures these hypothetic thoughts, not in order to state scientific facts, but rather so as to exercise "...the right to indulge your speculations...in order to give your imagination an airing, to give it a chance to develop into something that might be scientific"

(Bion, 1977c, p. 47). How, then, can we get in touch with these archaic mental states and how are we to communicate them?

From his earliest writings, Bion seems to be concerned with the capacity of an individual to communicate with an other that which is ineffable, irrepresentable. How can the baby communicate to his mother his hunger, fear of dying, loneliness, or dread? How is one to traverse the gap between psyche and psyche, between mind and mind? Bion begins by depicting projective identification as a primitive communication, and from here on, he seems to grapple with the question of how it occurs. He conceptualizes the notion of links between baby and mother, L,H,K,[1] focusing mainly on the *K* link: how does the mother know her baby's mind through knowing her own mind, on the way to baby knowing its own mind; and how does the baby know its mother's mind?

Much has been written on the various possibilities of the meeting of minds – projective identification, dream analysis, empathy, and even telepathy. However, Bion's notion of the caesura and its transcending has opened up a new and jolting vertex to a way of getting in touch with the analysand's internal reality.

I suggest that people seek our help so as to communicate their internal world and facilitate communication between cut off, dissociated, and encapsulated parts of their Self. This, I think, is what the young boy I cited at the beginning of the chapter was asking of me. This may be attempted through the function of dreaming, transforming barriers and incisions into caesuras.

"... Investigate the caesura", Bion pleads at the end of his *Caesura* paper, as if unfolding his creed towards the end of his life, "...not the analyst; not the analysand; not the unconscious; not the conscious; not sanity; not insanity. But the caesura, the link, the synapse..." (Bion, 1977a, p. 56). That is where emotional aliveness lies, but that is also where the threat of drowning lurks.

However, to get a better notion of the caesura, it is necessary to differentiate between Bion's alimentary model of thinking and his synaptic model. In the better-known alimentary model, thoughts are conceptualized as food and the mind as the digestive system. Transformations occur when primordial thoughts, raw sense impressions, are communicated to the mother through projective identification, where they are metabolized, detoxified, and digested by the mother's alpha-function, hence being returned to the infant through bearable communication.

The synaptic model is first mentioned in *Learning from Experience*. The word 'synapse' comes from the Greek and, although literally meaning *a link*, in effect the synapse is *a gap*, permitting a neuron to pass an electrical or chemical signal to another cell. It is a gap that is a link. Between the presynaptic and postsynaptic sites, there is extensive activity and powerful tension. The synaptic model differs from the alimentary one in that it takes account of the break in the continuity, the caesura. This break is what interests and inspires Bion: how do communication and transformation evolve between the two synaptic membranes in spite of the gap between them? Hence, I suggest, the notion of projective identification as primitive communication does not give a satisfactory answer since one has to ask *how* it occurs; what is the vehicle by which communication is carried from one mind to another?

Bion marks the caesura with a slash, inclined forward, indicating the gap between two mental states, signifying a potential dynamic change.

The caesura is therefore a model for the gap, that raging river between two banks. It is the place where catastrophic change occurs but where lies the danger of catastrophe as well. This is the almost impossible place Bion asks us to be in – the emotional turbulence – without gripping onto any of the banks in a way that halts movement. In fact, Bion not only asks us to be there, in the eye of the storm; he also asserts that when two personalities meet, an emotional storm is unavoidable (Bion, 1979).

The psychoanalytic quest is not traversing the caesura so as to arrive at a safe harbour, but rather widening the capacity for motion and free flowing between the river banks, between the various rims of the caesura. The mere movement and transition are what matters, and not its *direction*, hence there is no notion of moving forward towards a goal or cure. *The movement itself* is what expands the mind and facilitates psychic life. The movement is forever bidirectional, or multidirectional, for example between conscious and unconscious, and back again, and is made possible thanks to the 'contact barrier', a term used by Freud to describe the neurophysiological entity subsequently known as a synapse. The contact barrier, as indicated by its name, marks the point of contact and separation between conscious and unconscious. Being a selectively permeable membrane, it keeps conscious and unconscious separate, at the same time as allowing the flow between them. It protects contact with reality, avoiding its distortion by internal emotions in the way that dreaming protects sleep from outside distractions (Grinberg, Sor and de Bianchedi, 1975). Clinically, it manifests itself as something that resembles dreams (Bion, 1962a). The psychic movement between caesuras is made possible through dreaming, separating, and linking conscious and unconscious. Functioning in a placental economy (Aharoni, 2010; Irigaray, 1990), dreaming resembles the placenta which is responsible for feeding the foetus but also functions as an immunity system filtering dangerous matter and preventing its penetration.[2]

Dreaming goes on continuously, all through the day and night, thus creating a continuity of the mind's work. Just as dreaming protects sleep from external reality, enabling the working through and transformation of emotional experiences, so it protects that which is unconscious from penetrating consciousness in waking, allowing us to go on without being aware of all external and internal stimuli. Since dreaming serves to work through sense impressions threatening to overwhelm the psyche, it protects the personality from a psychotic state (Bion, 1962a).

In the same manner that dreaming protects and maintains the separation between sleeping and waking, simultaneously bridging them, so can one imaginatively conjecture how it creates a bridge and continuity between two minds, and yet always keeping in mind the unknowability of the other. However, this meeting of minds (as well as its inevitable failure) creates an emotional turbulence.

I will try to develop and illustrate Bion's ideas of reverie and dreaming, and Meltzer's (2005) further thoughts on counterdreaming, as means of penetrating the caesura, traversing and transcending the gap between mind and mind. Furthermore, in line with Bion's thinking, I would like to elaborate the notion that when the patient's dreaming comes to a halt, or encounters a caesura, it is up to the analyst to dream that which the patient cannot dream, thus setting the suspended process of dreaming back in motion and facilitating the generation of dialectical movement between different, and often remote, parts of the Self. Seeds of this notion are already evident in Freud's writings, notably in his *Revision of the Theory of Dreams* where he writes, "When the patient runs out of associations…we intervene on our own; we fill in the hints, draw undeniable conclusions, and give explicit utterances to what the patient only touched on in his associations" (1933, p. 12).

Different aspects of this theme have been developed by various authors (for example de M'Uzan, 2000; Ferro, 2005; Meltzer, 1986). Notably, Ogden (2004) has poetically written of the analyst participating in dreaming the patient's undreamt and interrupted dreams. While concurring with these thoughts, I will attempt in what follows to stress two points. Leaning on Bion's emphasis on the *process* of thinking, I would like to address not so much dreaming the patient's or analyst's foreclosed thoughts and feelings, but rather to think of the analyst's reverie and dreaming as facilitating the process of dreaming itself, *regardless of its content*. I will try to highlight the very function of dreaming that the patient internalizes, even if there is no overlap at all between the content of patient's and analyst's dreaming/non-dreaming. Furthermore, alongside the notion of the analyst's reverie as facilitating the analytic couple to get in touch with remote, seemingly unreachable parts of the psyche, I would also like to stress the *caesural* quality of reverie, encompassing the enigmatic otherness and the painful unknowability of the other.

Being a profound mode of thinking, dreaming facilitates the psyche to cope with emotional experience and to provide meaning. However, residing on the seam between conscious and unconscious, dreaming may afford a glimpse into the unconscious, thus threatening to subvert the psychic equilibrium and bring about a catastrophe as a result of the confusion it may afford between the psychotic and the non-psychotic parts of the personality. Hence, there is a tendency to try and evade it through a more saturated mode of thinking, often relying on external reality.

Reverie, dreaming, and emotional truth

> ...[S]ometimes Truth flashes up before us with daylight brightness, but soon it is obscured by the limitations of our material nature and social habits, and we fall back into darkness almost as black as that in which we were before. We are thus like a person whose surroundings are from time to time lit up by lightning, while in the intervals he is plunged into pitch-dark night.
>
> (Moses Maimonides, Jewish philosopher, 1191)

Dictionary definitions of 'reverie' are "a state of dreamy meditation" or "fanciful musing, a daydream" or "an instrumental composition of a vague and dreamy character" (Dictionary.com). Etymologically, it originates in old French so that in Bion's writings too, it has a foreign reverberation, designating a unique, strange, and ineffable state of consciousness. For Bion (1962a), reverie is a factor of the mother's alpha-function. It is that state of mind which is open and receptive to anything that comes from the loved object, and so receptive to the infant's projective identifications whether they are felt by the infant to be good or bad. Reverie is the mother's intuitive function, transforming the infant's emotional raw sense impressions, those as yet unmentalized emotional experiences (Mitrani, 1995), and affording them meaning by her mind. Mother's capacity for reverie rests on her capacity to tolerate frustration until able to make sense and give meaning to the infant's communication. "When the mother loves the infant what does she do it with?" Bion asks, and replies that "her love is expressed by reverie" (1962a, pp. 35–36).

Later on, Bion links maternal reverie and the analyst's dreaming. He describes the mental capacity 'to dream' an emotional experience whether it is in a waking or a sleeping state. He refers to "the person's sense impressions [of an emotional experience, which] have to be converted into elements such as the visual images commonly met with in dreams..." (Bion, 1992, p. 216). The analyst's reverie depends on experience that is not sensuous in the usual sense (seeing, touching, smelling, etc.) much like sensing anxiety, for example, that has no shape, colour, or sound. Bion (1970) therefore proposes the term 'to intuit' as a parallel to the physician's use of 'see', 'touch', 'smell', and 'hear'. The analyst perceives intuitively something from the mental happenings of which the patient is not quite aware, and describes this in an interpretation.

Bion (1977c) reminds us

> ...of this peculiar state of mind where we see things and go to places which, when our state of mind changes because we happen to do what we call 'wake up', then we ignore these facts, these journeys, these sights, on the grounds that they are only dreams.
>
> (p. 28)

I assume Bion suggests we allow more space for this state of mind of dreaming, in the analytic session, because it is there that the next creative thought might be concealed, making it possible to capture something of the analysand's psyche, or to communicate something we cannot do otherwise. Bion proffers that we have respect for the information gathered in this state of mind

> no matter what it is – whether it is a state of mind that subsequently you can assess by saying you dreamt it, or you hallucinated it or you 'doodled' it onto a piece of paper when you weren't thinking about anything in particular....
>
> (Ibid, p. 41)

That is what happens in reverie, and yet "[The analyst] must be able to dream the analysis as it is taking place, but of course he must not go to sleep" (Bion, 1992, p. 216). This is a simultaneous, paradoxical state of looseness of thought and dreaming, while the analyst is fully awake, akin to Freud's 'free floating *attention*'. From this state of mind of the analyst, the 'selected fact' emerges and crystallizes: "The selected fact is the name of an emotional experience, the emotional experience of a sense of discovery of coherence" (Bion, 1962a, p. 73). In the same vein, Bion says years later, in his *Italian Seminars*,

> If you can be wide open … if you allow [those wild thoughts] to lodge in your mind, however ridiculous, however stupid, however fantastic, then there may be a chance of having a look at them. That is a matter of daring to have such thoughts…and keeping them long enough to be able to formulate what they are.
>
> (Bion, 1977d, p. 44)

In a further attempt at depicting this state of mind, Bion imagines himself idling away his time, thinking in a way one might describe as being almost thoughtless. If as a child he had been caught at it, somebody would have said, "Why on earth don't you find something to do?" Then, after such laziness, he would like to have a look in case he had caught anything in the net of his idleness (Bion, 1977c, p. 32).[3]

This suggests a change of psychoanalytic technique, from an analytic technique of the left hemisphere to a technique of the right hemisphere (Grotstein, 2007). Bion (1977a) adds 'embryological' intuition as an additional sense and as a central element in analysis, alongside scientific thought, moving from content-centred thinking to a process-centred one. Following Kant, he assumes that intuition without a corresponding concept is blind (i.e. unbound and often fanatic), whereas a concept without content is empty (i.e. meaningless jargon). Hence, Bion (1965) suggests 'trained intuition', of which the analyst's own analysis is an essential component.

This is the way by which one can achieve truth. In order to meet the patient's emotional truth in the here-and-now of the session, and facilitate communication between analyst and patient, the analyst must possess 'Negative Capability', that is, he must be "...capable of being in uncertainties, mysteries, doubts, without any irritable reaching after fact and reason" (Bion, 1970, p. 125, citing the poet John Keats). Thus, one develops the 'Language of Achievement', an intuitive language affording a transient glimpse of the fleeting evolutions of the patient's truth as reflected by the emotional experience in the here-and-now. It serves to communicate something that is lurking, already present in the patient's mind but hitherto unknown to him (and the analyst). It is minute, subtle, and barely apprehensible. In a decisive moment, it is uttered. However, something nevertheless is unavoidably lost by the very act of verbalization (Sandler, 2005). This loss must be elaborated by the *analyst's* capacity for containment, tolerance of frustration, and ability to maintain the tension necessary to keep up his free-floating attention. Since the 'Language of Achievement' is supported by intuition and experience, it cannot be taught although it can be learnt (Ibid).

Bion implores that we listen to what is in the gap, listen beyond what is being said, and hear beyond the 'noise' of the words being uttered. The patient's words refer to the past and to the future, and so he avoids being in touch with himself, and with the pain and turbulence of being in touch with himself in the present. However, in order to hear beyond that which is *spoken* in the session, the analyst must live *in the present*, in the here-and-now of the session, and listen with his intuition, which may be an incarnation of that 'embryological' intuition.[4]

Intuition, says Boris (1986), is a process by which a second mind can realize what the first no longer can. This may be the embryological intuition we all once possessed, and whose potential we all carry and which must be restored to us and our analysands. This implies an exposition and elucidation of embryonic thought which forms a link between sense impressions and consciousness (Meltzer, 1978). For this to happen, we must 'blind ourselves' to the evidence of engaging in a conversation seemingly between two adults, and loosen the grip on familiar anchors of mature thought, so as to hear the "...incomprehensible, inaudible, ineffable...from which will come the future interpretation" (Bion, 1974, p. 127). Reverie makes it possible to listen to what happens in the gap, in the synapse. Thus, I suggest, it may serve as a bridge between the patient's free associations, and between these and the analyst's interpretations.

In effect, in addition to being a groundbreaking metapsychoanalytical paper, *Caesura* can be viewed as a paper on technique where Bion guides us as to the ways of traversing caesuras – guidelines stemming from his well-known emphasis on abandoning memory, desire, and understanding as a way to blurring the clear, yet deceiving, coordinates.[5] In *Caesura*, he articulates this, citing Freud (1916a) in his well-known letter to Lou Andreas Salome: "...I have to blind myself artificially in order to focus all the light on one dark spot..." (p. 45).

Encountering unmentalized experience

As mentioned in the previous chapter, Bion describes an unconscious mental state that has never been anything else, has never been conscious. He writes that in addition to unconscious and conscious states of mind, there may be another state of mind, one that might provisionally be called an *inaccessible* state of mind. It may become inaccessible because the foetus gets rid of it as soon as it can. Even the foetus has feelings or primordial ideas, like the awareness of its heartbeat, or an awareness of sounds in the outside world, which it tries to deal with by evacuating them, literally, into the amniotic fluid (Bion, 1977c). Alternatively, these are encapsulated and become unavailable for integration by the subject. Yet it is precisely here that the subject's capacity to approach these encapsulated areas of the mind crucially depends on a receptive object. The infant is dependent on its mother's reverie for internalizing and developing the function necessary for getting in touch with himself. Identification with the object's capacity for dreaming enables the infant to know itself, and make contact with what up until then had been encapsulated and inaccessible. Nevertheless, even then, something will forever remain untouched. It is this paradoxical tension that must be borne – the simultaneous striving to get in touch with the emotional experience through the Language of Achievement, alongside the painful awareness of its unknowability (reminiscent of Freud's discussion of the 'dream's navel' reaching down into the unknown). We can never fully have direct access to our emotional experience, for which we ultimately need the 'Language of Substitution' (Bion, 1970).

In the psychoanalytic experience, Bion writes,

> we are concerned both with the translation in the direction of what we do not know into something which we do know or which we can communicate, *and also from what we do know and can communicate to what we do not know and are not aware of because it is unconscious and which may even be pre-natal, or pre-birth of a psyche or a mental life*....
>
> (1977a, p. 54, italics added)

This is a bidirectional movement, not only from unconscious to conscious but also from conscious back to unconscious.

The possibility of surpassing the caesuras separating mental states so as to get in touch with those primal mental states is one of the greatest challenges of psychoanalytic work. When we attempt to get in touch with that primordial state of mind, we are not dealing with repressed psychic material but rather with unmentalized experience, psychic material that is mindless and often one-dimensional. In these unmentalized states, the analyst must perform the alpha-function that the patient as yet cannot. In order to get in touch with those non-mental areas, the analyst "must be capable of imaginative thought, or dream-thought, that embraces the intra-uterine experience as a 'world' quite different from the 'world' of projective identification" (Meltzer, 1986, p. 36).

By means of his free-floating attention and avoidance of preconscious assumptions, the analyst can begin to identify traces of representations that the patient was forced to evacuate from his mind (Parsons, 2005). However, one might add that this free-floating attention is destined to identify primordial, sensory *pre*-representations that *were never made conscious* but remained as unrealized, irrepresentable potential, described by Bion as 'proto-mental'. This may refer to the *unrepressed unconscious*,[6] as will be further elaborated in Chapter 3.

The attempt to get in touch with unrepresented areas of the psyche has been described by Cesar and Sara Botella (2005) as contact created when, unexpectedly and involuntarily, the analyst's mind regresses beyond free-floating attention, and the analyst unconsciously perceives the patient's experience of non-representation. The analyst's verbal thought regresses, and a rift is created with the world of representations. The analyst is exposed to something essentially irrepresentable. The void created may be dreadful. This is the rift that dreaming (or, at times, a nightmare) and the work of the analyst's mind may transform into a caesura, a gap *with continuity*.

Botella and Botella emphasize that the analyst's task is devoting himself to working as the patient's double: by opening his mind to a regressive movement, from verbal expression and object representations towards nonverbal experience and a quasi-hallucinatory kind of perception, the analyst reflects the patient's psychic world (Parsons, 2005). De M'Uzan (2000) calls this 'dreaming someone else's dream' which, he asserts, may occur, under a different form, when the analyst, thanks to quasi-hallucinatory phenomena, connects in a profound way with his analysand's discourse. Being a disturbing and uncanny experience for the analyst, there is a constant temptation to escape from the mirroring between analyst and patient.

The Botellas lean upon the hypothesis that the psyche has a normal aptitude for hallucinatory functioning.[7] This is expressed in dreaming while sleeping, whereas in waking mental activity, it is usually inhibited in the interests of reality testing. In the particular state of mind called for by the analytic session, the analyst can allow himself to regress along the axis of representation-perception so as to actualize the hallucinatory in his psychic functioning. This shift towards a more primal mental form takes place in response to the analyst's sensing that the patient's mind is in contact with the irrepresentable.

In fact, as Bion says (in Aguayo, 2013), it is like daring to use some kind of hallucination, on the off-chance that it may not be pathological. This might be the caesura between dreaming and hallucinating, acknowledging the similarity between them without denying the difference (in keeping with Bion's notion of a caesura, as opposed to a break, between the psychotic and the non-psychotic parts of the personality). Grappling with this question, Bion says in his *Commentary* to *Second Thoughts* that "the proper state for intuiting psycho-analytical realizations...can be compared with the states supposed to provide conditions for hallucinations. The hallucinated individual is apparently having sensuous experiences without any background of sensuous reality" (Bion, 1967b, p. 163).[8]

So, the analyst too must be able to identify something that cannot be perceived by any of the familiar senses, but rather through primordial intuition. In his later writings, Bion even goes on to say, "... It is not surprising that psycho-analysts are, almost as a function of being analysts, supposed to qualify for being insane and called such. It is part of the price they have to pay for being psycho-analysts" (1975, p. 113). Many patients, he adds, are afraid of ideas that may appear irrational and mad. And, again, I would like to take these words as intended for the analyst for he too is afraid. This does not mean that the analyst should hallucinate, but receptiveness to the psychotic parts of the patient's psyche exposes the analyst to the psychotic parts of his own mind, just as the mother, through her receptiveness to the infant's fear of dying, actually feels the dread of death herself.

Botella and Botella (2005) impressively illustrate this thinking with Thomas, a 4-year-old child in analysis. Up until the age of 20 months, Thomas had undergone numerous hospitalizations and surgical operations, developed slowly, and uttered only a few, barely intelligible words when first seen. Although described at first as presenting autistic traits, Thomas had certainly sought contact although incapable of maintaining a relationship. He would quickly drop the adult, taking refuge in a quiet corner. At the beginning of therapy, he ran off with a pot of glue and passionately breathed in its content, like a drug addict. At other times, he would lie down on the desk and absorb the sunlight with his eyes open, without even blinking. For long periods of time, he would throw and bang solid objects against hard surfaces of the room. He was fascinated by making noises and would go "Grrrr ... grrrr!"

On the basis of the smell, the light, and the noise, still holding onto higher-level mental activity (in effect, referring to the *repressed* unconscious), the analyst interpreted the strong smell, the bright light, and the noises in the hospital, where everything seemed to go 'Grrrr .... grrrr!'

At the end of the sessions, Thomas manifested depersonalizing anxieties. Interpretations, at whatever level, brought no relief. It seemed the child could not hear any content. He was beyond reach of all usual communication.

Botella goes on to say,

> Faced with this pale, immobile, haggard looking child, the very picture of terror, the analyst himself had, as it were, a nightmare. He then said to Thomas: 'Grrrr ... grrrr! Are you afraid of the wolf?' And without thinking about it, he spontaneously imitated the nasty beast that bites and claws. Terror-stricken, Thomas signalled for him to stop, but his disarray disappeared and he was able to leave. The time after ... [Thomas] propelled himself into the corridor and, wanting to frighten everybody, yelled out: 'Grrrr ... grrrr ... the wolf!'
>
> (Ibid, p. 32)

In retrospect, the authors realized that the sensuous experiences the child generated were not mental representations of infantile sensuous experiences. Rather, these were autistic shapes in search of numbing auto-sensuousness. The analyst's intervention, when he imitated the wolf, was not a dramatization of the child's internal world but an 'accident of thought', a work of figurability which lent meaning to Thomas's disarray and anxiety and relieved the analyst of the sense of torment and disappointment resulting from the failure of his usual analytic methods. We might say that the analyst's 'dream' is the parallel of the patient's inability to dream, his 'non-dream': "By...mimicking the wolf, the *analyst was not evoking the meaning of a phantasy in the face of loss, but was soliciting in the child a psychic work comparable to his own*" (Ibid, p. 33, italics added). It was not necessarily the content that came up in the analyst's reverie, or nightmare, that was significant, but rather the dreaming function which encouraged the child's psychic work, expanding the mind and facilitating the encounter with 'the void and formless infinite' from which the personality is won. The analyst's regression, his reverie which was cast in the form of a nightmare, enabled him to make contact with irrepresentable areas of Thomas's psyche.

This encounter with the irrepresentable is commonly met in work with autistic states when in touch with unrealized areas of the mind.

Alvarez (1999a) designates these mental states as *un*drawn as opposed to those *with*drawn mental states to which the patient regresses. Meltzer (Meltzer et al., 2002a) stresses that with patients in whom mental life has remained undeveloped, in the sense that symbolic thought has not developed adequately, the analyst should use his imagination and fulfil the alpha-function for the patient so as to meet his inaccessible internal world. The important aspect of this situation is that we are presented with an opportunity to think a bit for the child. As Bick (1962) writes in her paper on child analysis (also true, I believe, of adult analyses),

> ... One may have to sit with children for a long time completely in the dark...until suddenly something comes up from the depth... It imposes on the child analyst a greater dependence on *his* unconscious to provide him with clues to the meaning.
>
> (p. 329, italics added)

This reverberates with Freud's words that the analyst

> must turn his own unconscious like a receptive organ towards the transmitting unconscious of the patient. He must adjust himself to the patient as a telephone receiver is adjusted to the transmitting microphone. Just as the receiver converts back into sound waves the electric oscillations in the telephone line which were set up by sound waves, so the doctor's unconscious is able, from the derivatives of the unconscious which are communicated to him, to reconstruct that unconscious, which has determined the patient's free associations. But if the doctor is to be in a position to use his unconscious in this way as an instrument in the analysis, he...may not tolerate any resistances in himself which hold back from his consciousness what has been perceived by his unconscious.
>
> (1912a, pp. 115–116)

Unconsciously dreaming the psychoanalytic hour in this way may expose the analyst to a feeling that he is going mad himself. In order to encounter the psychotic part of the personality in the patient, our thinking too is required to be looser, so as to make contact with that part of the patient's mind. However, experience then becomes threatening. We may feel in our flesh that associative looseness, the danger of disintegration, and collapse of the contact barrier – and the tendency to get hold of some anchor strengthens. It is precisely then, when experience becomes persecutory, when one fears that thought might turn into action, that it is essential to remain in the caesura, in the synapse, *in the present*, despite the temptation to leave the immediate situation in the room, for example, by resorting to psychogenetic, experience-remote interpretations.

Already in *Attacks on Linking*, Bion (1959) describes the mother's experience of being exposed to the infant's primitive anxieties and fear of dying. Mother, in her receptiveness, through her reverie, takes into herself the psychotic anxieties of the screaming baby, an experience that evokes tremendously intense anxieties in her. She too fears the baby is dying and that she is driven insane, yet at the same time, retaining a balanced outlook, she knows the baby is not going to die. So the capacity for suspension in the caesura, in the midst of the raging river, necessitates faith in the analytic process, a belief that, despite being in the eye of the storm, we shall traverse the river and meet the other bank of the caesura ... until the next storm. This enables the mind's natural movement between dispersion and cohesion.

All this involves taking a different view about the psychoanalytic process. We must accustom ourselves to a different, transitive method of thinking (Bion, 1977a). It is this momentary encounter with the emotional truth in the present that is transformational, expanding the minds of both patient and analyst. For that to happen, it is essential to pay close attention to the never-ending change within the hour, to the influence of the patient's words upon us and not only to their content, and to lay a fertile ground for those embryonic, germinal thoughts emerging in us, even those experienced only physically, as yet unmentalized, without pushing them aside because they seem so irrelevant, and to view those seeming obstacles to the psychoanalytic process as communication.

Clinical material

The compression of the vast number of emotional nuances in every fraction of the session, and the continuous change in the patient and analyst's states of mind and of the emotional truth at any given moment, make it hard to record the unique and transient experience of the analytic encounter. Bion himself acknowledged the limitations of verbal formulations in trying to describe the psychic reality of the psychoanalytic session, and that any attempt at description is only a transformation or an incarnation, an evolution of the emotional experience. Bion (1962a) writes, "I have experience to record, but how to communicate this experience to others I am in doubt" (p. i). Meltzer (1988) adds that "compared to the complexity of what transpires in our consulting rooms, our descriptions of them are fairy tales... No amount of tape recording...will help, because the heart of the matter [...is] ineffable, infra-sensual, in the air..." (p. 23).

And yet I would like to try and describe such a moment in the analytic encounter, perhaps, a fairy tale:

Eric, a professor of Mathematics, has been in a four-times-a-week analysis for some years now. For long periods of time, I find it hard to remain attentive to him. Often, he overwhelms me with mathematical information which I find hard to follow, and at some point, I always lose him. I hear the words but cannot link the sentences or even the words; cannot comprehend what he is saying. I become numb in the face of the flood of words, which I experience as a spray of meaningless particles. Although he talks incessantly, I often feel it is not to me, and perhaps not even to himself. I articulate to myself that he is probably filling the emotional space gaping between us, and inside of him. He, in fact, feels he is trying to interest and fascinate me with the enormous information he provides me with. Over the years, I try to reflect on my experience with him, but mostly I try to remain attentive, futilely, and feel guilty for 'dropping' him. Lately, though, I noticed that I am looking forward to Eric's sessions, also wondering about not feeling bored any more. I find that I have a wealth of thoughts in his presence, even if not always directly related to the content of his words, and at times I am quite compelled by his physics and mathematical descriptions. Although I find it hard to articulate what is occurring between us, I feel that our encounter becomes more and more meaningful and emotionally present.

Eric rides a bicycle and usually arrives sweating heavily. I often wondered about the *absence* of his body odour, neither foul nor pleasant, even though he does leave a large, wet mark on the couch.

In the session I wish to describe, Eric is telling me about something that occurred at work, and again I try my best to listen. I feel my mind wandering and I fail to remain with him, but perhaps, this time, I allow my mind to wander off. I hear most of the things he is saying, and yet, simultaneously, my mind drifts to a boy I met and his difficulties at school. I think these might be due to some learning disability, an attention deficit disorder that has to be looked into. I realize my mind has wandered off and yet, again, I find myself visualizing some scenes from the movie *Eternal Sunshine of the Spotless Mind*, which I saw some years ago. To recapitulate, after a nasty fight, the main character's girlfriend hires a firm to erase all memories of their relationship. Upon discovering this, Joel is devastated and decides to undergo the procedure himself. The pictures from his life swiftly disappear but then, regretting his decision, he frantically chases after them, desperately trying to get a hold on the fleeting memories. I am not only reminded of these scenes but actually feel as if I am *in* the scene itself. I become dizzy and feel that my mind has emptied.

Somehow the scene foggily fits in with the situation I am in with Eric, and in the background I hear him telling me of a note he found in his drawer from a girl he was once in love with. He wondered how it was that he no longer thinks of her, as if he had completely erased her from his mind. He is reminded of other friends from different periods of his life, who too were eradicated from his mind. As he speaks, I realize he is occupied with something very emotional, internal, a rare occurrence in his analysis. I hear him saying that often, while speaking to me, he has pictures of various landscapes in his head. Again, I am aware that he is talking of something of great importance, from his internal world, and yet I feel tightly grasped in a cobweb of haze and find it hard to remain attached. Nevertheless, although I am not attentive, I seem to hear his words.

I manage to ask him to tell me more about the landscapes. He describes a picture where his parents and he once walked through a rocky terrain, with a water tower in the background. In another scene, he is walking through a junction in the mountains. However, he stresses that although all these pictures are taken from real events in his life in which real people were present, in the pictures in his head there is no one else. He thinks that one day he might recall our meetings too, visualizing them in a sunlit day, with me talking very passionately (and I think to myself that we usually meet in the evenings, and that I am silent most of the time...).

And then, while both hearing his words and being lost in thought, I say, "Here too you find it hard to keep an impression of me, and I fade away". He listens and nods, but I can sense that he is already far away. He too has faded away and is occupied with his work or with further plans for the evening – a familiar experience with him. I tell him of the picture I recalled from the movie, and in response he says: "It's funny that the faces disappear. There are people I remember in every other sense, but the faces are gone. I can remember where I parked my car in huge car parks or specific corners in enormous airports around the world, but the *faces* seem to disappear". Hearing these words, I abruptly regain my senses and describe to Eric my feeling during most of the session, and in fact throughout long periods of the analysis. I say: "You are making a tremendous effort to remain present here with me, to keep an impression of me and my words within you, of the feelings evoked in you by my interventions. Yet, the experience seems to slip away and you don't seem to be able to capture it. You remember the words, but the feeling dissolves away".

Just like the odourless sweat, the faceless object that cannot keep an emotional impression within it is very present in this session, as it had probably been in previous occasions, but now it has suddenly jumped out of the two-dimensional picture and has become a three-dimensional figure. This is the hole, or the void, that the patient seems to fill with endless information. He says, "I can't filter the frenzy of thoughts about work, they simply fill me up. Perhaps it's a thought disorder, something that's not in my control".

"The frenzy of thoughts" is probably all those sense impressions, beta-elements that the patient cannot dream, cannot perform alpha-function for them, hence they overwhelm him. Without the capacity to dream them, they cannot be repressed and stored in the unconscious. They remain as unmentalized experience. This illustrates the need for an object who can dream that which the patient as yet cannot.

The clinical vignette described in the analysis of Eric is the outcome of a long and painful suspension in the experience of being eradicated, of being incapable of keeping anything in mind, of dropping, and of being dropped, until gradually the sensuous experience becomes a mental one. This can be visualized as a photo negative emerging clearer and clearer out of the darkness, won from 'the void and formless infinite'. Often, this happens initially in the mind of the analyst through his reverie. In Eric's analysis too, even though there seems to be a content-related link between the thoughts evoked in my mind and the content of Eric's thoughts characterizing his internal world, the significant thing was not the 'discovery' of the faceless and mindless object, but rather Eric's growing capacity to dream, with the analyst, in the session. Only when I loosened the effort to struggle against my thoughts from wandering off and from the attempt to understand the content of his words, could he begin to dream in a way that expands his mind, enabling him to think from different vertices, rather than the actual concrete thing. *The element that the patient internalizes is the function of dreaming, the function of seeking meaning, and not a specific meaning.* In this thinking, the expansion of the mental container is at the heart of the psychoanalytic process and not the uncovering of unconscious content. Just as the milk, no matter how essential, is not enough without the mother's love, so is the content of the interpretation, however meaningful, not enough to generate a transformation without reverie and a long-enough suspension in the synapse.

These new thoughts that emerged in Eric's analysis, embryonic 'thoughts without a thinker' (Bion, 1970), are quite obvious once they have found a mental space in someone's mind. 'Thoughts without a thinker' are thoughts that are discovered, not invented. They surprise us by coming into the mind unobstructed by memories, desires, judgements and opinions, thoughts that 'occur' in the mind, as it were unbidden (Davison, 2002). Bion links these to truth that simply exists: "Nobody need think the true thought: it awaits the advent of a thinker who achieves significance through the true thought" (1970, p. 103). *Even though the moment of discovery seems to emerge out of nowhere, it is, in fact, the fruit of a long suspension in the unthinkable, undreamable, and inarticulate, reflecting a great deal of unconscious work that has taken place by the analytic couple, but primarily in the analyst's mind, until able to offer it as an interpretation to the patient.*

We cannot invite or try to create such an occurrence and cannot take this presence that Bion and Meltzer propose, as a practical proposal. It must surprise us. All we can do is try to be open and receptive to its appearance and refrain from brushing it aside as an unwelcome noise or distraction.

Discovering new caesuras

Emotional growth and the possibility of encountering emotional truth require not only traversing caesuras, but creating, or discovering, new, surprising, and unexpected ones too. The tendency to move aside a new, emergent thought is derived from its very nature that threatens to subvert the psychic equilibrium. Its unexpected and uninvited appearance renders the person "...naked, incongruous, alien, without a point of reference that ma[kes] sense" (Bion, 1975, p. 27). Bion develops this thought throughout his writings, notably in *Attention and Interpretation* where he describes the relationship between the group and the mystic emerging from within it. Bion describes the group's resistance to accept the mystic, the creative genius born from within the group, because of the catastrophic change and the emotional turbulence that his new, and often subversive, ideas entail.

Bion (1977c) refers to Freud as "...one of these peculiar people who seemed to think that dreams are worthy of further consideration" (p. 28). Freud dared to listen to something else, and so the whole world of psychoanalysis opened up. Someone has to dare and be psychotic, or insane, and hear the wrong thing... (Bion, 1975 in Aguayo, 2013).

The fear of catastrophic change often emerges at the point where new caesuras are created, at the place where a new incision is created that is not the obvious one. The discovery of new caesuras entails deconstruction, or destruction, of the familiar thought or idea and necessitates mourning the loss of the old perception, hence the tendency to hold tightly onto the familiar. However, this is the potential for growth. Analytic transformation is possible through a *breakup* of the familiar meaning and a *breakthrough* of the new discovery. Often, this entails a threat of catastrophic *breakdown* (Bion, 1977a).

A good illustration of this is Bion's (1970) well-known vignette when he suddenly hears the ice/cream as I/scream. After some years when the words 'ice cream' appeared sporadically, Bion suddenly heard these words as 'I scream', cutting the syllables differently, later, becoming 'no - I scream' (no ice cream). And, again, it is not only the discovery of the new words that are significant but the *movement* between the words, the link between the objects. This movement, Bion conjectures, is akin to the course undergone by the good object on the way from being a good, nourishing one (ice cream) to an 'I scream' object, ultimately becoming a 'no – I scream'. Despite the large gaps in time between the patient's associations, they are related and linked. The new caesura created enabled the resumption of the movement of associations and of dreaming. From this and other vignettes, like the one in his paper *Evidence* (see p. 175), we can think of the analyst's inhibition to offer such an interpretation to the patient for fear of it being just a pun, an unfounded free association of his own, one that the patient could never accept. I suppose this is a familiar experience to all of us when a new idea emerges and surprises us, felt so real, and yet we hesitate and dare not express it out loud. Often, we may be embarrassed, even ashamed to have thought it. We may react somatically, swamped by a wave of heat, accelerated heartbeat, perspiration, and disquiet. All these may be signs heralding our sudden descent into the raging caesura and an imminent, threatening catastrophic change, and the temptation to step aside may be impressive.

A fragment from an analytic session

The catastrophic experience may often seem small or minor to an outside observer and yet, for the participants in the analytic experience, it is shaking. Again, I would like to refer to the catastrophic experience from the analyst's vertex:

Simon has been in analysis for a number of years, consistently avoiding recognizing his dependence and his deep attachment to me. Throughout the analysis, unwittingly, I try to overcome a persistent feeling of being redundant. I feel, but do not really perceive, do not 'suffer', to paraphrase Bion's description of the patient who "feels the pain but will not suffer it" (1970, p. 9). In one of our sessions, after a weekend break, Simon describes the distress he had been feeling over some issue, and how a friend had been able to calm him and explain why he had been so anxious. The friend also managed to help him get out of the difficult situation in which he found himself. His talking about the friend's thoughts is fluent and then suddenly truncated in mid-sentence. I find myself completing the sentence in my head, and I recall that this was a sentence I had said to him some weeks ago. I feel certain he had stopped his words after he too perceived, in a fraction of a second, that these were words I had said, but something in him was compelled to attack this recognition for fear of having to acknowledge that he has taken in something from me. Only then am I struck by pain, sorrow, frustration, and a severe feeling of exclusion. As I mentioned, this all occurs in a fraction of a second, and Simon goes on talking. I am shaken, I feel my heart beating very fast, and I feel certain I must stop and relate to what has just occurred. But Simon is in distress and occupied with his story, and I wonder if it's just my need to protest and declare my presence, my significance. I feel inclined to renounce, to move on and hear the rest of the weekend's distress, but I also feel the turbulence and the wish to stop, and the fear to do so. I fear appearing as someone preoccupied with himself, and that the patient will again attack and nullify my words. This time I *suffer* the occurrence, am able to think about it, afford the needed space in my mind. The occurrence becomes meaningful in the here-and-now of the session. My emotional turbulence facilitates my getting in touch with the patient's emotional turbulence that he fears he will not be able to bear.

I think this illustrates the fear evoked in the face of catastrophic change. This is the fear of deviating from the familiar, safe but numbing route ... and endangering oneself. The catastrophic experience described is brief and occurred mainly in the mind of the analyst. Nevertheless, I am of the opinion that a brief catastrophic experience often heralds the coming of an intense experience further along the analytic road, in the same way that its occurrence in the mind of the analyst is a precursor of its emergence in the mind of the patient. With Simon, within a few days the patient experienced intense and paralyzing anxiety that informed the beginning of a stormy period in which he felt his wife was going to leave him and that he was about to lose his job due to his dysfunction. Only weeks later could he bear to think that the intense anxiety that struck him was evoked by the head-on encounter with his dependence on the analytic relationship, which he could no longer deny.

Bion (1967c) stresses that a patient will accept an interpretation only if he feels that the analyst has passed through an emotional crisis himself as a part of the act of giving the interpretation. Hence, internalizing the analyst's transformational and dreaming function enables the patient to achieve closer contact with himself.

Concluding remarks

Dreaming, which is, in fact, unconscious emotional thinking, serves as a container for the emotional turbulence in the caesura and facilitates tolerating the catastrophic change. The capacity to bear the distress, uncertainty, and fear of breakdown thus depend on the analyst's capacity for dreaming. Again, I would like to stress the importance of the *analyst's* dreaming which holds and contains *his* mind while traversing the raging caesura river. I have tried to portray the analyst's dreaming as a primary means enabling him to be at-one with the emotional truth of the session, as opposed to knowing more about the patient's mind.

Meltzer (1986), who also seems to think that one of the main indications of Bion's theory is technical, says we cannot expect to deal with unmentalized material by interpretation of content. We must set ourselves an entirely different task, namely that of discovering the emotional experience which the patient is unable to dream about and do this dreaming for him. It is quite clear, he says, that we cannot perform this function intellectually. It requires an unusual degree of identification with the patient, an unusual depth of reverie in the session, and an unusual degree of tolerance of feeling mad oneself.

In effect, we are invited to be in a paradoxical state, designated by Meltzer (2005) as *counterdreaming*. He writes,

> It is difficult to explain the technique of counterdreaming. It is not enough to fall asleep while the patient is talking. It requires a process of working over the material, focusing and selecting interpretive configurations awaiting a state of satisfaction (rest). The state of observation is essentially a resting state. It is also a state of heightened vigilance. I compare it with waiting in the dark for the deer, grazing at night, seen by their flashing white tails. This nocturnal vigilance is on the alert for movement of the quarry, part object minimal movements which with patience can be seen to form a pattern of incipient meaning 'cast before'. This catching of the incipient meaning cast before is a function of receptive imagination – open to the possible, unconcerned with probability. Being rich with suspense, it is necessarily fatiguing and fraught

with anxiety. It is a trial of strength – and faith – that gives substance to terms such as resistance or retreat. However, it is a poetry generator.

(p. 182)

Notes

1 Bion (1962a) asserts that an emotional experience cannot be conceived of in isolation from a relationship. The basic relationships he postulates are Love, Hate, and Knowledge, designating them as *L*, *H*, and *K* links, respectively.
2 Placental economy is a primitive registration, prior to birth and to the link between mouth and nipple. It suggests a primordial, paradoxical form of linkage-separateness. Albeit commonly thought of as a mutual product, half maternal and half foetal, the placenta is, in fact, a tissue created by the foetus, differentiated from the endometrium, although deeply embedded in it. Even though it is created by the foetus, it behaves almost independently of it. Even in the womb, there is no fusion between mother and foetus, nor is there an empty space between them, but rather a semi-permeable membrane of linkage and separateness (Irigaray, 1990). Thus, it seems that the placenta serves as an apt metaphor for understanding the function of the contact barrier and of dreaming.
3 For that he had articulated 'the grid', to facilitate mapping, after the session, those wandering thoughts, and for conceptualizing his intuitions.
4 In denoting intuition as 'embryological', Bion was also influenced by Buber's reference to Jewish myth, saying "…in his mother's womb man knows the universe and forgets it at birth" (in Bion, 1977a). This concept helps Bion to conjecture how the foetus perceives the intrauterine environment or becomes aware of feelings of terror, of sound, of sight, etc. (Bion, 1977c). The usefulness of making conjectures about a continuity between prenatal and postnatal functioning is that it allows us to widen the field of clinical observation and understanding of certain manifestations, seeing them as traces of the first stages of emotional development (Tuckett and Levinson, 2010). Moreover, this speculative imagination serves to produce the conditions in which the germ of a scientific idea can flourish (Bion, 1977c).
5 Civitarese (2008) elaborates the notion of 'caesura' as Bion's discourse on method.
6 For Bion, Freud's conceptualization of the unconscious in terms of the *repressed* unconscious is not sufficient. Among other reasons, this is due to the expansion of psychoanalysis and the encounter with patients whose thinking and dreaming capacities are defected (Lombardi, 2009), as can be seen in autistic states, for instance.

7 Freud (1917), too, writes that at the beginning of our mental life, we did, in fact, have the capacity to hallucinate the satisfying object when we felt the need for it. But we soon had to give up hallucinatory satisfaction of our wishes and set up a kind of 'reality-testing'.

8 Freud (1917) writes that "The formation of the wishful phantasy and its regression to hallucination are the most essential parts of the dream-work, but they do not belong exclusively to dreams" (p. 229). He differentiated between the hallucination of the schizophrenic and the hallucinatory delirium of amentia. In the latter, resembling a daydream, he says, one might speak of a 'hallucinatory wishful psychosis' and attribute it equally to dreams and amentia. In *On Hallucination* (1958), Bion differentiates between hysterical and psychotic hallucinations. He refers to the patient's experience at times as a hallucination and at other times as a dream. Already here, Bion moves within the caesura between a dream and a hallucination.

Chapter 3

Beyond the spectrum

Fear of breakdown, catastrophic change, and the unrepressed unconscious

> ... It's wrong what they say about the past... about how you can bury it. Because the past claws its way out....
> (Khaled Hosseini, The Kite Runner)

To what extent, Bion (1967a) asks, can we rely on the luxury of sticking to a part of the total experience which is verbally communicable? Bion makes use of the spectrum of the electromagnetic waves as an analogy for emphasizing the limits of our sensory apparatus, which receives only a small part of the spectrum. The wavelengths visible to us fall in a narrow strip of visual perception in between the infrared on the one end and the ultraviolet on the other. We cannot see the ones that fall off these ends, but they are nevertheless there. Using that as an analogy, Bion suggests that, thanks to verbal capacity, there is a certain realm of mental life, which we can speak of in terms like personality, mind, and so forth. This is the small part of the spectrum, in which one could talk about it as being verbally communicable. However, the psychoanalytic encounter compels us to observe and meet those areas of the mind that lie beyond that narrow sphere. We see a patient who seems an ordinary neurotic patient, Bion says, but as the analysis goes on, he seems to have what one might call a psychotic breakdown. Alternatively, the analysis takes a turn in that what we are accustomed to regard as psychotic elements become much more visible. "Can we make some corresponding extension of our...mental capacity, to take in a little bit more of...the invisible aspects of the spectrum?" (Ibid, p. 60).

Guy, aged 30, a young painter, is in his third year of analysis which had begun as a twice-a-week psychotherapy. He is a good looking, suntanned, and muscular young man. His body is usually very exposed. He arrives to our sessions wearing shorts, a sleeveless vest, and clogs. From the very start, he became very attached to me, in a somewhat undifferentiated manner. He finds it hard to leave at the end of the hour, asking, allegedly humorously, if there's no 'double session'. I feel him very adhesive, intrusive, always arriving early, walking around my backyard, once even standing at the door when I opened it for the previous patient to leave. He talks very emotionally, weeps, moves incessantly. He wants to tell me of the panic attacks he had experienced some years ago but cannot find the words. He's afraid the attacks might reappear, and he will do anything to prevent them from coming back. He remembers his greatest fear was of falling. Fainting and falling. He relates the panic attacks to his use of drugs at the time of their first occurrence. Up until then, he says, his life was terrific: he would fall in love twice a week, smoke grass and felt great, organized parties for all his friends, and everybody sought his company. He says he was in touch with his feelings, very active in a lot of sports, and there was no sign of anxiety. The first panic attack came out of the blue. He describes a clear "cut" between his life until he began using drugs and that after the first panic attack.

In one of our initial sessions, he tells a recurring dream where he is in a stormy river with his mother, and he fears she is about to harm him. He explains that his mother is very emotional and stormy. In the past, she was depressed and anorectic. She is very attached to him, very offended if he doesn't call often enough. Father is described as more practical, organized, impermeable, and blocked.

Guy is still intensely involved in various extreme sports, even though he feels these activities no longer suit his age, and I realize he needs these thrills, being afraid of growing up. He says he has not had a meaningful relationship with a woman for years.

In time, I hear more about his nocturnal activities – he drinks a lot, picks up a girl, and takes her home. He is known around town as a "great lay", and the girls seek him out. None of them really interest him; he's afraid to lose himself in an other. He says, "I'm good at beginnings but not at relationships". He's afraid of getting bored, afraid of endings, of death. He says, "I want to stay with you here in the room for hours". Although his enthusiasm seems histrionic, it is contagious, and I too look forward to our sessions. After a few weeks, I offer him the use of the couch and suggest he come four times a week. He accepts. But the move to the couch brings along a dramatic change.

The sessions become surprisingly deadening. He recounts over and over the load he has on his shoulders, the disappointments from close friends, the despair and hopelessness he feels of any possible change. He stops taking girls home, stops drinking, says he masturbates several times a day, needs to feel alive. I realize that the masturbation, much like the physical and mental overactivity, is not an expression of pleasure but an excess of excitation. He is compelled to unburden himself of the unbearable, unmentalized stress he has inside of him. 'A slave of quantities', as described by de M'Uzan (2003).

He keeps arriving exactly two minutes early for his sessions. I feel it drives me crazy. He moves constantly on the couch, bounces his legs frantically, stretches them as if to feel the limits of his body, incessantly puts on his glasses and takes them off. At the end of the sessions, the couch looks like a battlefield. The napkin is wrinkled besides the pillow, the small mat is crumpled, and the pillow is upside down. During the sessions, he picks his nose, his ears, takes out secretions from his eyes and puts it in his mouth, scratches himself, digs into wounds in his skin, peels the scab off, and reopens them. Lying down, his body is even more exposed than before. His vest is pulled up, his shorts stretched down, and his pubic hair is revealed. He seems to need to cling to me and cannot bear any gap or barrier between us, not even the napkin or any clothing.

And amidst all this movement, I can hardly keep my eyes open. I feel an unfathomable sleepiness descending on me. At first, I assume I am trying to defend myself, or silence the hostility I feel, or perhaps the rejection, disgust, homosexual anxiety, or excitation. Perhaps I am trying to preserve my boundaries from being breached. I do not want him to come anymore, and I feel immense guilt over the harsh feelings I have for him.

The analysis is hard for him too. He is despaired, and yet the time between sessions feels to him like eternity. I think that he might be better off going to another analyst, someone more competent who could bear him.

From time to time, he wants to sit. He goes over to the armchair or sits up on the couch, and miraculously, the experience returns to what it was at the beginning of our sessions. He goes back to being moving, attractive, fascinating, and my heart goes out to him. My fatigue completely disappears.

As soon as he goes back to lie on the couch, the deadness prevails.

I realize this is a crucial communication, however in the state I am in, I can hardly think. My thinking is anesthetized, and I am barely alive – not even dead, just numb, a kind of stupor.

The months go rapidly by, and his condition deteriorates. He feels utterly desperate. Nothing interests him anymore, and he hardly works. I am surprised to realize that he's already three years in analysis. It seems hardly a year. I feel guilty for not being able to help him, and even more than that, I feel that the analysis itself is responsible for the deterioration and worsening of his condition.

In one of the sessions, after speaking and weeping, while I remain silent and immersed in a state of opacity, I hear him ask: "Are you dead?"

I startle and 'wake up'.

I think I may have unconsciously become identified with the deadening mother who could not stand his aliveness. Alternatively, I think of him as saturated with his mother's total presence, which completely imbues him, drowning and deadening him. I feel him inducing a feeling of death all around, and I realize he has to move incessantly so as not to feel his deadness, and mine. It seems I am both the dead and the deadening mother. Transference here is not a kind of displacement as it is traditionally described, but a form of turnaround in which the patient inflicts on the analyst what he has been subjected to without being able to integrate it (Roussillon, 2013).

For several months, I struggle with the sleep threatening to overwhelm me. I succeed not to fall asleep, but once in a while I drift into a dream, perhaps a daydream, and leap in a startle, trying to get hold of a shred of the dream, sensing that something very valuable is concealed in it, if only I could capture a glimpse of it. But the dreams quickly fade away and disappear. I get tired of struggling, and it becomes increasingly clear that the very effort to keep awake is, in fact, what prevents me from encountering something deeper in Guy's inner world. I feel more and more convinced that I must let go, and that whatever will be – will be! And yet I am afraid, and I feel it will lead to catastrophe. It can demolish the analysis.

I feel a growing aversion to Guy, to his pungent body odour, to the way he slides his bare feet over the couch, or peels off dry skin from his feet, letting it drop on the couch. He leaves a large oil stain on the couch after a visit to the garage, and I feel him adhering to me and suffocating me. He, or his residues, remain on the couch, which has become the place where he lives. I am reminded of the dream from the beginning. I seem to have become the mother who wants to harm him, perhaps abort him? And yet I think this is what must probably happen. He will have to fall, to collapse, to be dropped, but I dare not.

The sessions I will report are obviously the ones I was able to be more attentive or the ones in which we could transform something from the psychotic part of the personality to a symbol, a verbal formulation, or mentalize an unmentalized experience (Mitrani, 1995).

A session

Guy begins by saying, "I'm trying to tell you what I think in various ways, but I'm afraid you'll think all kinds of bad things about me and then it's hard for me to think about it. I keep trying to fill up my time so as not to have any … I don't even know what … the more I fill myself up like this, the emptier I feel … I try to think rationally so that I can get things in order. My emotional part is in chaos! I don't have a clue as to how to deal with it all! I feel I so much want to connect but every time I try – I panic!"

He sobs, frustrated, and moves agitatedly.

"Connect to what?" I ask, trying to help him articulate his feeling.

"To what I really feel! To something real!"

He goes on to describe how he goes crazy at work, screaming at people. "I can't take all this shit! Nothing is working out! I have these scenarios in my head running in loops, bringing on panic. I can't decide anything. I don't know who I am, what I am! I tried to think if there's anything specific that brings on the panic. I think it usually happens when I'm with someone I know, and then all of a sudden he says something odd, something that doesn't fit, something in his behaviour that seems strange…".

He gets stuck, can't explain, becoming very frustrated.

He tries to go on: "It's as if I don't know him, as if there's something I don't get, something I can't understand rationally, can't connect. I feel I'm dissociated, 'besides it', and I get into a loop. Phew! How can I explain it??!"

He presses hard on his temples, and his whole body is on the move. He's in a terrible distress, sighs, sobs, snuffles, "It's hard for me to think!"

"Try...", I say quietly.

He weeps, but goes on: "Okay. I'll try to think. It happens step by step. First, something odd happens, and then, just before I panic, I think about the very fact that I even noticed it, and I don't understand: why do I even pay attention to these things? Why do I observe what's happening? And then I start to criticize myself, and I think that I always *observe*, but I never *feel*, and then I panic – and out of the panic, everything just rolls on!"

I say, "You feel something begins to come into being and you sever it at the root...".

He says, "Yes. I don't want to let it in. It's bad. I don't want it to happen but I can't control it".

He begins to speak coherently about a specific time when he began to feel the fear spreading inside him, and he succeeds in articulating a fear of going mad. He speaks of his fear of remaining alone and dying. However, the affect has changed. He doesn't move restlessly anymore, and I feel he is more connected, and calmer. I realize that the effort to capture what he is drives him mad, and yet the capacity to put this amorphous experience into words is plenty for now. The fact that I managed to keep him in mind is an indication for me that his speech was more meaningful – not a beta-screen, but rather a contact barrier that has been constructed from alpha-elements and dream-thoughts.

The session illustrates for me the strenuous struggle Guy is immersed in, between trying to communicate his inner experience of non-existence and the fear of the recurrence of the terrifying experience; the fear that if he succeeds in connecting to the feeling he is trying to describe, and articulate it, he will collapse and fall. But then I think, as Winnicott (1974) says, that the breakdown he and I are afraid of, has already occurred. Perhaps now, it can be experienced. I realize that the amorphous experience may be that same experience of non-existence Winnicott writes about. This is his greatest fear. This is an experience he is living for the first time in the analysis – an experience that has already occurred, encapsulated in the *un*repressed unconscious, an experience of a world where it is impossible to feel. This is an amorphous, meaningless world, in which the threat of falling into an infinite and formless void lurks at every minute.

I feel we have come a long way. The amorphous experience is present in the here-and-now of the analysis. However, we have still not encountered something essential that we both seek to meet and yet we both seem to dread too. The session described above is an exceptional one amidst the experience of deadness and nothingness that dominates the analysis with Guy. I still struggle not to drop him, still have to make an enormous effort to remain attentive, to find words, to make sense, and not to hate him.

In time, I feel that I am getting to the limits of my capacity. Guy doesn't give up. He keeps arriving early, soiling the couch, and anesthetizing me.

It was at that time that I came across a poem by Octavio Paz:

> …listen to me as one listens to the rain,
> without listening, hear what I say
> with eyes open inward, asleep
> with all five senses awake…
>
> (1975, p. 134)

These words echo Bion (1976d) who writes that in order to be able to pick up signs of some archaic, irrepresentable psychic element

> we have to be in a peculiar state of mind; the margin between being consciously awake, able to verbalize one's impressions, and being asleep, is extremely small. It is easy to be in a state of mind where you slip over into sleep, actually in the office when you are supposed to be working. It is equally easy to slip over into a state of being horribly intellectually awake. The border between the two, the correct state of mind, is very difficult to achieve… Being on the right wavelength, which has to be experienced to be recognized, is unfortunately comparatively rare.
>
> (p. 288)

Nevertheless, it is there we must strive to.

Perhaps that's how I must be – 'agree' to sleep "with eyes open inward", to relinquish the demands of the super-ego, to agree that what will be – will be, to stop grappling with the numbness and the amorphous experience.

Another session

I arrive at one of the following sessions in utter despair. I feel I cannot struggle any more. If a catastrophe has to happen, then so be it! I feel the analysis is stuck anyway. Guy arrives early as usual, with an inappropriate grin. My heart is pounding, and I feel a great turbulence. I hate him, I hate my work, my professional identity is subverted, and I feel all hope is lost. I sink heavily in my armchair.

Surprisingly, I am wide awake.

He begins jokingly, "Some mother I have! Calls me up first thing in the morning, and even though she can hear I'm still asleep, she talks to me as if I'm awake. I had just woken up from a crazy dream".

He goes on to recount the dream: "I don't know where it was, a hotel or somebody's home. I was with a friend and another girl. Can't remember whom. I look out of the window and see a pool and many stairs leading down, like some kind of a resort, and the only way down is through the stairs outside. I follow my friend till we reach the end of the stairs. The rest are all broken. No way through. Everything's broken and you can't reach the pool. But *he* succeeds. He jumps and makes some kind of a somersault, hangs onto the railing. *I* am too scared and I also don't want to lose the girl. I'm afraid that if we go there she'll never find us. He hangs onto the railing and passes easily, as if it's something he does daily, but *I* couldn't. And then mom called. It was really weird".

"Weird?" I ask.

He says, "Don't know. When we went down to the pool, we arrived somewhere else, a big square in the centre of some city. The railing led us *further* then the pool, *beyond* it. What amazed me was that I said to the other guy 'How will she ever find us? We're not at the pool. She'll never find us', and then he magically disappeared for a second, jumped over to the other side and fetched her".

"I know what I think about this dream", he goes on to say. "This guy is sure of himself, he has money; he has everything. When he slides down the railing, he overcomes the obstacle in a second, but *me*, I just see it all from above. *I arrive unnaturally*, and even then, I don't get to the pool. The pool means water, feelings, and I skip over it to another place, feeling that something is missing. And then there was the call".

I wait a while and then ask about the resort.

He says, "It was somewhere in Europe. I pass from one level to another lower one, and the pool is in between – and up there everything was good, and down there, everything was … well, rock bottom, nowhere else to go. When I got there I could go either straight or sideways, there was nothing further down.

I felt lost. I didn't know where I was".

He is silent for a minute and then begins to sigh deeply, inhaling and exhaling intensely, as if he's having trouble breathing.

He says, "When I woke up I was afraid I'd die".

We are silent for some minutes. In my mind, I associate the dream to birth more than death, and I feel very turbulent. I want to interpret, but I fear it is only an overvalued idea I latch onto. And then I just say, "I actually thought more in the way of birth…".

He is reflective for some minutes, and then he says, "I know it took a long time until I was out, at least 12 hours. Finally, I arrived unnaturally because my mom had to have suction so that I would come out. I was born in the evening, relatively small. It was a hard delivery. My mom used to smoke a lot. She hadn't smoked during the pregnancy, just got fatter and fatter".

"Why did she get fatter?" I ask.

"Because she ate…", he replies cynically.

"And why did she eat?" I ask.

"Why did she eat??! Because she was hungry!! Because *I* was in there! … After that she would eat and throw up … I feel uneasy talking about my mom". He becomes silent. After a few minutes, he goes on: "She never told me, but I knew. It wasn't normal the way she threw up all the time. Damned illness! … It doesn't feel right talking like that about my mother".

"Why?" I ask. "What are you afraid of?"

"My mother had a fucked up life", he cries out loudly. "All her life she's had to deal with all this shit! She's getting old. Soon I'll have to deal with her wanting plastic surgery!"

"*You* will have to deal with it??" I ask.

Guy: "It's just a way of speaking".

"It sounds like when a mother talks about her child", I say.

He yells, "Because my mom is a baby! That's it! I said it! There's nothing I can do about it!! My mom is an insecure little baby! Her centre is herself! It's getting harder and harder for me to deal with it. It's hard to deal with an apathetic dad and a 4-years-old mom!"

Crying forcefully he says, "You know what just went through my head?! I thought what would happen to me when my parents die. Sometimes I think I'll get into a crazy breakdown that I won't be able to deal with. I'm weak!! I have no one except my family! I'm sick of it all!"

He breathes heavily, sighing, and he says, "I'm panicking a little now".

I ask him to describe his feelings. He cries and says he's confused. I try to understand more, and he just says, "I feel I'm going mad!"

He presses his temples, exhaling, trying to organize his breath, inhaling and exhaling heavily as if he's suffocating. He is agitated and moves restlessly on the couch. He's crying and cannot speak. He stammers, chokes, and says, "I must calm down! I can't go on anymore! I'm trying to stop my thoughts and that only makes me panic more. I'm disconnecting again!"

I say, "what is it that you don't want to think?"

He doesn't reply, just exhales forcefully. I am afraid he might be having a heart attack. I am very tense, and after a few minutes, he says, "I've just had a panic attack like I haven't had in years! I was scared I was going mad. I couldn't think what I was thinking. The very fact that it happens *here* only amplified the panic. That's it! Enough! I can't go on anymore!"

It's time for us to stop. He asks for a glass of water. He drinks and leaves relatively organized.

The caesura between breakdown and breakthrough

Is Guy having a breakdown or a breakthrough?

What would we think, Bion (1976d) asks, if we knew someone carved holes in human beings – if we could not excuse the behaviour on the grounds that he was a surgeon? And what would we say when this successful surgeon, who has done surgical operations for years, had what we call a 'breakdown', and cannot face the operating theatre? Is it a 'breakdown', Bion asks, or break-up? Break-in? Or break-out? Or breakthrough? Might we think that the surgeon is seeing something he has never allowed himself to see before – how cruel, how brutal, how violent he is?

Bion proffers we observe from different and unconventional vertices. What appears like a breakdown from one vertex may be a breakthrough when looked at from a different vertex.

One might therefore ask if my despair and difficulty in keeping and bearing Guy in my mind is an expression of a breakdown and a collapse of my analytic capacities, or might it be a caesura on the way to encountering the deadness in Guy's inner world? Could we think that my struggle to keep thinking, to stay awake, is actually an expression of my *resistance* to encountering the emotional truth present in the room, and to my attempt to defend against a formless and chaotic experience, against 'becoming O', and as an attempt to prevent Guy's inevitable breakdown? "The aspect which we perhaps share most with patients is *avoidance* of mental pain beyond a certain threshold and the search for acceptable solutions or defences" (Ferro, 1993, p. 927).

To my mind, Guy's panic attack is saturated with meaning and is the most meaningful event at this stage of the analysis. A breakdown is no doubt a tragedy, but it can become a transformative experience leading to a breakthrough (Bollas, 2013).

To this day, I cannot say what exactly precipitated Guy's anxiety attack in this session. Nevertheless I think that my utter and absolute despair, my very renunciation of the struggle against sleep and detachment, my mere collapse, are the elements that created the conditions for Guy to get in touch with himself, with the roots of his being and with the primitive *agonies* in him (since, as Winnicott says, anxiety is not a strong-enough word here). These primitive agonies may be felt as a return to an unintegrated state, falling forever, loss of psychosomatic collusion, loss of sense of real, loss of capacity to relate to objects, etc. They are realized in states of disintegration, self-holding, depersonalization, autistic states, and so on (Winnicott, 1974). One does not encounter primitive agonies in themselves but rather their shadows (Eigen, 1999), much like our limited capacity to only *approximate* at-one-ment with O, unknowable, absolute truth. We can only make contact with the intersection of the *evolution* of O with the domain of objects of sense (Bion, 1970).

The analyst's participation

Winnicott writes, "At length, dependence becomes a main feature, and then the analyst's mistakes and failures become direct causes of...the outbreak of fear of breakdown" (1974, p. 103). I suggest that "the analyst's mistakes and failures" are not a mishap in the analytic process, but may rather be an expression of the analyst's receptivity to the patient's illness and his primal communication. The patient 'knows' his analyst's state of mind. Only when the patient senses the analyst's receptivity to the emotional experience in its entirety, does he know that the analyst has relinquished his own method of verbal communication and has opened himself to the *patient's* method of primitive communication. Only when he perceives the analyst's internal struggle to bear the unbearable, does he know that he has touched the analyst deeply, and only then does he feel capable of encountering something unbearable and encapsulated within himself. When confronting the psychotic parts of the personality, the analyst's experience is an integral part of the patient's material. It is the analyst who must feel in his flesh the fear of breakdown and the fear of potential catastrophe *in the present*.

We are thus required to take upon ourselves a dissociated part of the patient's psyche which the patient cannot as yet assume authorship of. At this phase of the analysis, it was the psychic deadness inside Guy's psyche, the deadness that existed but was not experienced, but most of all, the hateful, deadening aspects of the inner object. Receptivity to this facilitates something from the unrepressed unconscious to emerge – not something that has been mentalized and repressed, but something that has never been registered "for want of a poet ... [since] as yet the poet hadn't turned up; so the recording tape was a blank!" (Bion, 1975, p. 120). The analyst's tolerating the countertransference involves his making links (as well as breaking links) in *his* mind, and it is this which allows the patient to do likewise (Carpy, 1989). It seems that the link *I* made between the dream and the experience of birth, albeit being *my* association, created a profound and as yet unformulated link in Guy's mind.

The following session

For the following session, Guy arrives pale, without his usual smile, and sits in the armchair. He says he can't lie down today. He breathes heavily and says that since our last session, he doesn't function. He feels he cannot live with this anxiety anymore. He says he's afraid to lie down because he's scared it'll happen to him again. He says he told a friend about our previous session and how he was overcome by panic. The friend thought it might be a breakthrough(!).

He says, "I feel I'm losing it! It's awful. It reminded me of the panic attack I had when I felt I was going to die, except that this time I thought I was going completely mad".

He describes his agitation, the constant attempt to keep the thoughts away, the muddle he has in his head. He feels he's grinding thoughts all day, severing them, scared he'll end up in a "loony bin".

Gradually he begins to describe his experience of disconnectedness, talking very emotionally: "I feel I'm disconnected from myself, not feeling things from here! (pointing to his chest). Right now I *do* feel, but usually I'm not connected to what I feel. I have no control over it. I'm cautious – I try not to be too happy, not to get too excited, to keep very still! I keep hearing criticism from inside of me!"

I intervene only to try and help him go on. He says, "I'll give you an example: I was with friends and the whole time I'm terrified I'm going to panic. Everyone asks me why I'm so restless, why am I not calm. I don't want another thought to emerge ... I'm terrified when I think back about things that happened in the past. I think of things I went through, memories, and I feel so disconnected from them, as if I've never experienced them, and that drives me to panic of being so disconnected!"

He's in a storm, and his body is trembling. "I can't connect to good experiences either. I feel I've missed so much along the way. I'm scared to think. Scared of anything that might disrupt my equilibrium. I'm scared of drinking (alcohol). Sometimes I feel heat waves and I'm scared something might happen to me!"

I try to put in words what I have understood so far, and I say, "It seems you're afraid the panic and anxiety will take hold of you. You then disconnect yourself so as not to feel the panic, but then you panic for fear of being detached and disconnected".

"Yes", he says. "But the anxiety of being disconnected is something new. In the past, I could detach myself and everything was okay. Now

I'm scared it'll lead to madness. Last time the panic attack came on because I thought you could see I was going mad, that my brain is twisted, that my thinking is fucked up! I can't sit down quietly and think. I'm afraid of thinking!!"

He goes on: "Last time I began imagining that you were thinking I'm mentally ill and that I need medication, and then everything went blurry and I was paralyzed and really anxious! I haven't had such feelings in a long time!"

After some time, he says, "Here, right now I'm beginning to feel the anxiety rising".

I am aware that my mind has drifted, that I had lost him.

He says, "I lost the thread of thought".

And I think that it is *I* who has lost the thread and that he had been dropped.

I say, "You may have lost the thread of thought because you didn't know where I was. You were alarmed because I didn't look at you and you felt I wasn't there, that I didn't keep you in my mind, that I had dropped you – and then you felt you were losing the thread of thought, and began to feel anxious".

He's quiet. He says, "Yes", and remains quiet.

A few minutes later, he seems calmer. He says, "Somehow now, I managed to get over the panic. It was about to erupt, and then I felt I was back in place. I'm a little relieved now. I can breathe a little. I heard you and I felt safe again".

I think he felt safe being back in my mind.

He goes on talking but confuses the words. He says something about knowing I used to work in a hospital, but then he hesitates, gets muddled up, stammers. I ask what had frightened him. He tries to diminish his words and says he only *assumes* I worked in a hospital.

I say, "you were afraid to say you looked me up...".

He laughs hysterically, embarrassed, and gradually begins to say that he googled me: "But just three or four times. I saw you worked at the hospital, wrote a few papers, and that you don't have Facebook...". He can't stop laughing and says he feels guilty for being a Peeping Tom.

It seems that when I am impenetrable to him, when I don't keep him in my mind, he tries to intrude secretly, stealthily, sometimes violently. Perhaps now he felt he could *tell* me about it, without having to *act*.

*

For the neurotic, the couch can be symbolical of the mother's love. However, when encountering the psychotic parts of the personality, it would be more true to say that the couch *is* the analyst's womb or lap (Winnicott, 1947). The earliest anxiety, Winnicott (1952) suggests, is related to being insecurely held. I now realize that lying on the couch, Guy was regressed to a primordial and primitive state, feeling unheld in an actual womb or lap. This state awakened primary catastrophic anxieties of unintegration, falling forever and death. Sitting face to face, we again meet the non-psychotic parts of his personality, and the experience is then completely different – for both of us. This may be a reflection of the acute split he makes between his life up until the first panic attack, when he held himself with his intellectual and social skills, constant activity and an efficient False Self organization, and the life *after* the panic attack and the collapse of the omnipotent self-holding.

The unrepressed unconscious

Both Winnicott and Bion echo Freud who maintained that our psychoanalytic investigations have directed our interest too exclusively to the repressed. Freud (1923b) writes,

> We recognize that the *Ucs.* does not coincide with the repressed; it is still true that all that is repressed is *Ucs.*, but not all that is *Ucs.* is repressed. A part of the ego, too—and Heaven knows how important a part...undoubtedly is *Ucs.* And this *Ucs.*...is not latent like the *Pcs.*... [W]e find ourselves thus confronted by the necessity of postulating a third *Ucs.*, which is not repressed.
> (p. 18, italics in the original)

Later on, he says, "Pathological research has directed our interest too exclusively to the repressed" (p. 19).

Freud (1920) referred to the tendency "to repeat the repressed material as a contemporary experience" (p. 18). However, in light of his reservation that "not all that is *Ucs.* is repressed", it would be more apt to speak of the tendency to repeat the *unconscious* material as a contemporary experience, and the unconscious in this respect is rather the *un*repressed unconscious.

Winnicott writes of the fear of breakdown and the pull towards it, and Bion writes of catastrophic change and the fear of it. Both meet in the realm of the *unrepressed unconscious*. Both focus on the dread of encountering emotional truth encapsulated in the unmentalized, unrepressed unconscious, threatening the mind with a psychotic state. Yet both contend that this encounter, facilitating the integration of remote and unmentalized parts of the self, can save the personality from mental catastrophe, or alternatively from psychic death as a defence against it.

Winnicott, as we know, refers to a fear of breakdown that has already happened, an unthinkable fact encapsulated in the unconscious.

> The patient needs to 'remember' this but it is not possible to remember something that has not yet happened, and this thing of the past has not happened yet because the patient was not there for it to happen to.
>
> (1974, p. 105)

Furthermore,

> The unconscious here is not exactly the repressed unconscious of psychoneurosis... In this special context the unconscious means that the ego integration is not able to encompass something. The ego is too immature to gather all the phenomena into the area of personal omnipotence.
>
> (p. 104)

In this thinking, the traumatic experience is *that which could not be elaborated psychically* (Botella and Botella, 2005). An essential characteristic of the fear of breakdown as depicted by Winnicott is the compulsive pursuit of an event from the past – in the future. As always, we return to Freud (1895), who described the core of the anxiety neurosis being an anxious, compulsive expectation of a catastrophe in the future. This anxiousness may appear as an anxiety attack consisting of the feeling of anxiety alone, without any associated idea, or accompanied by the interpretation that is nearest to hand, such as ideas of the extinction of life, or of a stroke, or of a threat of madness. Freud too writes that the anxiety is often of a recurrence of an anxiety that has already happened.

Bion likewise addresses those encapsulated areas of the psyche, and the individual's capacity to dare to communicate with those unconscious, irrepresentable areas of his psyche. The analytic stance capacitating the encounter with these areas of the mind is described by Bion (1970) as "an 'act of faith' [that] has as its background something that is unconscious and unknown *because it has not happened*" (p. 35, italics added). He says,

> we [are] dealing with people who…dare to come to a psychoanalyst, but who really need some sort of assistance which would enable them to penetrate their own resistance, or which would enable them to penetrate whatever this thing is which seems to get in between themselves and themselves.
> (Bion, 1975 in Aguayo, 2013, pp. 65–66)

And this thing which gets in between themselves and themselves is not something that has been repressed, but rather that inaccessible part for which Bion adopts the metaphor of the caesura of birth and the mental events that lie *beyond* it.

The capacity of an individual for being at-one with oneself, for 'becoming O', is experienced as a catastrophic change. It is catastrophic because it subverts psychic equilibrium. It is catastrophic because it is experienced as "death to an existing state of mind" (Bion, 1970, p. 79), hence arousing fear and pain. "Mental evolution or growth is catastrophic and timeless" (Ibid, p. 108). However, when it is contained in the analytic setting, it may be controlled without bursting the mental container. It can then lead not to catastrophe, but rather catastrophic *change*.

Thus, Winnicott refers to the fear of breakdown as fear of encountering an experience encapsulated in the unrepressed unconscious. It is my understanding that catastrophic change is capacitated through an encounter with the unrepressed unconscious *in the present*, in the transference. Since it is unconscious and yet unrepressed, it cannot be known, but one can only 'become' it. One cannot get in touch with these remote parts of the psyche through interpretation alone. These experiences must first be *lived* in the present. This is a transformation in O, a paradoxical, caesural experience in the here-and-now of the analytic setting, perhaps echoing a past experience, which has occurred but as yet not been experienced. It is an experience entailing a loss of identity, simultaneously enabling psychic growth. Paraphrasing Bion's notion of a thought without a thinker awaiting a thinker to think it, one might consider an experience without a self to experience it, awaiting an other, an analyst, to experience it, hence facilitating the patient to experience it and 'remember' it. This experience that has not been experienced, that has not been registered and is absent from the mind, becomes a present event in the here-and-now of the analytic process and acquires *a posteriori* [Nachträglich][1] memory status (Sapisochin, 2013).

Returning to Bion's metaphor of the spectrum of the electromagnetic waves, we might think of those irrepresentable, imperceptible experiences, not part of the sensuous reality that is verbally or mentally communicable. This may be the unknowable 'ultimate reality' that can only be approached through its derivatives in sensuous reality. One can only *become* it.

Guy's anxiety attacks appeared from somewhere beyond the spectrum. The attempts to understand or interpret them dynamically and verbally led to an impasse. Guy's anxiety seems to have been an expression of an inexorable upsurge of tension, a surplus of unbound and intolerable quantity of excitation, originating in primitive unmentalized experiences that the mental container could not contain due to its embryonic, primitive, and immature nature and/or the absence of an external object able to facilitate the transformation and elaboration of the experience.

*

Already at the beginning of his writing, describing the anxiety disorder, Freud (1895) was aware that the anxiety does not derive from a repressed conflict, but rather from primal, almost biological experiences. It seems that we can already find here the buds of the notion of an unrepressed unconscious. However, at this phase of his thinking, Freud had left that which was not repressed outside the realm of psychoanalysis. He writes, "…the affect does not originate in a repressed idea, but turns out to be *not further reducible by psychological analysis, nor amenable to psychotherapy"* (1895, p. 97, italics in the original). However, the anxiety disorder seems to have continued to occupy his mind. He wrote quite a bit about it and seems to have had the intuition that it would *not* be possible to place it outside the realm of psychoanalysis. Without formulating it in so many words, it seems he may have laid the foundation for a differentiation between neurosis encapsulating the repressed unconscious and the part of the personality that is encapsulated in the *un*repressed unconscious. In a letter to Fliess, he writes, "…in hysteria it is *psychical* excitation that takes a wrong path exclusively into the somatic field, whereas here [anxiety neurosis] it is a *physical* tension, which cannot enter the psychical field and therefore remains on the physical path" (1894a, p. 195, italics in the original). He goes on to suggest that anxiety disorder is related to an accumulation of excitation and one cannot find traces leading to a psychical conflict. Freud seems to suggest that in the absence of an appropriate mental capacity, the somatic excitation (beta-elements?) could not be transformed into the psychical sphere and remained as intolerable excess. It has remained in the somatic field and not entered the psychical field.[2]

The traumatic situation then seems to be an excess of excitation, unable to be transformed even in the form of a neurotic symptom. The individual remains as a 'slave of quantity' condemned to the dominance of quantities of excitation he cannot monitor or elaborate mentally. The individual is rendered in extreme helplessness, franticness, agitation, and confusion which can only acquire meaning *in retrospect* through the mind of an analyst.

Clinical experiences with the psychotic parts of the personality have led Bion and Winnicott to pick up the gauntlet left by Freud. Both related to essentially somatic, or almost somatic, experiences, those that have yet not been *experienced* psychically – in Winnicott's writings due to the immature psyche that could not encompass the surplus and gather it into an area of personal omnipotence, and in Bion's writings due to a defected alpha-function and an incapacity to dream.

Hence, the way to psychic transformation is pinned in the possibility to experience the past in the present, for the first time, in the transference. This, I suggest, is possible primarily through the analyst's capacity and willingness to experience the agonies of breakdown in his flesh. It is the analyst who must 'agree' to experience a catastrophic change, to lose his identity, even if momentarily, hence enabling the patient to dare and approach the breakdown that has already occurred and the psychotic part of his personality. Hence, both patient and analyst can experience catastrophic change.

Speculative imagination

Speculative imagination is an expression of the analyst's dreaming and a means of capturing something from the ineffable, irrepresentable emotional truth. "These speculative imaginations, however ridiculous, however neurotic, however psychotic, may nevertheless be stages on the way to what one would ultimately regard as scientific, psycho-analytic formulations" (Bion, 1977c, p. 41).

Could we speculate that Guy is compelled to repeat a primordial trauma that has been burnt and encapsulated in his psyche before it could be experienced or registered as an emotional experience, perhaps even before he was born? Could the dream in which he is in a stormy river with mother, fearing she is about to harm him, tell of his mother's death wish at the time of his coming into being? Could it be that being immersed in psychic deadness herself, she had no space inside her for a foetus experienced as too greedy and needy? Alternatively, could the dream tell of an unconscious phantasy of his?

Reflecting on the way in which Guy severs his nascent thoughts, forbidding them to sprout and develop, I wonder – is he reliving, over and over again an experience of disruption? A phantasy of abortion? Are we, Guy and I, compelled to repeat and relive the trauma – I as the aborting object and him as the aborted foetus? Could this be an unthought thought captured in the unrepressed unconscious awaiting a thinker to think it? Or is this my overvalued idea (Britton and Steiner, 1994), an anchor protecting *me* from drowning in the raging river of caesura?

I assume we will never know what 'really' happened *then and there*, and it is probably of no importance that we shall. Nevertheless, neither one of us, Guy nor myself, have any doubt about the experience in the here-and-now of the analysis.

Notes

1 'Nachträglichkeit' (deferred action) is a term frequently used by Freud in connection with his view of psychical temporality and causality: experiences, impressions, and memory traces may be revised at a later date to fit in with fresh experiences or with the attainment of a new stage of development. They may, in that event, be endowed not only with a new meaning but also with psychical effectiveness (Laplanche & Pontalis, 1973).
2 This is known as the first theory of anxiety, in which Freud related the origin of anxiety neurosis to an excessive accumulation of unsatisfied sexual stimuli, i.e. pure physical tension directly turning into anxiety due to an absence of a capacity for psychic elaboration. Some 30 years later, Freud (1926) developed the second theory of anxiety in which he claimed that anxiety is caused mainly for fear of losing the object and of separating from it. He thus placed the origins of anxiety in the psychical sphere.

Chapter 4

On boredom
A close encounter with encapsulated parts of the psyche

In his introduction to Winnicott's *Holding and Interpretation*, Khan (1986) mentions an incident in which, some six months before Winnicott's death, a group of young priests invited him to give a talk. They asked him how they might differentiate between a person whom they could help by talking to him and someone in need of professional psychiatric help. Winnicott, taken aback by the simplicity of their question, paused a long time and then answered:

> If a person comes and talks to you and, listening to him, you feel he is boring you, then he is sick, and needs psychiatric treatment. But if he sustains your attention, no matter how grave his distress or conflict, then you can help him.
>
> (Ibid, p. 1)

On this note, Winnicott seems to signify boredom as the area which we analyse, the underlying reason why many patients come to analysis, even if unable to pinpoint their unease. Boredom is therefore inherent to all analyses, and will manifest itself sooner or later, if the analyst enables it.

The analyst's experience of boredom

The analyst's subjective experience of boredom can be seen as ranging between lazy, affable daydreaming, empty limpness, and free-floating mentation on the one hand, and troublesome states of emptiness in the face of lifeless silence, or monotonous, intellectual droning on the other. I would like to refer specifically to these states in analysis, in which the patient seems immersed in circular mental activity, going over and over the same stories, sometimes in a begrudging, embittered tone. One patient, at a stage when he could already observe this, aptly called it 'dribbling'. The analyst feels time is standing still. He is weary and his thoughts wander, often feeling guilty. Frequently, he feels he is losing his mind. At times, he feels so emotionally numb that the boredom no longer bothers him; he simply feels nothing, lifeless.

Khan (1986) regarded boredom as a form of character defence, an attempt at petrifying mental space that strives to nullify any effort to make something happen, out of fear of a catastrophe or a regression which the patient deems to be irreparable and from which he fears he might never recover. Moreover, following Winnicott, he saw boredom as reflecting that which is inherently inauthentic. These could be situations in which patient and analyst sink into the comfort of pseudo-psychoanalytic associations and interpretations, but do not touch upon primal anxieties. This could be boredom resulting from dissociation between emotion and cognition, as one sees in Asperger syndrome or obsessional disorders. These are also states in which the patient replaces the environmental holding with a mental self-holding by disconnecting mind and soma (Winnicott, 1949). In these states, the patient becomes his own 'therapist' out of a strong need for control, and the analyst feels superfluous, distant and often, bored. For example, Dana, a young woman in analysis, indefatigably engages in constant 'thinking', seemingly interested and curious about everything, but she leaves no chink in her armour of thought for the analyst to touch her. During one of her sessions, she says, "If I stop thinking, I will die". So used to caring for herself, this patient finds it difficult to wish for someone to make contact with. She has come to analysis out of "intellectual curiosity".

Boredom can emanate from the analysand's massive evacuation of irritability, grievance, and meticulously recited, undigested, unsymbolized stories of his external life, apparently making it very difficult for the analyst to explore the transference or the patient's internal world.

Meltzer (Meltzer et al., 2002b) suggests that with practically all patients there come moments when they bring material that as such is of very little interest, very superficial, that has lost all value as communication. And yet he goes on to say that when we get bored, we can be sure that what is going on is some kind of acting *within the transference*.

I would like to suggest that the experience of boredom in analysis may signify an encounter with a hidden, encapsulated part of the psyche, an area of bidimensional experience. This is a place where unexplored emotional potential lies, impeded from *becoming*, in the absence of suitable primary environmental conditions. In this area, mental activity has been suspended, and experience is rendered meaningless; others are not recognized as existing, essentially there is no *two*. This is a barren area of lack, an encounter with the autistic core of the psyche. The experience of boredom thus emanates from the patient's adhesive identification (Meltzer, 1974), 'sticking' to the analyst who, in contagion with the patient, experiences a sense of nothingness, mindlessness. However, boredom, subjectively experienced by the analyst, may also be an experiential expression of despair, a reliving of primal object relations with an emotionally non-existent primary object. These encapsulated experiences with a dead inner object are often transformed into psychic deadness and emptiness, experienced by the analyst through projective identification, and relived by the analytic couple in the transference situation. This emptiness, I suggest, must find its place in the mind; otherwise, a whole piece of the individual's inner experience is torn off, leaving a black hole in its wake.

I shall try to elaborate on these two forms of narcissistic identifications, i.e. adhesive identification and projective identification, and the interplay between them, the former relating to bidimensional mental functioning whereas the latter relates to tridimensional mentality.

Bidimensionality

Klein (1946) described the internalization of an object already from the beginning of life. However, Bick (1968) observed that not all infants seem to have internalized a containing object. Lacking an internal containing object which can hold the different parts of the personality, these infants seem unable to project into an external object which functions as a container. It seems that a skin object must be incorporated very early on in mental development to allow a space within the self to develop so that projective identification, as a primary means of nonverbal communication between mother and infant, is able to function without impediment (Mitrani, 2001). Bick postulated that the contact of the infant's skin with the mother's, especially between mouth and nipple, creates a sense of a primary containing object. When the mother is not experienced as a safe-enough containing object, the infant creates a phantasy of a skin which has a secondary containing function, replacing dependence on the object with pseudo-independence. Bick developed the notion of a *second skin* with its adhesive quality as a result of her work with children lacking an internal mental space.

Through his work with children with autism, Meltzer (Meltzer et al., 1975) tries to demonstrate certain aspects of compromised mental functioning, which are, in his view, connected to the difficulty in creating a tridimensional conception of self and object, a precondition of the formation of a containing function. Contrary to Bick, who emphasized the faulty character of the maternal container, Meltzer, at first, also describes a structural defect of the subject in his incapacity to form a conception of the object as a container. In other words, the subject remains in a state in which cognition and experience are bidimensional.

The bidimensional experience, which characterizes children with autism, represents a mental functioning in which there is no internal space; only the surface of the object and the self are experienced. In bidimensional object relations, the object is perceived as no more than the sensual characteristics of its surface (similar to the way at the beginning of development that the object is experienced as a sense of softness and warmth emanating from the tactile sensation of the infant's cheek on its mother's breast. The sensation *is* the object). The self is thus also experienced as a surface with no inner dimensions. (It is experienced only in terms of its external properties; no capacity to recognize its inner space exists.) In this bidimensional mode, pain can neither be contained nor experienced. Objects and events cannot be taken in and thought about, since there is no inside; the object is experienced as having no mind capable of reverie, and there is no space within the self for phantasy, thought, or memory. This mode of bidimensional functioning is illustrated by Alvarez (1992) through her patient, Robbie. She writes,

> … He had latched on to a repetitive, highly sensual…type of language; he would, if left to his own devices, go on for years

repeating the same phrases or stories. My mistake in the early years had been to think that because he was repeating them, they still had as yet ununderstood meanings... Gradually, I faced the fact that the emptiness and unbelievable staleness of these stories were filling me with impotent rage, disgust, despair and, worst of all, unutterable boredom. In fact, what meaning there was, lay in *the sensual qualities of the words themselves,* not the stories. Robbie was excited and tickled, not by the content of the stories, but by particular words which he loved to roll around on his tongue. He was fascinated...by the colour and texture of people's voices... Sounds were felt, quite literally, to touch him, caress him, tickle him... I simply began to know that the stories were utterly dead.

(p. 52, italics added)

Boredom, primitive mental states, and the analyst's alpha-function

In these primal mental states, and in the absence of an experience of an internal space, no sense of separate identity has developed. Out of catastrophic anxieties of unintegration, the patient adheres to the analyst, through adhesive identification, for example, by taking over some of the analyst's *external* characteristics, such as certain words, intonation, manner of dress, even the analyst's smell, and making it his own. Thus, there is no sense of twoness. Since it takes two to create something new, the analysis is rendered sterile. This sterility results in a sense of futility and boredom.

Often, the analyst's sense of boredom derives from the use the patient makes of him as an autistic object, trying to turn the analyst into a part of himself, an object with no life of its own, and so strives to avoid becoming aware of separateness and to deny life with all its uncertainties. In this state, the patient omnipotently creates an analysis in which no real contact with another person takes place, contact which might entail the anxieties associated with dangerous human errors and misunderstandings (Ogden, 1995). Therefore, the patient produces material that call up banal, stale interpretations. The analyst finds himself repetitively reproducing the same old interpretations that feel like gravel in his mouth, and finds himself bored while repeating them. In effect, the analyst has been turned into an autistic object, under the patient's omnipotent control, feeling lifeless. With children, this often takes the form of pseudo-playing wherein the patient dictates to the analyst exactly what to say, how to behave, and how to play, to the point at which the analyst feels like an inanimate object in the patient's hands. The analyst may feel surging anger while trying to stay alive or, worse still, may be grasped by a sense of utter exhaustion. Sometimes the patient turns *himself* into an autistic object and sinks into repetitive activity stifling any unexpected emotions. The child or adult, who is not autistic, may perpetuate repetitive behaviour or endless chatter, so as to hold on to the object by keeping it busy, and is also bored, but is afraid to stop lest he lose the object. Alvarez (1992, 1999b), Tustin (1992), and others working with autistic states stress how important it is for the analyst on the one hand, not to force himself to feel interest yet on the other, not to turn into a lifeless autistic object that has lost his capacity to think and feel. These authors suggest relating to the anxiety that lies at the bottom of the desperate clinging and boring, repetitive behaviour, and to the patient's deadening of himself.

With children with autism, and with those for whom mental life has remained undeveloped, in the sense that symbolic thought has not developed adequately, the analyst should use his imagination and fulfil the alpha-function for the patient. It is different from the function of interpretation, which consists of uncovering the symbolic meaning. Here, no meaning has yet been generated, and the process of symbolization has not been set in train. This kind of work consists of filling with meaning something that is void of meaning. While giving them meaning, the analyst is also giving them symbols until they are capable of forming their own symbols. One supposes that this is what the mother's alpha-function does, later allowing the child to introject his thoughts and develop his own symbols (Meltzer et al., 2002a). This is a very hard task since often words are not yet heard as symbols but as concrete objects.

Alvarez (1992) has argued that active reclamation of the lost capacity for hope of the child with autism and his lost ego functions requires a change in technique. Meltzer (Meltzer et al., 2002b) gives an example of an adolescent who draws only geometrical shapes, and when the therapist asks him what he is drawing, he gives geometrical answers: "This is a square, this is a rectangle...". In this situation, says

Meltzer, "There is nothing left but the [therapist's] imagination to give any meaning to the drawing... One of the factors that most inhibits the therapist is the fear of making a mistake" (Ibid, p. 50). However, the important aspect of this situation is that we are presented with an opportunity to perform the alpha-function for the patient, in the sense of searching for meaning. As already stressed in Chapter 2, the element that the patient internalizes is this function of *seeking* meaning, and not a specific meaning or an object that *knows* the meaning. Often, the patient does not respond immediately; therefore, we have no way of establishing whether what we have said bears any meaning or is mere nonsense for the patient. In this kind of work, Meltzer says, we must allow our imagination to roam wild, and we must speak as much as possible. Out of a boring state, we must create something. Anzieu (1989) calls this 'a bath of words'. He describes a patient who had difficulty speaking and remained silent for hours on end. Anzieu recounts how he slowly, through trial and error and guesswork, tried to envelop her in a bath of words that seemed vital for her to be immersed in. From time to time, he says, he was even right in his hypotheses ...

I would like to stress that the experience of boredom when working with encapsulated, withdrawn, or undrawn states is both meaningful and communicative, and yet presents us with difficult questions as to the (un)developmental level and psychic or mental functioning which give rise to this experience in analysis.

A powerful paradigm of the experience of boredom in analysis is conveyed by the analyst trying to survive the repetitive, deadening activities of children with autism. The first example is therefore from the analysis of a little boy with autism, where the need to revive and reclaim him is more evident.

Daniel

Daniel is now in the third year of his four-times-a-week analysis, which he began when he was four. Daniel is an exceptionally sweet child, adorable and immediately lovable, with a misleading, bashful smile, which makes it all the more difficult not to yield to his insatiable need to be cuddled, held and have things done for him, thus denying any separateness between him and his object.

He was breastfed until the age of 13 months, though mother felt that he didn't need her while breastfeeding. She had felt he fed without relaxing and yielding, as if interested in the milk, not in her. The parents felt that there was 'something missing' from the start. He displayed behaviour that the parents found worrisome such as drumming continuously with his hand, crawling in circles, and erratic reactions. At the age of three, he was diagnosed with autism and placed in a special kindergarten. When I first saw him, he was uttering clear sentences, although often in a rigidly repetitive way and tended to repeat and recite sentences he has heard. Often, he will repeat a question in order to elicit a desired and known response. When we met, he did not use the word "I" but referred to himself as "you".

Our relationship began instantly upon meeting. I came to fetch him from the kindergarten, and from the start, he came willingly. On the way, he would recite lines from a children's story, or only *begin* to recite, and wait for me to continue the rhyme. In the room, he did not play symbolic games but repeated actions over and over. Despite this fact, initially, I felt no two sessions were exactly alike, and there was always something different (for example, the force with which he threw things, sprayed water, and so on). I took this as a good sign.

During the first two months of analysis, he scattered everything off the shelves onto the floor. At first, the toys seemed to drop from his fingers, but as time passed, he began throwing them with great force and kicking them around. He would often repeat sentences I had said, such as "Oh, everything is all scattered". Although I remained helpless in the face of the scattering, I decided to wait and see how things would develop. A few months later, he had stopped scattering toys but started to squirt water. This was obviously not play. It seemed as if his experiences were literally spilling out through the holes of his porous envelope. I was there to hold this outpour and begin to assign meaning in my mind to all this. He was not listening, or could not listen, to my words which felt to me to disappear into thin air, just as he must have felt about his experiences, or parts of himself.

As time went by, I felt that my holding these experiences in my mind was not enough. He was sinking into his autistic activities, and I was drifting away in my mind. I realized I must regulate this outpour concretely, for example, by insisting we *both* put everything back in place or wipe the wet floor and furniture before the end of the session, even though he absolutely ignored me when I said it was time to end. Moreover, I needed to introduce new elements that might be attractive for him. Daniel is enchanted by numbers. A 'game' that developed between us during these weeks was when he asked me to count aloud the numbers painted on a toy he found. I complied but, in order to turn it into a game, I counted each number in a different intonation. Suddenly, I would pronounce a certain number in a very loud tone, or in a gruff voice, and Daniel would burst out laughing, drooling out of enjoyment and excitement. He would often ask to repeat this game, which ultimately became repetitive and dead.

In the second year of analysis, Daniel began to use acrylic paints. Session after session, he would fill a jar with water, placing the blue, green, and black paints in a row. He would then pour exactly four spurts of each colour into the water jar. He would stir the water with the brush until it turned into the colour he wished, and then carry it to the sink, pour the coloured water down the drain, exclaiming "black!", "blue!", or "green!" He would accompany this activity with a compulsive repetition of certain phrases such as "one more colour and that's enough", "soon we will have to finish", or "we meet *every* Tuesday". These phrases seemed to give him a sense of omnipotent control, and their repetitive nature helped him conserve sameness and deny any spontaneous, unforeseeable events that might confront him with 'not-me' reality. During these endless sessions, he would use me mainly to help him pour out the paint from the container when he couldn't manage it or when he needed a stronger hand. I seem to be there only to regulate concretely the stream of water or the amount of paint, maintaining the frame. This went on for weeks on end in an exhausting and compulsive way, and, needless to say, extremely boring.

Once, while he was busy with his ritual, I got lost in my thoughts, not even looking at him. Suddenly, he turned to me and asked, "Are you thinking about something?" I was awakened, astonished, and, even though I knew the question was a recital I have heard before, I couldn't help noticing how appropriate it was to the situation. I replied, "Yes, I was wondering why you always use the same colours, and thought what a shame it is that you don't sometimes use the red or yellow". He again responded with an appropriate but parrot-like phrase: "Just asking! Don't talk!" I laughed because it sounded so appropriate and mature and he looked so cute. He enjoys my laughter and so immediately repeated the phrase "just asking!" in an attempt to elicit the same laughter again. Again, this short dialogue soon becomes repetitive and lifeless.

However, the next day he takes out the red, yellow, and white paints and adds them to his usual repertoire. It seems that, when I withdrew, it was he who reclaimed me with his question and impressed upon me his need that I remain an alive object even when he sinks into his autism. After my response, he could resume his repetitive 'play', possibly knowing that I had resumed holding the thinking.

He now continued his repetitive activity, this time using six colours. Sometimes he would ask me to help him pour paint into a jar, insisting that I, too, put in exactly four spurts. When I refuse and propose using a different number of spurts, he yells, saying, "But I want four!" (Suddenly, he says "I" and not "you" while speaking of himself, as if, in face of my "no", he succeeds in better defining his selfhood.) I say, in between his repetitive yelled recitations: "It calms you that it is always the same number, and that I think exactly the same as you, but we don't have to have four. We can use a different number every time. It can be fun when it turns out different each time." He seems to ignore me, but I feel I must speak up, not give in, and not give over to tedium and deadness. I insist on not ceasing to exist as a separate being. Daniel was overjoyed when he felt he had omnipotent control over the colours, but it seems imperative not to grant him omnipotent control over his analyst, so as not to turn into one of his lifeless autistic objects. Sometimes I interpret the terror that surges in him when I am different, when I don't act according to his wishes, since then he feels that I am ruthlessly torn from him. Other times, my existence as an alive being expresses itself through my sincere excitement at the sight of the vivid colours on the backdrop of the stark white sink. This sight is at times enthralling, and I can feel part of a marvellous aesthetic experience, which for a moment creates a sublime feeling of oneness. In this sense, in the context of the infantile transference, I respond as would an ordinary mother to a much younger infant.

In the infantile transference, babyhood feelings which are being stirred up by the analytic situation become directed towards the analyst (Tustin, 1990). However, motherhood feelings are also being stirred up in the analyst and become directed towards the patient. The analyst then responds towards an older child, or even an adult, as if he were an infant, participates or initiates play appropriate to early development, regulates and modifies tantrum, explosiveness and ecstasy, and by doing so, sets arrested development in train.

Daniel reacted almost immediately to my live presence, and his repetitive activity turned more and more into play. He began to experiment with mixing different colours together, discovering which combinations create which new colours. I felt that I too waited in suspense to see which colour would be revealed, and liveliness would at times be restored. Even though every such game would quickly become repetitive, there *is* movement.

Although it is hard to remain alive in the face of persistent deadness, in these cases, especially in the analyses of children with autism, an overly passive stance, trying not to assert one's subjectivity, does not enable life to begin to grow inside the patient, and the analyst then retreats and becomes numb.

The analyst's mind and the patient's deadness

Experiences that should have been registered by the primary object are registered by the analyst by means of countertransference and in this manner become tangible to the patient. I wish to stress that in the same manner, *the experience of void and desolation*, as a central experience in the inner world of the patient, appears first in the analyst's experiential world. As with confusion, anxiety, and other emotions which are hard to bear, so does boredom enable the analyst to feel, sometimes intensely, the forgotten double messages, pain and distress of the small child, who was forced to learn to deaden his inner vitality in order to survive (McDougall, 1989). Therefore, I propose that, while taking into account the vital importance of creating aliveness from within the desolate void, and *in addition* to being compelled to facilitate the realization of the hidden potential of the individual through the libidinal action of psychoanalysis, it is just as important that the analyst be able to bear the experience of boredom and emptiness, without trying to revive the patient in a manner which often seems artificial and forced.

Mariela

In a moving paper, Cecchi (1990) writes of the analysis of Mariela, a little girl aged 28 months, who developed an autistic syndrome as a reaction to a traumatic situation. Mariela grew up in Argentina in the midst of a brutal military dictatorship, where people were abducted, tortured, and murdered. Her development was described as normal until she was 20 months old, when her mother became pregnant under difficult circumstances. Both parents were deeply worried over the political situation and the possible consequences for them. The mother, in particular, was frightened and depressed. Mariela began to change, became withdrawn and sad, played less, and had no appetite. When Mariela was 25 months old, a group of armed men broke into her house and, before her very eyes, beat up her parents and dragged them away bleeding. Mariela was found by a neighbour, crouched in the corner against a wall, panic on her face. A few months later, she was brought to therapy by her maternal grandmother.

At the beginning of her five-times-a-week analysis, Mariela did not speak, walked slowly with rigid movements, did not fix her eyes, and looked like a lifeless doll. She remained frozen and did not respond to any attempt made by the analyst to make contact with her. The analyst made enormous efforts to reach her, never took her gaze away from her, focused all her attention on her all the time. But to no avail. Mariela remained frozen and silent. At some point, during the 16th meeting, the analyst reports that she felt utterly exhausted and discouraged. She did not speak or even look at the girl. Suddenly, this suffocating atmosphere was broken by a sound, the first sound uttered by Mariela since she had come to analysis. The analyst recognized the musical tone 'D'. Mariela was still motionless, and the analyst sang another 'D'. Following this, the analyst was told by the grandmother that Mariela's parents were both musicians and that her mother sang to her on every occasion, with the exception of the last months, when she was depressed.

The analyst then decided to change her technique and to try and actively reclaim Mariela's lost parts, a change which did indeed enable Mariela to take important steps forward and emerge out of her autistic state. The analyst started to sing to the child, songs which Mariela's mother used to sing to her, and also asked the grandmother to bring photographs and objects that belonged to the mother into the analysis.

However, it seems important to pay close attention to the moment at which the child first responded. This was a moment at which the analyst reported that she was feeling dejected and, for the first time since she began to treat the child, did not speak or even look at her. Cecchi feels that at that moment of abandonment, Mariela resorted to her internal good object and cried for it. I would like to suggest that before the analyst could reclaim the lost parts of the child, she had to be with the child in the lost parts themselves, to experience the loss, the despair, and the depression herself (this despair often appearing experientially in the form of unutterable boredom). In this way, Mariela could connect to the depressed primary object, to the mother that was depressed even before the terrible trauma that the child and her parents had suffered. The sound that the child uttered, writes Cecchi, "was an expression from the most hidden traces of Mariela's bond with her mother" (Ibid, p. 407). In other words, only when the analyst abandoned her efforts at reviving the child, only when she 'agreed' to make contact with the depressed and withdrawn object of the *pre-trauma* era, only then could the child relinquish the adhesion to the depressed part and revive in herself the life and hope, the libido and creativity, out of a sense of recognition and integration of the depressed object within her.

Even if we aim at enabling the patient to live psychically, we must first be present and willing to receive psychic communications of deadness. Mariela needed to make prolonged transferential use of the analyst as a dead, depressed, and despaired object, before she could allow the analyst to challenge her.

Thus, it seems vital that the patient find an object that can meet the gap, the emptiness, the desolation, and can bear the fear of loss, finality, and death – out of faith in the possibility of continuity. This is the ability to bear the caesura, a break after which there is continuation, as opposed to a gap experienced as a cutting-off, a chasm. (The capacity to bear the gap resembles the mother's ability to bear the gaps while breastfeeding, to remain in waiting, and still enable the infant to dally, until the moment at which he wants to resume nursing. Similarly, although in a completely different way, sinking into autism may stem from a need to take a breath of air, to rest.) This may be the basis for hope – a moment of suspense in which a promise lies hidden. Absence, therefore, is also potential presence. Phillips (1993) writes, "Boredom…is a precarious process in which the child is…both waiting for something and looking for something…the child is reaching to a recurrent sense of emptiness out of which his real desire can crystallize" (p. 72).

This seems true of the analyst too, as an object carrying the patient's projections and as a new object facilitating the growth of the patient's mind.

When the object too experiences the emptiness as unbearable and catastrophic and tries to artificially enliven the subject, the individual is compelled to turn to protective autistic mechanisms in order to deaden his awareness, so that the lack will not become a chasm and the fear – a dread.

Therefore, it is my view that it is of the utmost importance to make space for the experience of emptiness that resides in the patient, because *it is a part of him.* Through bringing the emptiness and desolation into analysis, the individual makes room for the empty, blunt, dead inner object which resides within him, and which he must find a way to integrate within his psyche. This inner object is a vital part of the patient's inner world, part of his history, and cannot be erased, or filled, so that its emptiness is eradicated.

Ron

Ron, aged 13 years, was initially seen by me in a once-a-week psychotherapy. He was described by his parents as unhappy, listless, and disinterested in his surroundings. He refused therapy because "people cry there", but ultimately turned to his parents and said he was willing to try three sessions.

At our first session, I saw a cute youngster, slightly dishevelled, unfashionably dressed, and silent. To my queries, he simply answered: "I don't know". He mentioned something about wanting to transfer to another school, but then murmured: "What's the use? It'll be the same everywhere". I barely managed to scrape up a few short responses from him. He said he was "plonked in front of the television most of the day … I go to some afternoon spots to pass the time". During most of the session, he was silent while I talked, feeling I needed to put into words what he could not say. I spoke of his feeling alone, sad, hopeless; how he found it impossible to explain what he was feeling and how he felt no one seemed to understand him. He listened. As I continued to speak, tears began to roll down his cheeks. At first, he tried to wipe them away with his finger, afterwards with a tissue he took from the table.

For the next two years, he attended sessions regularly. Initially, as noted above, he was willing to come once a week only, and I realized a lot of work would have to be done before he could commit himself to analysis. I began to think of these long gaps between the sessions as equivalents of the holes within his mind, and that I would have to carry and hold the continuity in my mind in order to facilitate a psychic skin to be formed in him. He was usually silent, always tired, sleepy, with nothing to say. He answered laconically with words like "Okay" or "fine". He didn't feel there was any point in telling me about himself. "I don't feel a need to talk to you", he would say. I tried to describe the feeling of living in an objectless world, or the pain and the loneliness associated with relating to an object unreceptive to his inner experiences. Another time I said that I sometimes felt him so far away, as if in a deep pit, where no one knew he was. I said he felt nothing, not even the need to cry out for help. Maybe he even felt protected. He could be left there, and no one would know. He usually listened, unresponsive or mumbling "I don't know", or smiling, with an expression that spoke of non-comprehension. At times I was silent, thoughtful, sometimes relating to the stubborn entrenchment I felt within him. Often I felt despair, pining for the smallest sign of hope.

I offered to play with him. He replied that it was all the same to him if we sat there in silence or played, and didn't care what we played. As far as he was concerned, "everything was fine". I found it hard to understand what I was doing with him, and felt I had nothing to offer, but he kept on coming, and never missed a session. If he had a test or a school trip, he would call and try to reschedule. That encouraged me a bit. I thought that maybe he was getting something out of the process after all. In the midst of the numbness in the sessions, I often felt sadness, which was also a sign of life to me.

He arrived at one of the sessions with an MP3 player. I asked what he was listening to, and he answered, "Nothing special, I was listening to some music in the cab, a song called *Numb*". I 'jumped', as if

I had come upon a treasure. At last, some meaning in the midst of all this emptiness, and I related to the numbness that *he* felt. He listened but then said that he didn't know what the word 'numb' meant anyway. I asked to hear the song, and he offered me his earphones. The words spoke of feeling numb, tired, not feeling anyone there, hoping to be more like oneself and less like the other...

We developed a routine in which we played for part of the session. He taught me a card game that I wasn't familiar with, and I enthusiastically took to the game. While playing, there was a bit more vitality in the room: competition, provocation, some laughter. At our sessions, I was eager to play the card game and enjoyed it. But then he wanted to play a different game, a monotonous game that bores me to death. We 'played' this for weeks and weeks, and the life slowly seeped out of the room.

It was then, after months of trying to revive him, that I began to realize that it must be important for him that we remain in the midst of this boredom, numbness, and deadness, and that I should not try to enliven, cajole, or try and get us out of those feelings in a forced or artificial manner. He was uninterested in lively games and, on the contrary, seemed to want us to be in a lifeless area. As in the song, he was asking for us to be more like him and be less like me.

However, despite this intuitive awareness, our time together was unbearable. Not only because of the lifelessness but also due to the feelings of rejection that I felt projected into me. I met with his parents who told me that Ron now had many friends and had become very active and popular in school, spending most of his afternoons with friends. Only his school work was deteriorating; nothing interested him. His parents saw nothing of what I was experiencing during our sessions, and I realized that my experience with Ron was unique.

Yet I felt a growing sense of dread about having to get through another hour with him. When he asked to reschedule his hour, I struggled with my desire to give up on the session altogether. We had stopped playing. I felt playing had become forced. He was tired, often silent. His silence felt like an auto-sensual armour, as was his constant handling of his mobile phone. I felt bewildered, ultimately interpreting that when I too am silent, he feels me detached and abandoning and yet, when I speak, he feels I am forcing myself onto him and insensitive. To this he raised his eyes at me but soon retreated to his shell.

I tried to walk the thin line between remaining in this experience of lifelessness and yet without emotionally retreating from him.

As T.S. Eliot writes,

> ... I said to my soul, be still, and wait without hope
> For hope would be hope for the wrong thing ....
>
> ('East Coker', 1952, p. 186)

At times, I spoke of how difficult it was for him to feel a desire for something, even a desire to come here. He said he came only because his parents wanted him to come, but he thought we could end therapy. The difficulty I felt bearing the sessions won through, and I agreed that we should end a few weeks hence, at the summer holidays. I felt very bad about this, but lost hope in my ability to help him.

We arrived at the last session. He was silent. I was in despair. He said he was tired since he had spent the day at the beach. He lay sprawled on the armchair, hardly responding to my words. It seemed as if it did not matter to him that this was to be our last meeting. I felt I had to gather my forces, not to let things die like that. I spoke of my heavy feeling, about how hard it was that we were parting.

I tried to hold on to the theories I believe in, of primitive mental states, of the potential self that has yet to be born, of the need for a live presence. I thought to myself that I must survive this experience, to imbue it with meaning, not to recoil, but had trouble believing in it myself. I felt that some other analyst might help him more, that I couldn't reach him.

He said we had done nothing anyway, so it didn't really matter if we parted. I felt much grief and sadness. I looked at him, he had grown so much since we had first met, and I thought fondly of how much time we had spent together.

I mustered all my strength and said that I thought we had done a great deal together; that I thought he had brought a very important part of himself to our meetings, the tired, numb part that takes no interest in anything. I continued, saying that I thought he had actually shared a great secret with me, that no one apart from me knew. That maybe he had only been able to tell me about it by being with me in this way. I added that I thought he hoped that somebody would recognize this part, and maybe here, that was made possible. Maybe that was the meaning of our meetings. He seemed apathetic, as if saying: "well, if you say so ...", but nonetheless I felt he had been listening and that I may have touched something deep within him. In spite of previous realizations, it seemed I too needed to reach the bottom of the pit of despair, to ultimately awaken on the edge, a hair's thread from the death of the analysis.

I said that I felt it was a shame to part now, and that I wished we could continue, but not against his will. I added that it was hard to meet only once a week and that I thought it was best if we met more, at least twice a week, maybe even every day.

To my utter surprise, his eyes lit up. He looked at me with a gaze full of life, and said that he couldn't think of any other free day for another session. I asked if he would like us to try, and he answered that he was willing to give it a chance. I asked on which days he could come for more sessions (we were meeting on Sundays), and he said he didn't have many options, he could come only on Thursdays and Fridays, and actually on Mondays too ...

I was very moved, a bit confused. I suggested he think about it during the week, and that we would meet again. He assured me that that wouldn't happen, since from the moment he goes out the door, he stops thinking...

I spoke with his parents, and we added three more sessions a week. At the next session, after more than two years in therapy, he arrived in a more alert state. He showed me some scars he has over his body: one on his forehead since he was a baby, one on his back from when he was five years old, and one on his foot from last year. The one on his foot, he says, is the "coolest". He remembered how a nail pierced his foot and twisted inside his skin. He remembered the sound of the skin tearing "flack" ... I felt a shiver down my spine and thought how impervious he was to pain. He added how every time he gets hurt he gets a tetanus shot because he has no record of his vaccinations, and no one knew if he had been vaccinated or not. Now, he said, he can't be given any more tetanus shots since his body was so full of immunizations ...

At another session, he mistakenly arrived two hours early. He waited outside, with nothing to do, but did not give up on the session, only to fight off an oppressive urge to sleep the minute he walked in the room. The boredom and emptiness still dwell in the room, but now they have meaning, thus facilitating our survival.

Still, alongside the boredom, more transference associations appear in the material, and increasingly more emotionally meaningful experiences can be felt. Once, during one of the long silences, I noticed him smiling and asked him what had happened. He didn't want to say. Finally, he told me, in a manner that was not possible till now, that he had been fantasizing an imaginary conversation between us: "I [Ron] would say: 'I was thinking of seeing the movie *The Sixth Sense*', and you [Analyst] would ask: 'What reminded you of it?' I would then say: 'We talked about it at school today'. You will probably say: 'I think there are other reasons. Maybe because the movie is about a boy who goes to a psychologist because he sees dead people, and you feel that you are dead amongst the living ...'".

I was stunned, moved, and said that what he said was amazing. He laughed and said, "Don't take it so seriously, don't get all worked up. It's too far-fetched. But, you see? I can be a psychologist too...".

Ron retreated from anything that could arouse feelings. He sank into a libidinal freeze which produced a sense of boredom and death in the analyst. For Ron, the vital heart of his self and the active quest for object relations have been paralysed, resulting in a predicament out of which Ron could not extricate himself. He was barely able to signal for help but by very faint, fading signals.

Sinking into a narcissistic shell enabled Ron to avoid finding an object that could awaken libidinal longing. Fear smothered his desire to live and love. He forfeited his spontaneous outpouring into object relations, and the outflow was replaced by a longing for absolute withdrawal from life, not into death as non-existence, but into the living death of oblivion, an escape into passivity and the inactivity of sleep, or staring at a television screen. There he felt safe. However, this was secretly experienced as psychic death (Guntrip, 1968).

The difficulty encountered when facing such a closed off, silenced, deadened inner world, with the autistic and schizoid mechanisms that surround it, can cause the analyst to retreat and decathect the patient. Ron found himself at the edge of a precipice he could not cross. However, if *the analyst* can and does cross this gulf when he shows the patient that he knows about it, this is of the highest importance in analysis (Guntrip, 1968). The patient's chance for realizing his life-potential depends on the extent to which *the analyst* is capable of preserving his emotional investment in the face of the patient's retreat. The analyst's capacity to hear the patient's vivid need of emotional relationships and the fear of such relations is of the utmost significance. However, as I have learned from Ron's analysis, it was important that I also recognize the experience of boredom and make space for it as a valuable emotional experience, as an area in which Ron could rediscover his passion or, alternatively, enable it to emerge. Yet the line between contemplation and waiting and between abandonment and loss of meaning is a thin and fine one.

In my view, the numbness Ron projected into me was not an attack. However, even if regarded as an attack, as Bollas (1987b) writes,

> In attacking the object, the infant brings to bear, in reality, a self-state which up to that point has been primarily internal. As the object allows for this misuse of it, its capacity to survive is appreciated by the infant, who needs to externalize and to actualize this self-state.
>
> (p. 119)

Discussion

In these situations of suspension of the patient's mental activity, of boredom, or of emptiness and psychic holes, the analyst may respond with an intense effort of thought in order to try to think that which the patient cannot think, so as not to be overtaken by this psychic death. However, if, as Green (1975) emphasizes, one fills the emptiness prematurely through interpretation, one is repeating the intrusion of the bad object. If, on the other hand, one leaves the emptiness as it is, one is repeating the inaccessibility of the good object. If the analyst goes mad along with the patient, he is no longer in a position to contain the overflow. Green suggests that the analyst give the patient a ventilated space, an experience which is neither meaningless nor saturated with meaning, always keeping in mind the multivalency of meanings. Also, I might add, to remain in a position of searching and questioning. One could say that it is important *to keep in mind* simultaneously the two facets, even if at times we overreact with meaning, or overly withdraw to a meaningless state, so long as we can fluctuate, at least in our mind, in the dialectic space, between the neurotic and psychotic parts of the personality, between interpretation of the defence or avoidance on the one hand, and reclaiming and realization of the unrealized potential on the other, between emotional deadness and aliveness, without denying any part. Phillips (1993) suggests that the analytic stance is in effect 'attentive boredom'. This may be seen as a position comprising this dialectical movement.

In order for the patient to reclaim his aliveness and pull himself out of his frozen state, it is up to the analyst to recognize the patient's hidden aliveness and bring it to light. The knowledge of the existence of this potential aliveness enables the analyst to survive and allows the patient to dare to give life and love the opportunity to peer beyond their frozen barriers.

And yet, as many of those working with autistic states will bear witness, in many analyses, as was the case with Ron and in the analysis of Mariela, it does not suffice to recognize the abyss wherein the patient lies and to attempt to revive him to life. In frozen emotional states, it is for the analyst to search for the hidden aliveness and yet, at the same time, surrender to the experience of numbness, deadness, and boredom. In this dialectic space, boredom, emptiness, and deadness can begin to exist, not only as a thing-in-itself that cannot be thought about, not only as an inanimate object lying in the psyche, but as a feeling (Ogden, 1995).

There is, therefore, an elusive dialectical movement between searching and restoring aliveness and between being in lifeless emotional areas. Collapse in one direction or another, which is expressed by an over-active or over-passive analytical stance, narrows the patient's internal space.

In all three clinical illustrations, the experience of boredom, deadness, and despair was dominant. At times, it was the bidimensional, undrawn states which prevailed, thus demanding a more active technique wherein the analyst tries to reclaim the patient's potential capacity for mental life, as was the case with Daniel. At other times, as was gradually realized with Ron, the analyst must bear these deadening states of anti-life, often experienced as boredom, and facilitate their integration through interpretation. Yet these states must first be allowed to exist. I suggest that in all cases, this experience signifies an encounter with encapsulated parts of the psyche. In the former, it is predominantly due to lack of mentalization, whereas in the latter, it may be a reliving of early experiences with an undifferentiated and undifferentiating, dead, absent, or obtuse primary object. However, it is never one *or* the other. A child suffering from deficit can at other times become an avoidant child. When he becomes avoidant, reclamation by the analyst will be experienced as intrusive. It will then be crucial to approach him with care, delicately; otherwise, he will sink deeper into autistic manoeuvres. In these states, taking over the patient's aliveness might in effect be repeating a major part of the patient's psychopathology within the transference as described by Joseph (1982). It then seems that the pull towards life is split off and deposited in the analyst. The analyst tries to enliven the patient, who reacts slightly and then retreats so that the next step is left for the analyst, and the splitting is perpetuated.

At first, Ron seemed to need me as an alive presence, who could reach deep into the pit in which he lay and attract him to the world outside, and yet, as time went by, and his mind grew, we both encountered the primal object relations that lay encapsulated within his psyche, but never experienced. Ron needed us both to live through and *experience* these primal object relations *in the transference*. The analyst's ability to bear the boredom and experience it as a signifier of a meaningful emotional area enables the patient to begin *experiencing* the boredom. During the times I felt emptiness and boredom with Ron, he himself did not feel bored. He was in a sort of numb existential state. The notation of this experience in *me* enabled *him* to begin *experiencing* it.

Looked at from this perspective, one could say that the boredom undergoes a transformation. It does not disappear; rather, it becomes transformed from psychic deadness into a valuable and meaningful experience. In part, it turns into something more alive and, in part, it remains a potential space in the internal world, a place that can be lived with, a place that was never permitted as valid. Thus, there is, within the wilderness of the psyche, a tiny movement that may occasionally appear in the psyche of the analyst. This is the slight movement that is between an active hope to revive or cure the life forces and an accepting suspension within the boredom, in recognition of it being a part of the psyche.

Chapter 5

Attacks on linking or a drive to communicate?

Tolerating the paradox

In his *Fragment of an Analysis of a Case of Hysteria*, Freud (1905) recalls bringing forth the assumption that Dora was reproaching herself for her masturbation. Dora denied flatly that she could remember any such thing, but a few days later, she arrived wearing a small reticule at her waist. As she lay on the sofa and talked, she kept playing with it – opening it, putting a finger into it, shutting it again, and so on. Freud explained this as a symptomatic act: an act that people perform automatically, unconsciously, without attending to them, as if in a moment of distraction. Closer observation, however, will show that these actions, in fact, give expression to unconscious thoughts and impulses. Freud writes, "He that has eyes to see and ears to hear may convince himself that no mortal can keep a secret. If his lips are silent, he chatters with his finger-tips; betrayal oozes out of him at every pore" (1905, pp. 77–78). Freud seems to identify the urge to reveal one's innermost secrets and communicate one's deepest desires and experiences. This, to my mind, is an illustration of a drive to communicate.

The urge to communicate, alongside the difficulty in communicating, seems to be the Ariadne's thread running throughout Bion's work, from his *War Memoirs* (1997) to his very last seminars, and to my mind, this duality is a very powerful driving force in Bion's need to write.

Intimate experience with disturbed thought processes in the psychotic mind led Bion to develop a theory of thinking in which the container-contained relationship is central. The concept of containment is rooted in Bion's traumatic experiences in World War I

(Szykierski, 2010) and in a need to communicate the experiences of horror to a receptive other. His *Diary* (Bion, 1997), written to his parents in 1919, at the end of World War I, was offered as a compensation for his having found it impossible to write letters to them during the war – even though, as Francesca Bion notes, his *Diary* has none of the nightmare quality he so vividly depicted in his autobiography *The Long Week-End* (1982). "He would have been unable to express his very recent painful experiences, especially to his parents, but it is evident that he had them in mind throughout" (F. Bion, 1997, p. 2). She recalls that during the first occasion they dined together, Bion spoke movingly of his experiences as if compelled to communicate haunting memories.

Already at the very beginning of *Diary*, Bion laments his inability "to be absolutely accurate in some things" (1997, p. 5) and writes that he can only describe his *impressions* of various actions and try to portray his feelings at that time. Further on, he writes,

> I am at a loss now to tell you of our life. Such worlds separate the ordinary human's point of view from mine at that time, that anything I can write will either be incomprehensible or will give a quite wrong impression.
>
> (Ibid, p. 94)

However, the difficulty of communicating is also deeply rooted in the inability or refusal of the significant other to hear and take in unbearable experiences. In his autobiography, Bion (1982) describes a fellow officer's repeated attempts to tell how he tripped into a shell hole filled with a "human soup" made up of body parts, blood, and mud, while his peers repeatedly refuse to listen to him.

Elsewhere, he writes,

> The behaviour, facial expression, and poverty of conversation could give an impression of depression and even fear at the prospect of battle. Fear there certainly was; fear of fear was, I think, common to all – officers and men. The inability to admit it to anyone, as there was no one to admit it to without being guilty of spreading alarm and despondency, produced a curious sense of being entirely alone in company with a crowd of mindless

robots – machines devoid of humanity. The loneliness was intense; I can still feel my skin drawn over the bones of my face as if it were the mask of a cadaver.

(Bion, 1997, p. 204)

In his psychoanalytic writings, Bion often seems to go out of his way to describe the frustration and suffering he feels in the face of an inability to represent and communicate the emotional experience in general, and in the psychoanalytic encounter in particular.

> The experience of the patient's communication and psychoanalyst's interpretation is ineffable and essential... What has to be communicated is real enough; yet every psycho-analyst knows the frustration of trying to make clear, even to another psycho-analyst, an experience which sounds unconvincing as soon as it is formulated. We may have to reconcile ourselves to the idea that such communication is impossible at the present stage of psycho-analysis.
>
> (Bion, 1967b, p. 122)

Furthermore,

> I do not feel able to communicate to the reader an account that would be likely to satisfy me as correct. I am more confident that I could make the reader understand what I had to put up with if I could extract from him a promise that he would faithfully read every word I wrote; I would then set about writing several thousand words virtually indistinguishable from what I have already written... In short, I cannot have as much confidence in my ability to tell the reader what happened as I have in my ability *to do something to the reader that I have had done to me*. I have had an emotional experience; I feel confident in my ability to re-create that emotional experience, but not to represent it.
>
> (Bion, 1992, p. 219, italics added)

Bion writes this in reference to a patient who talked in such a way that he (Bion) could not reconstruct his patient's words and could not repeat them. Indeed, Bion did have an emotional experience but had to have this experience in such a way that he was unable to learn from it. Nevertheless, he wonders if one might not, after all, attribute meaning to the similarity between the analyst's predicament and the patient's situation when he is unable to think. In other words, despite the patient's fragmented thinking and the fragmentation that comes along in the analyst's thinking, does this attack on thinking not tell, in retrospect, some kind of story? The patient's material seems incoherent, but incoherence might be the communication that the patient is trying to convey (Bion, 1970).

It seems to me that Bion is stressing the operation of the non-psychotic part of the mind in the psychotic patient's personality – that is, the communicative aspect in the part of the personality that seemingly cannot think or communicate. Yet it is in the analyst's mind that a new story, one that has not existed before, can be created.

In contrast to his conception of K as a process of getting to know, Bion (1962a) conceptualized −K (minus K) as a process of mis-knowing, mis-understanding, and mis-representing derived from envy. Leaving aside the question of whether this experience of −K originates in the mother or in the infant, and observing *the link* between them, as Bion himself proffers (1959, 1977a), one might observe that a −K *link* in analysis tells the story of an internal object relationship saturated with envy and hate[1] between mother and infant. Hence, one might presume that this relationship, portraying the psychotic part of the personality, communicates an experience in which sense data cannot be transformed into dream thoughts, or a psychic state in which nothing can be known (Schneider, 2005). The patient is thus rendered in a condition where he is flooded with stimuli that cannot be mentalized and that remain as an irritating franticness of foreign objects inside his mind and body. The patient feels he is being driven insane. The psychotic part of the personality cannot or does not want to learn from experience and acquire knowledge. However, it is my understanding that *the urge to communicate this unwillingness, or inability to learn and to know, remains.*

Bion says,

> Certainly, in analysis itself, one does get a sort of feeling that there is something important that the patient is trying to communicate.

He doesn't come and waste his time and his money just about nothing, although he very often says so or even wants to make you believe that it is so.

(1975, in Aguayo, 2013, p. 63)

Just as the link between container and contained in an experience of K – that is, a state of a fertile and emotionally growth-promoting relationship – may tell a story of the internalization of a fruitful relationship between mother and infant, so may a destructive relationship, as in an experience of −K, tell of the internalization of a destructive, projective-identification-rejecting relationship between an infant and its primary object (see also Eaton, 2005). This is a relationship where the emotions were too intense for the precarious self and so were experienced as violently attacking it, or else where the self attacked the part of the personality able to perceive the emotions, in order to protect itself from intolerable psychic pain. The important thing is that they tell a story and are thus communicative (and again, my interest does not lay in the question of whether this originates in infant or object, which is unknowable, but rather in the link between them, which is now an internal link).

Schneider (2005) writes that under certain circumstances, the attack on thinking is a desperate attempt to get rid of all thoughts and not to know, so as to protect the individual's sense of continuity of being – for example, when a person feels that truth will kill him (or those whom he loves and depends upon). Attacks on linking is then a mental function in itself, safeguarding the individual's sanity from breakdown due to it being overwhelmed by internal and/or external reality more than can be borne or contained. Thus, one might explore manifestations of −K driven not by envy, but that rather serve the non-psychotic parts of the personality. This may communicate the prohibition on knowing and the psychic state derived from the person's fear that knowing will bring on psychological catastrophe.

In the first papers of *Second Thoughts*, Bion writes that psychotic thinking is a product of the interaction between environmental and inborn factors, yet predominantly disregards the former. However, in the last three papers of that book, *On Arrogance* (1957), *Attacks on Linking* (1959), and *A Theory of Thinking* (1962b), he moves on to describe the infant's link with the environment and the latter's contribution in the production of the psychotic part of the personality.

Furthermore, it is here that Bion conceptualizes projective identification as a primitive, or rather primal, method of communication and not only as an omnipotent phantasy and a psychotic defence. Bion (1959) distinguishes between "a normal degree of projective identification", sometimes referred to as "realistic projective identification", which is the infant's method of communicating with the receptive mother, and "excessive projective identification", when the infant is left to bear its intolerable emotional experience on its own and is compelled to evacuate in order to survive. The capacity for communication is founded upon a good relationship between the infant and the breast, on the primary object's receptivity to realistic projective identification, where the mother succeeds in actuality to take in the infant's primal communication – for example, the fear that it is dying – and transforms it into a bearable emotion for the infant's psyche.

I suggest that attacks on linking may be a (re)living, in the transference, of a disturbed primal link between the infant and its environment. I would further like to suggest that the notion of attacks on linking, as depicted by Bion, may describe the patient's unconscious, primal communication of an emotional experience to the analyst – an experience that he cannot otherwise communicate. Moreover, this experience in which the patient's and/or analyst's thinking is being attacked in psychoanalysis is thus not only an attack on communication but is also itself a communication.

Hence, attacks on linking may be a manifestation of the drive to represent, as described by Bollas (2002), or the truth drive, as described by Grotstein (2004) – or a drive to communicate, as I propose.

A drive to communicate

Bollas (2002) writes of a drive to represent the self. The desire to represent the self presupposes the self's belief in a good object, which is based in turn on the self's communications of early infantile states to a mother who, to a lesser or greater extent, received and transformed these communications. Thus, the pleasure principle of representation drives the self to communicate with the other, and part of this complex action is the self's unconscious investment in seeking its own truth. The psychoanalytic process of free association, Bollas asserts, incessantly serves the drive to represent the self's unconscious.

Grotstein (2004) assumes a truth drive underlying the quest for emotional truth, which has the fortitude and characteristics of an instinctual drive. This assumption helps us understand why the patient is able to accept interpretations from the analyst, even though these work in favour of the reality principle and against the pleasure principle. Grotstein leans on Bion (1962a), who writes that truth is essential for psychic health. The effect on the personality of deprivation of truth is analogous to the effect of physical starvation on the body. Bion (1992) adds that, at first, the patient cannot find his emotional truth without the analyst's aid.

When speaking of truth, I do not refer to *The* Truth, but rather to truth in transit, suggesting that truth becomes a dynamic feeling related to what is taking place at a certain point in the transference, depending more on intuition than on by-products of sensory perception (Horovitz, 2007). This is not necessarily an empirical truth, but rather a sense of truth that emerges at a moment when different views of an emotional experience are "observed" from different vertices and conjoined in a way that feels *truth-ful*.[2]

And yet this truth is often disturbing and difficult to bear since it entails the *break-up* of a familiar meaning and the *breakthrough* of a new discovery. This in turn threatens the personality with a catastrophic *breakdown* (Bion, 1977a).

I suggest that in addition to the need to meet one's inner truth and to represent it, and in addition to one's need to know oneself, one also has a deep and essential urge to communicate this truth to another and to be known by him. This is one's appeal to the other in order to know and to become oneself. Indeed, the revelation of emotional truth is dependent on an other to facilitate this search and the process of transformation, but this is an essential and yet insufficient condition. We require the other not just to facilitate the discovery of truth; we need him as someone whom we can communicate with and with whom we can share this emotional truth. We need him as an open and receptive container able to hear the truth and take it in – not so as to rid ourselves of it, but rather out of a compelling and uncompromising need to find a receptive object who might hold the intensity of the experience of encountering truth.

Referring to Bion's last three papers of *Second Thoughts*, Britton (2013) describes the original disaster that occurred when there was an attempt to form a link between infant and mother through normal projective identification. Instead of a prototype of communicative understanding being established between infant and mother, misunderstanding created a primitive superego that was hostile to empathic projective identification. This notion, according to Britton, gives *instinctual weight* to the wish to be understood – or, more accurately, the desperate *need to feel understood*. By instinctual weight, he means that, for such a patient, it is survival that is at stake, either literally or existentially.

I suggest that the drive to communicate depicts the urge as well as *the imperative* to communicate one's inner truth. By designating it a drive, I would like to call attention to its fortitude as a powerful motivating force in the functioning of the psychic apparatus. Again, it is psychic survival that is at stake.[3]

A powerful illustration of the drive to communicate one's inner truth is found in Laub's (1992) description of his experience of listening to testimonies in working with Holocaust survivors and their children. He writes,

> The survivors did not only need to survive so that they could tell their story; they also needed to tell their story in order to survive. There is, in each survivor, an imperative need to *tell* and thus to come to know one's story... This imperative to tell and to be heard can become itself an all-consuming task. Yet no amount of telling seems ever to do justice to this inner compulsion. There are never enough words or the right words...to articulate the story that cannot be fully captured in *thought, memory, and speech*. The pressure thus continues unremittingly, and if the words are not trustworthy or adequate, the life that is chosen can become the vehicle by which the struggle to tell continues.
>
> (p. 78, italics in original)

*

An emotional stance of tolerating paradoxes is at the core of the psychoanalytic attitude in general, and at the heart of Bion's psychoanalytic thinking (Sandler, 2005). The notion of attacks on linking, to my mind, depicts a paradoxical, caesural experience in which the attack on linking is also a link in itself. The possibility of moving among different vertices without collapsing to linear, one-dimensional thinking facilitates psychic transformation and growth.

If Bion had simply wished to describe an attack on the analytic process out of aggression, inborn envy or hate, he would not have needed to coin a new concept. Theories of destructiveness, primary aggression, and the like have existed since the outset of psychoanalysis. However, Bion suggests a new, dialectical, and paradoxical thought, which as such remains unsaturated, inviting more and more meta-psychological and clinical thinking, making it possible to approach irrepresentable and ineffable emotional truth.

Bion's patient[4]

Bion (1957) describes a patient with whom the establishment of an analytically potent relationship by means of verbal communication at a certain period in the analysis seemed to be impossible. The patient's speech lacked coherence and consisted of sentences that were remarkably deficient in various aspects of English grammar. Analyst and patient together formed a frustrated and impotent couple. The patient himself observed that the method of communication was so mutilated that creative work was impossible, and he despaired of the possibility that any transformation would come about.

It was tempting to assume, Bion says, that the patient could not bear any creative relationship as a result of envy and hate, yet such interpretations did not lead any further. Bion (1959) writes, "Increasing intensity of emotions in the patient...originated in what he felt was my refusal to accept parts of his personality. Consequently he strove to force them into me with increased desperation and violence. His behaviour, isolated from the context of the analysis, *might have appeared to be* an expression of primary aggression. The more violent his phantasies of projective identification, the more frightened he became of me. There were sessions in which such behaviour expressed unprovoked aggression, but I quote this series because it shows the patient in a different light, his violence *a reaction* to what he felt was my hostile defensiveness. The analytic situation built up in my mind a sense of witnessing an extremely early scene. I felt that the patient had experienced in infancy a mother who dutifully responded to the infant's emotional displays. The dutiful response had in it an element of impatient 'I don't know what's the matter with the child'" (p. 104, italics added).

In time, it became clear that the analyst's insistence on verbal communication was felt by the patient as a refusal to serve as a container for the patient's projections and as a mutilating attack on his method of primal communication; the analyst was identified with an obstructive force that could not tolerate the patient's methods of communication. Bion deduced that he was felt by the patient to be curious about him, but unable to withstand the patient's need that he be a receptacle for his projections. This was experienced as an attack on linking.

The patient's ability to profit from analysis lies in the opportunity to split off parts of his psyche and project them into the analyst, in the hope that their dwelling in his psyche would enable their transformation. This possibility is felt as a primitive link providing a foundation on which, ultimately, verbal communication depended. Bion (1959) writes, "The link between patient and analyst, or infant and breast, is the mechanism of projective identification. The destructive attacks upon this link originate in *a source external to the patient or infant, namely the analyst or breast*" (p. 105, italics added).

The psychological catastrophe experienced by the patient was not only a mutilating attack on his primitive link with the object but also the introjection and identification with a communication-rejecting internal object. This was the experience the patient was desperately conveying in the only way he could, through primal communication. Being identified with a destructive internal object, he was inflicting on the analyst what he himself had been subjected to without being able to mentally integrate it (Roussillon, 2013). Realizing this, and by referring to the transference as a total situation, Bion could ultimately experience what happened in the analysis as itself a communication, and not simply as an attack on communication.

Again, it is important to note that it is not a question of who is guilty or responsible for the obstruction. The significant issue at hand is not to identify the obstructive object, but rather the obstructive *link* relived by the analytic couple, whose realization is facilitated by both parties. Analyst and patient are both cast as characters in the patient's internal world, relived on the analytic stage.

My patient

Tom sought treatment as a result of feelings of emptiness and loss of meaning. The patient, 40 years old, is married with two daughters. Soon after his birth, his mother died abruptly of cardiac arrest, and he was sent to live with her unmarried sister in a distant town, since his father, a depressed holocaust survivor, could not handle raising him. Without going into the details of this analysis, I will say that Tom is very absorbed in his analysis, hardly ever misses a session, and that analysis has become a life-giving experience for him. He has made significant steps in deepening his relationship with members of his family, has widened his social milieu, and has begun to feel much more meaning in his life. Yet the atmosphere in the analysis is often tough, tiring, and at times despairing, especially as a result of his obsessive and laborious speech, with which he fills every minute of our four weekly analytic sessions. He talks incessantly, explaining and developing piles upon piles of theories about himself. Tom is a very articulate person, loves to talk, and often seems to get sensuous and voluptuous pleasure from his words.

Maiello (2008) gives a strikingly similar description of a patient of hers, and I can only quote her words:

> He tended to put in sequence several almost synonymous substantives or adjectives to describe one and the same thing. His conscious intention was to get as closely as possible to the central meaning of what he wanted to express. But the effect was the opposite. My countertransference sensation was of saturation and suffocation, and his circular verbal wrapping up of the content of his message immobilized my mind... His rotatory language induced an almost irresistible sleepiness... I occasionally felt...an equally irresistible impulse or urge to shout or to scream.

Tom often talks for some 30 minutes, then stops and waits for me to respond. When I remain silent or find it hard to gather myself after the barrage of words, he is hurt, withdraws into himself in silence, at times filled with rage – and at other times he falls asleep. Lately, I have begun to feel that Tom has lost his capacity for judgement and insight; he has begun to raise heretical questions about analysis, and elementary assumptions of the therapeutic alliance are beginning to crumble. It seems we are talking in two different languages. He has become very curious about my motives and is obsessed with getting a direct answer as to what I feel or think. When I decline to respond, he withdraws in silence or falls asleep.

The two sessions I will report are clearly ones in which we managed to transform an unmentalized experience (Mitrani, 1995) into a thought, a symbol, or a verbal formulation, as opposed to the many sessions in which we were both caught up in Tom's blurring and numbing functioning.

A session

As Tom enters his session and lies down on the couch, I realize I have forgotten to lay his cloth napkin on the pillow. I go over to the drawer and take out his napkin, he raises his head, I place the napkin on the pillow, and I sit down behind him. He is silent for a few minutes and then says, "I thought I'd ask something, but I know I would have to answer it myself". A few more minutes of silence, and then he says, "I wanted to ask if you mark the napkins in any way and if you keep a specific napkin for each patient, or do you randomly take one out".

I feel an urge to answer and yet I wait. He says he assumes these are not disposable napkins because that would be too much of a bother.

I ask if he has any thoughts about this and he, as always, replies with many words, while building abstract, remote, multistory theoretical constructions. He explains he has no answers, and that answers are of no interest to him. He thinks of it in principle and as reflecting thought processes. He assumes I have all kinds of complex thoughts out of which I arrive at my decisions. The answer in itself does not interest him, but rather the array of thoughts, the way in which they connect until they generate a choice.

I suggest it is important for him to know that my choice is driven by my thoughts about him and are not random or arbitrary.

He says it is nothing to him if it is one way or the other, and that he is only interested in *the principle* by which specific thoughts generate specific choices.

He goes on like this for some 20 minutes, developing his thoughts in an obsessive and exhausting manner, and I feel the threads of thoughts slip through my fingers. I try to break through his obsessive thinking and suggest we think about the feelings he has about the napkin, his relationship to it, what it may represent for him, but I fail to receive any emotional response.

At a certain point, I say, "But what do you *feel* about the napkin!??"

Tom replies spontaneously and very surprisingly, as if something is erupting from a very deep and encapsulated part within: "I can't answer this question, just as I can't answer you about what it feels like to grow up with a mother! I have no idea how to begin to answer this!"

I am stunned by his reply.

I realize the napkin has become equated with mother (and its absence with her absence), and after I recover, I say, "When mother died, you must have felt that nothing made any sense and that your capacity to generate meaning simply collapsed".

My strong urge to answer him at the beginning of the session makes sense now, and I realize that I felt he was turning to me as a curious child turns to his mother. The absence of the napkin seemed to have evoked a multiplicity of questions about me and my inner state of mind. Not receiving any response from me, he must have felt as he had at all those times during his childhood when he failed to receive a meaningful response to his questions – for example: "Why did mother leave me?" or "Why does father not want me?"

In these situations, Tom is drawn into circular, unending thoughts that leave him with nothing. I now understand his obsessive and rotatory talk. His abstract, distant speech has often been experienced as an attack on my capacity to think – as sand in my eyes, as a smokescreen. However, I now realize that the way I feel in the face of his meaningless, obsessive thoughts, may, with the aid of my mind, tell the story of how he used to stand in the face of the vague, blurring answers to his crucial queries. In the absence of a real object with whom he could confront his meaningless experiences, he had remained alone, with nothing and no one but himself. He was caught up in a circular way of thinking by which he tried to explain and elucidate an unthinkable reality, resulting in explanations that are more evacuative than mental.

I interpret[5]: "Each person has his own napkin. I don't mark them, but no two are alike. I know each napkin and to whom it belongs".

Tom listens attentively and remains silent. After some time, I ask if that is the reply he expected, and he says he did not expect any reply, but the one I gave him has touched him.

These are not usual words from him, and I ask him to say a little more. He says that when I responded, all the possible replies were nullified. That is not the reply he expected, but it is the one he *wanted* to hear.

I say, "So you had some possible replies in your head...", but he insists he had none whatsoever.

Indeed, I realize that the minute I replied, all other possible responses, which until now could not be thought, crystallized *in retrospect* – were there and yet were not. They were thoughts without a thinker, awaiting a thinker to think them. This is an illustration of the transference as a new creation in the here-and-now, not simply a repetition. The contemporary happenings in the transference generated something that could not have been realized in the past (Faimberg, 2012).

Tom recalls a barber whom he used to go to as a boy. The barber would take a cloth sheet from the previous customer, shake it, and put it around Tom's neck. Years later, when he visited as an adult, the barber would open a drawer, take out a sheet, and wrap it around him. He assumes that when he left, the barber shook it and returned it to the drawer to use for the next customer.

"This is what you thought I do, too", I say. He confirms.

I say, "And yet you didn't think of this option before". He says he had not.

The absence of thoughts that Tom described was not the result of an attack on his thinking, but rather indicated that the thoughts did not exist for him until my thinking generated/found them in retrospect. This demonstrates the need for an other, an analyst, who by moving among different vertices might set the patient's halted dreaming back in motion.

Needless to say, Tom did not talk obsessively or circularly until the end of this session, and in fact he spoke in an experience-near and moving manner. I could now see clearly that his obsessive thinking – or perhaps his unthinking – was not just an attack on thinking, but rather a specific mode of being, relived in the session with me, presumably telling of an earlier, infantile mode of being. It was an uncompromising attempt to tell me we were speaking in two different languages. In that period of the analysis, it was I who tried with all my might to communicate in verbal, experience-remote language, while the patient unconsciously communicated in a more primal form, reliving early experiences with me. It was he who unconsciously made me feel in my flesh his infantile experience, hence communicating experiences he could not do otherwise, except through primal communication. It was not he who attacked my thinking, but I, in my refusal to hear the occurrence in the room as a communication and, with my stupidity to think he could describe his feelings in a language that was unavailable to him, was the one who was attacking his primal communication. This recreated *and communicated* a −K link in the here-and-now of the analysis. Both of us, analyst and analysand, were on two rims of the caesura, so as to capacitate the realization of this specific link on the analytic stage.

Tom's obsessive speech immobilized my mind, inducing numbness and exhaustion, and could be seen as distancing us from encountering an internal emotional experience. Nevertheless, as Bion writes, "Thanks to the beta-screen, the psychotic patient has a capacity for evoking emotions in the analyst" (1962a, p. 24). These emotions lend themselves to psychoanalytic investigation and equip the analyst with a psychoanalytic vertex of what is going on (Sandler, 2005). The analyst can then identify the emotions evoked in him so as to understand the function of the beta-screen, that is, the story hidden in the specific atmosphere evoked in the psychoanalytic situation. The confused state then becomes dreamable and communicative.

Another session

Tom begins the following session by saying he is still thinking of what I said the day before about the napkin and of the way I said it, and that there was something very kind in it. Something in my voice, a certain nuance that was pleasant – and yet it was hard for him to

Attacks on linking 113

believe it. He feels it is momentary and ephemeral, and he wonders whether to surrender to it or whether not to pay too much attention to it since it is temporary anyway.

He goes on to speak of a neighbour whom he had loved and who he felt loved him too. He would talk to her and she would take an interest in him. He remembers a certain softness he was otherwise unfamiliar with. After a time, the woman got married and left town, and he never heard from her again.

He says that the things I said the day before reminded him of that woman.

I suggest that something in my voice reminded him of a motherly feeling.

He confirms but immediately adds that he must beware not to get addicted to that feeling.

After some time, he adds, "On second thought, so what if it's just momentary – it's still something". And, after another minute, "I had to go through quite a bit to be able to say that. It's not trivial for me. I want to say", he adds, "that I don't think I ever expressed in words the feeling that she was motherly to me. I remember the sadness and disappointment when she left".

We remain silent for some time, and then I say, "Whenever something *is there*, you're immediately afraid you might soon lose it".

Nothing has now acquired meaning. It has become a *no-thing*. This may be a reliving of primal object relations with an emotionally non-existent primary object. As described by Rose (2007), communicating to the analyst an experience of nothingness, of absence, may compel the patient to be in some sense absent. In this way, nothingness as it exists in a patient is symbolized and communicated in the transference. The paradox of nothingness is that it is full of desire, a desire to communicate, but it can appear that the subject communicating nothingness in the transference wants nothing or wishes to nullify whatever there is.

Tom says, "Yes, because when there's nothing, there's no confrontation, just an experience of nothing. The disappearance of what there was opened up a huge abyss, a black hole. The only way to deal with it must have been to ignore it, and in some lengthy process I managed to annihilate it from my experience, but at the same time I annihilated myself. I didn't know this would be the result. I'm held up by some very thin threads – the rest is gone. With just that, I had to build myself up, my whole being".

I am deeply moved by his articulate speech, which succeeds in moving me – in contrast to the distancing and circular articulation we have been used to.

We sink into a long and reflective silence. There is no trace of his obsessive manner of speech. I notice that tears are running down from the corners of his eyes.

After some time, I ask him if he is thinking of something. He says, "I wonder if I could find that woman today. She must be in her seventies. But why do I even think of looking for her? It's as if I need to thank her for something. But why? For what?"

I say, "It's not her you're looking for". And after a moment, I add, "You must miss the feeling you once had, the kindness and the love you felt, the hope you had".

*

Tom communicated his internal world in a primal and unconscious way, the only way that he could. He had relived, or perhaps lived for the first time, an essential, unconscious[6] experience from his internal world in the analytic setting. This was an internal link that was actualized and lived through over and over again throughout his life, until mentalization in the analytic situation could, even if momentarily, stop the vicious circle. Thus, in the analytic setting, at times he was identified with a young boy standing bewildered and helpless in the face of meaningless actual and emotional experiences, when all that remained for him to do was to try to fit in with his environment in a pleasing manner, while I was experienced as an obstructive and attacking environment. At other times, it was I who was identified with the baffled, desperate boy, left numb and unable to think, being confronted by a blurring and dulling object. What at times appeared as an attack on thinking was, in fact, a profound expression and a primal mode of thinking, stemming from an unrelenting drive to communicate.

"To some this reconstruction will appear to be unduly fanciful", Bion (1959) writes of his patient, "[but] to me it does not seem forced and is the reply to any who may object that too much stress is placed on the transference to the exclusion of a proper elucidation of early memories" (p. 104).

Epilogue

Steiner (2000) writes that sometimes the material confronting the analyst is chaotic, and he stands before various types of dissociation, splitting, and fragmentation of both the patient's and analyst's thinking and verbalizing. This may leave the analyst in various states of confusion and helplessness. Nevertheless, the potential to understand arises if the analyst recognizes that the disturbance is itself a clue to what is happening. Once recognized, chaos or contradiction in the patient's material, or an upsurge of feeling on the part of the analyst, may be used as a marker that alerts the analyst to the need to look in a different way at what is being communicated.

Many doors have opened up in Tom's life, but the essential experience of standing behind a closed door has not disappeared and continues to accompany him in many ways, in and out of the transference relationship. Painfully, he acknowledges that he will never be able to decipher something fundamental in our relationship and will never be able to know fully what goes on in my mind.

In one of the sessions that followed the ones I have reported, Tom spoke in an exceedingly incoherent way, and I could not comprehend what he was saying. The sentences were disrupted and referred to material from previous sessions. He spoke as if we both knew what he was talking about, denying the separateness between us, but I had no idea. This had been common in Tom's analysis, but up until that moment, I had not been able to capture it. I felt a growing sense of distress, detachment, and consequent alarm, with no anchor to hold on to, and despite Bion's demand to eschew memory and desire, I was stimulated to make futile attempts to recall what it was that he was talking about. I felt the growing gap between us and the pull to give up and withdraw.

After some time, I said that he assumed we both know what he was talking about, but, in fact, we do not *meet*. He replied with much sensitivity and insight: "Perhaps this is what I do over and over again. I create an experience in which we can't communicate. Perhaps, more than the closeness I say I want to achieve, I want to arrive at a deep conviction that this is not possible. This is the place I'm at. It's a sort of dance and, at its climax, one might feel the longed-for closeness – but then again, it's gone! I keep coming back to the recognition that it's impossible – it's a fracture I can't stitch together. It's the fracture of my mother's death! It's a break at the heart of my consciousness, the place that I pump myself up from".

I say, "It's a place you cannot give up because giving it up will be giving up something essential of yours".

The possibility of encountering unbearable emotional truth and communicating it has a tremendous impact on the mind and on its capacity to grow, and is at the heart of the potential for change.

Notes

1 Although nestled in Kleinian terminology, I suggest that when Bion talks about hate and envy, he is actually referring to "increasing intensity of emotions", more than the individual can bear and metabolize. Consequently, these emotions, *whether love or hate*, are experienced as painfully excessive and violent.
2 Bion offers a paradigm of this notion when he writes,

> A sense of truth is experienced if the view of an object which is hated can be conjoined to a view of the same object when it is loved and the conjunction confirms that the object experienced by different emotions is the same object.
>
> (1967b, p. 119)

3 We recall that a drive (Trieb) is a "dynamic process consisting in a *pressure*...which directs the organism towards an aim; ...and it is in the object, or thanks to it, that the instinct may achieve its aim" (Laplanche and Pontalis, 1967, p. 214, italics in original). The word *Trieb* is of Germanic origin and retains overtones suggestive of pressure, drawing attention to the irresistible nature of the pressure. Following the distinction – already evident in Freud – between the wholly psychic Trieb on the one hand, and on the other, *Instinkt*, with its biological connotations, one might imaginatively speculate that having been transformed into the mental sphere, the instincts might have lost some of their strength and been split into their "by-products". One might further speculate that the transition, or caesura, from instinct to drive may entail what Bion conceptualized as a catastrophic change, thus changing the state of the instincts. In this vein, one might speak of life drive*s* and death drive*s* in the plural, and in this sense, one might refer to the drive to communicate as a derivative of the life and death instincts.

4 It seems that Bion is describing the same patient in both *On Arrogance* (1957) and *Attacks on Linking* (1959). I shall therefore refer to these two descriptions as complementary and will note which paper I am relying upon whenever I refer to one of these descriptions.
5 I deliberately say "interpret", not "say" or "reply". A major function of an interpretation is to illuminate something so as to help the patient release further material. This may often be known only in retrospect, after observing the patient's response to the analyst's verbal formulation.
6 When using the term unconscious, I am referring to the unrepressed unconscious as elaborated in Chapter 3. To recapitulate, repressed unconscious experiences may be represented; hence, they can appear in dreams, slips of the tongue, symptoms, and so on and can be brought into consciousness by interpretation. However, when we speak of the unrepressed unconscious, we refer to impressions that are without representation and so do not require specific mental activity to keep them from consciousness. This is akin to Freud's (1915a) conception of primal repression (or to Bollas's (1987a) notion of the unthought known). However, primal repression is a difficult concept, partly because the label has an unsatisfactory and misleading implication that something mental had been or is being actively primally repressed (Kinston and Cohen, 1986).

Chapter 6

The painful vicissitudes of the patient's love
Transference-love and the aesthetic conflict

> ...we are never so defenceless against suffering as when we love....
> (Freud, 1930, p. 81)

Psychoanalysis began with the treatment of Anna O., and one might say that it began at the point where the analyst could *not* contain and bear his patient's love for him. In the more widely known version, Breuer who had become increasingly fascinated with Anna O.'s treatment is thought to have ignored his wife and consequently evoked her jealousy. Belatedly recognizing her discomfort, Breuer abruptly terminated Anna O.'s treatment. Shortly thereafter, he was called back to find her in the midst of a hysterical childbirth. He calmed her down and, the next day, took his wife on a second honeymoon. Freud recounted this story to his wife, Martha, who

> identified herself with Breuer's wife and hoped the same thing would never happen to her, whereupon Freud reproved her vanity in supposing that other women would fall in love with her husband; 'for that to happen one has to be a Breuer'.
> (Jones, 1953, p. 225)

Freud, it seems, denied the possibility that one of *his* patients might fall in love with him, whereas Martha seemed to intuitively understand the universal nature of the phenomenon. Freud's delayed recognition of the widespread potential for transference-love (Freud, 1915b) may reflect its very force and threat, then, and to this very day too (Spector-Person, 1993).

Initially, Freud regarded the passionate demand for love as the work of resistance in the face of remembering some particularly distressing piece of life history. Yet, he recommended that the analyst "take care not to steer away from the transference-love, or to repulse it or to make it distasteful to the patient" (1915b, p. 166). Kohon (2005) adds, "Can we conceive of an analysis without transference, without the love generated by transference? Love is at the centre of transference... which helps the subject open up his self to another subject and form a relationship with him" (p. 78).

I would like to suggest that one of the essential elements in psychoanalysis, promoting growth of the mind, is the analyst's capacity to contain the pains of the aesthetic conflict (Meltzer, 1988) and tolerate the patient's love. Furthermore, I suggest that transference-love may be stimulated by the aesthetic conflict relived in the transference. The aesthetic conflict, described by Meltzer, emerges between the aesthetic impact of the mother's external beauty on the infant and her enigmatic inside, her mood, tone, or expression, which can change mysteriously, arousing anxiety and uncertainty in the infant. The encounter between mother and infant is described by Meltzer as a moment imbued with beauty and pain:

> [Mother's] outward beauty...bombards [the infant] with an emotional experience of passionate quality... But the *meaning* of his mother's perception, of the appearance and disappearance of the breast and of the light in her eyes, of a face over which emotions pass like the shadows of clouds over the landscape, are unknown to him....
> (Ibid, p. 22, italics added)

Mother wears the Gioconda smile, but the infant does not know what she feels inside and what makes her come and go. Mental pain seems to overwhelm the infant as he is confronted by the fact that the love object, arousing an ecstatic and sublime sense of oneness is also ambiguous, separate, and outside his omnipotent control. Whereas in classical theory it is the *absence* of the object that creates a state of frustration and stimulates thought and knowledge, Meltzer emphasizes the need to discover the inside of the *present* object, and to bear its otherness as essential for psychic development. And so, Meltzer gives love a primary place in emotional development, thus conceptualizing a new attitude to the problem of mental pain (Bégoin, 2000). Meltzer writes, "The psychopathology which we... allege to treat has its primary basis in the flight from the pain of the aesthetic conflict" (1988, p. 29).

I would like to present clinical material from two analyses, representing different facets of the difficulty bearing the patient's love. In the first case, I will describe an analysis characterized, from its onset, by an intense emotional attachment, at times overwhelming in its fortitude, and by open revelations of love, neediness, excitement, and arousal of the patient in relation to me. These powerful emotional expressions aroused intense counter-transferential feelings and dilemmas. I too felt warm and loving feelings towards the patient. However, I was often overwhelmed, bewildered, worried, and persecuted by his love. In a second, shorter vignette, I will try to reflect on an analysis in which I found it very hard to be receptive to the patient's adhesive and intrusive love, and often remained indifferent and distant.

Dave

With Dave, a 27 years old blacksmith, the transferential force was prominent from the beginning. He came to our initial meeting after having smoked grass, feeling he couldn't bear the tension, and at the end, found it difficult to leave. I felt he had stuck to me, and that I had adhered to his excitement. Subsequently, when he asked if he should come twice a week, I hesitated for a moment, perhaps alarmed by the intensity between us. He immediately reacted to the rejection and said that coming once a week was, in fact, a lot...

Dave is the third of five children. Between him and his younger brother are an exceptional number of years which brought up the question as to what had transpired with his mother after his birth. He said he wasn't happy, derived no satisfaction from work, and wasn't sure whether he wanted to be a blacksmith like his father. Above all, he said, he doesn't know if he should marry Donna, his girlfriend, with whom he has a very turbulent relationship.

Since the age of 15, he smokes a lot of grass. When he doesn't smoke, he feels bored, "time just doesn't seem to pass". He spoke of very dangerous, criminal behaviour, and said he likes to feel the adrenalin run through his blood. I said he needed these experiences in order to feel himself, that he fears getting lost, feeling dead. He replied that he knows such states in which he sits mute, and then: "I don't feel a thing. No hunger, no thirst, nothing". In sessions, Dave was preoccupied with our relations. It was something he had never experienced. He spoke of his relations with *his* clients, and how sometimes he becomes "emotionally attached to them". Once, when I said I noticed he finds the separation at the end of the session difficult, he replied that if I noticed such things, perhaps *I* too had become emotionally attached *to him*. He often phoned me between sessions, felt he just had to hear my voice, and that a mere word of mine was enough for him to feel better. He found it hard not to smoke, despite his wish not to. It seemed he needed me like he needed grass, yet I wasn't as available as it was.

When I offered him to begin analysis, he was very moved and excited, and immediately, with no hesitation or question, wanted to set up four sessions. I suggested we continue to reflect about it the following week, and again, he responded immediately to the experience of rejection and said it was fine, and that perhaps I could also tell him more about analysis so he'd know what he was getting himself into. He added how he feared that "Dave the killer would emerge".

In the first analytic session, Dave said he had waited impatiently to see me. He wanted to phone but thought he'd wait. He began reading the book 'When Nietzsche Wept'. "It's about psychology", he said. (He finds it hard to read and didn't say the name of the book quite right, and I realized that he began reading for me and in honour of the analysis, something which deeply moved me.) He said he found himself walking around, laughing, and added he didn't understand what it was that was bursting out from within.

Analysis became the centre of his life. He wasn't interested in seeing anyone; he only waited for our meetings and found it very difficult when we didn't meet. At the same time, he was worried he was burdening me, that I wouldn't have patience for him. He spoke about Donna, how he felt addicted to her like a drug. He disclosed his fears in relation to her, thus unfolding the drama that was to be between us. He spoke of how much he loved her and how much he feared she'll abandon him. He couldn't bear not having complete exclusivity over her. He said he couldn't rely on her love, since love always comes to an end.

He spoke of a premonition that he would have to sacrifice his firstborn. "Donna doesn't deserve to lose a son…", he said. I understood the fear, aroused with such force now, that he had to protect the object of his love from the death he felt he could bring it (perhaps this was "Dave the killer" he feared). He also felt he had to bring dramatic and arousing material to analysis as a way to revive and enliven me, and so assure my wish to continue treating him. Often, he would succeed. I was aroused by the material he brought up, would feel, think, and be alive.

I felt an abundance of material, but at the same time, I was troubled about his immediate responsiveness. Anything I said immediately aroused in him many feelings, thoughts, and memories. He was very attentive as to what moved me, trying to decipher what occurs in the mind of others, what hides behind the other's overt behaviour. He tried to become like me, to connect to me by way of similarity between us. He said that until he met me, he was preoccupied with "all sort of insignificant beliefs", and today, he knows "only a psychologist can really help". He curbed any attempt on my part to say something about the way he cancels himself, feeling that he must be identical to me. I came to understand his need for idealization without, at least for now, any interpretation.

In a way I could not yet understand, his relations with Donna improved, and he could feel his love for her. He was in a state of tremendous excitement towards the analysis and his contact with me. He felt "surging powers, incredible power to create and work". He complimented the analysis to no end and expressed great love towards me. After such an eruption of feelings, he would become silent, alarmed, embarrassed, "soaking in sweat". He found it hard to leave me, and after the first summer break, he returned 'stoned' and unavailable. He spoke endlessly. I related to the way the break had left him feeling injured after he had become so attached to me, feeling I suddenly left and so he felt he had to become immune by being 'stoned'. He said, "the grass is a 24 hour friend", and spoke of how he smokes to feel less vulnerable.

He felt very spiritual and began attending religious classes. He barely ate or slept, wandered the streets at night, gathered a homeless person and gave him a bed in his work shed, adopted an immigrant family and gave them blankets, a heater, some clothes. He gathered around him a group of 'believers'. He was intoxicated and felt he had exceptional powers to read the souls of others. He didn't work, only smoked, wandered the streets, and saved souls.

Dave felt all powerful. I, on the other hand, felt powerless, worried, barely able to speak.

Those about him were worried too. Friends told him he had to stop analysis. His brother wanted to come and see me. I visualized situations in which his relatives break into my office to take revenge on me and my family. I became very paranoid and overwhelmed with very difficult feelings.

Gradually though, I realized, the turbulence Dave was experiencing was due to his feelings of love towards me and the hope these feelings aroused in him. He felt that if he had me, he could do anything. And yet, the relationship with me filled him with deep pain. He was preoccupied with a possible separation between us. He said he thought about me all the time and felt that I am the only one who cares for him. These feelings he had towards me deeply confused him. He said he had once felt such respect towards his father, and now he felt it towards me. The revelation of his love aroused complex feelings within me too. Yet in time, I learned from Dave how important it was that I be able to contain his love. Through these positive feelings for me, he began to get in touch with feelings of love towards his father. He spoke with longing of the many hours they spent together working in the smithy, how he had learned so much from him. He consciously felt a link between his father and me, with the maternal transference remaining primarily unconscious for the time being.

He was overwhelmed with the feeling that he didn't know what was happening *within* me, what *I* was thinking. He tried to interpret every movement I made, every whisper of mine behind the couch, tried to penetrate my mind, and I realized that he couldn't bear not knowing what transpires in the mind of another.

I thought of his mother, whom he barely spoke about. She appeared as someone present in her silence, someone who, it seemed, he could never know what was occurring within her. I said that when he doesn't know what goes on within the other, he goes mad, becomes filled with cruel fantasies, flooded with anxiety that he may be deserted, that who he is, just isn't enough. He listened attentively. Surprisingly, he too, began thinking of his mother. It seems he felt he was unable to decipher what she thought or felt and was helpless in the face of her silence. The following weekend, he spoke with Donna, heard about her past, and felt he understood her more. This time he succeeded in actually talking, and not just knowing the other through primitive communication. I now understood the paranoid anxieties that were aroused in me. It seemed I had responded to his powerful intrusion and his desperate need to penetrate the mind of the other.

He feared being alone over the weekend, and on Friday's session he fell asleep and found it hard to wake up and leave. He felt physical pain all over and on the weekends sought some substitute, once a tarot reader, another time a priest. He felt that only I remained there for him, and he feared I might suddenly disappear, perhaps die, and then he would remain all alone. He was very depressed, unsure as to whether analysis could help him. I also felt helpless in the face of his terrible pain. The analysis was a home for him, and he felt homeless when he left. He felt he had only now begun to live *his* life, yet he was alone. I said his feeling of aloneness, his lack of belongingness, had accompanied him throughout his life, but that perhaps lately, since his feeling at one with me, he has come face to face with the intensity of these feelings.

The analytic frame was too narrow to contain him. He wished to be constantly present in my mind. He wanted to come more, six times a week, perhaps three times a day. "So I can enter your stomach", he said. He felt he needed more and I wasn't always able to respond, realistically and perhaps also emotionally.

Over time, I began to feel in the grasp of a terrible fatigue, a sense of deadness, and struggled to stay awake. During sessions, I was barely able to think, everything felt numb. *Between* sessions, I tried to give meaning to this fatigue. At times, I felt like a child facing mother's silence and deadness, felt that I too was dying. Other times, I was identified with this same, silent, absent mother. I thought he might be conserving something from his childhood, the presence of an opaque, unavailable object.

The more he longed for me, the more mother began to appear in the analysis. His pain was enormous. His need of me and it seems, the primary longing for his mother, flooded him. His mother began to appear in his dreams. He dreamt he drove with a friend's mother to a spectacular lake. The lake was lit with a glowing green light. He drove to pick Donna up, to show her. When she arrived and looked at the lake, the light went out…

I thought about Donna's extinguished, extinguishing gaze, which seemed to reverberate his mother's glance. I said he was finding his mother, dreaming about her, speaking to her, feeling he could approach her more, going out on trips with her and perhaps into a deeper layer within himself. He listened and fell into a deep sleep. I felt there was a lot of devotion and trust in this sleep. When he woke up spontaneously a few minutes before the end of the session, he said that he had wanted to delve deeper within himself for a long time. He thought that's what had just happened. And thus, every time we encountered the empty, numb, extinguished place within, he seemed calmer and felt he could breathe.

He recounted many dreams, trying hard to give meaning to emotional events, felt it was what enlivened him. He said he felt that I didn't say much yet when I spoke, he felt it was precise. I said that when I say something precise, he is moved, has a sense of wholeness, almost ecstasy, as if there is perfect harmony and we are connected. He corrected me and said, "I feel I am connected to *myself*", thus articulating a growing sense of internal unison, a re-experiencing of continuity and the beginning of integration and recovery from interruptions of being. He began to discover the possibility of closing his eyes, detaching his adhesive, clinging attention from the external object, and turn to events of his own mind (Balint, 1959).

In time, I noticed he was now more capable of seeing the other in actuality. When Donna was in a bad mood, for example, he would not be as angry at her, or feel attacked, deserted, or guilty. He was more able to encounter the extent of his ability and responsibility and met the other as an entity outside his omnipotent control. He said, "Analysis let me feel depression and pain and get to difficult places I hadn't the courage to approach before... I even think analysis let me love myself".

Discussion of clinical material: the analyst's capacity to tolerate the aesthetic conflict

I would like to discuss a few thoughts in relation to this analysis and the analyst's capacity to bear the patient's love and the aesthetic conflict (see Young, 2004).

I use the word 'love', although I am unable to define it. I turn to Freud (1921) who writes,

> Even in its caprices the usage of language remains true to some kind of reality. Thus it gives the name of 'love' to a great many kinds of emotional relationships which we too group together theoretically as love; but then again it feels a doubt whether this love is real, true, actual love, and so hints at a whole scale of possibilities within the range of the phenomena of love.
>
> (p. 111)

Or Bion (1962a), who states that "two adults may mean widely different things by the same word 'love', yet this word is one I must use to describe part of what I believe to be an infant's experience" (p. 33).

For a long time, especially during the second year of analysis, when he was at the height of regression, Dave was overwhelmed by the analysis, by his relation to me, infatuated. We were both intoxicated by the analysis. In retrospect, I think it was essential for us both to be immersed within such ecstasy, as any other stance would have been experienced as an intolerable and sudden separateness, leaving him anguished, leading him to encapsulate his true self within the autistic shell he knew so well.

Tustin (1992) stressed the idea that the overflow of ecstasy of at-one-ment, resulting from a sublime sense of 'oneness' experienced by mother and infant, can only be borne if adequately contained by the mother herself. Yet, one must not forget that the breast that enlivens the baby is the one that painfully overwhelms him too. Tustin goes on to say that if the mother's capacity to bear such extreme states is muted, then the infant is left to bear such states alone, and experiences a catastrophic sense of premature twoness. The introjection of the containing capacity, initially felt to be located in the *external* object, leads to the development of an *internal* object capable of sustaining and bearing feelings of ecstasy and love; an object that might form the basis of the patient's own self-esteem (Mitrani, 2001). Hence, the infant is absolutely dependent on another's mind to be able to bear the extremes of love and hate as a 'normal' condition, a condition which generates the 'ordinary madness' of the infantile state (Waddell, 2005). This is the personal madness present later in all forms of love, clearly visible in transference-love. It is the madness of pleasure and desire, of narcissism and idealization (Kohon, 2005).

I am not asserting that this ecstasy is the same as mature love. Yet, I do think that it is an archaic, primitive form of such love, and a precursor to that expressed in later periods when Dave's capacity for integration came to be developed.

At the end of the third year, Dave frequently and openly expressed his love towards me. Even now, I find it hard to quote many of these remarks, maybe a remnant of the difficulty I had in bearing his love, and in acknowledging the intensity and concrete reality of the transference. He said, "I'm lucky I met you in this life. From the beginning, I trusted you as if I've known you for 20 years. I think you gave me new life, brought my soul closer to my body".

This experience that "we've known each other for 20 years" is characteristic of the lovers' certainty that they already knew each other long before they met, and pleads in favour of the psychoanalytic conception that in love, the lovers do not *find* the object of their love but *re-find* it after having lost it in the remote past (Green, 2005).

At the end of the fourth year, Dave recounted sitting on the beach, enthralled by merely gazing at the horizon, not lacking anything. He added, "I feel I'm beginning to gain joy from inside myself, yet I'm also overwhelmed by it. It's as if it's something I've had and someone took it away from me". Again, Dave seems to express his recovery from a broken line of being, through a re-experience of continuity (Winnicott, 1988).

Yet, in order for a space inside the self to be created, where Dave could retreat periodically for reintegration, and for him to bear close intimacy with another person and the beauty of the world, Dave had to tolerate the aesthetic conflict this entailed. That is, tolerate the fact that the person he loves so is the same person who is separate from him, not within his power, an ambiguous person with her/his own independent thoughts. He had to suffer and contain the unknown. This is the apprehension of beauty with all its mysterious and terrifying aspects.

Dave's regression derived, I suggest, from a forceful and painful encounter with the aesthetic conflict. On the one hand, his falling in love with me (and I with him, by way of aesthetic reciprocity[1]) and the beauty he found in our work, and on the other hand, the madness he experienced as a result of not knowing what was going on within my mind, what was going on within Donna's mind, and what had transpired within his mother's mind. The capacity to tolerate uncertainty, not knowing, is constantly called upon in the passion of intimate relations and is the heart of the matter of the aesthetic conflict (Meltzer, 1988). Yet in order for us to meet the aesthetic conflict, and in order for Dave to be able to find anew the 'beautiful mother', it was imperative that I too be able to tolerate the aesthetic conflict, to receive his love and bear the pain of such love.

The ability to experience beauty and love depends on a containing object with a capacity to endure not only our painful experiences but our joyful ones and feelings of love towards it as well. Our capacity to love depends largely upon the way in which our loving feelings have been dealt with, accepted, and validated by an other (Mitrani, 2001). If the mother is unable to tolerate the love of her baby, or is unable to feel she deserves his love, the infant introjects an object that is unable to feel loved or worthy of love. His love fails to be validated.

Dave seems to have been identified with the encapsulated, depressed part of an object experienced as 'dead'. Often, I envisioned a child running towards someone to be embraced, coming up against a brick wall. In one of our sessions, he said with deep embarrassment how he would have wanted me to give him a hug. In retrospect, I think what was even harder for him to say, was that he would have wanted to give *me* a hug. I think of him as a child who remained with a hug harboured within him, with no release, and how this discouraged excitement remained as disquiet, as hyperactivity, as a franticness and tension that needed to be evacuated.

In the fourth year of analysis, Dave said with embarrassment, "I love you", and I was reminded of Winnicott's quote of the subject saying to the object: "'Hullo object!' 'I destroyed you.' 'I love you.' 'You have value for me because of your survival of my destruction of you.' 'While I am loving you I am all the time destroying you in (unconscious) *fantasy*'" (1969a, p. 90).

Dave needed an environment that would allow for the developmental process from object relating to object use, entailing a growing awareness of separateness. The analytic process facilitated his love for the object to gradually go through different incarnations. The love he spoke of in his fourth year of analysis was different from the one that overwhelmed him during the earlier years, and was, I suggest, a more mature form of love.

Some further theoretical considerations

The difficulty tolerating the patient's love is also related to the analyst's own narcissistic conflicts. The analyst must believe he deserves to be loved and that what he has to offer, is valuable to the patient, like the mother who must feel that she really is beautiful as Meltzer says. As in Tamir's (2003) beautiful metaphor, she must really believe that her kiss can magically cure the child's injury – a belief that has more to do with her *playfulness* than her grandiosity.

And yet, it is essential that the analyst be prudent and monitors his countertransference, as the narcissistic needs of the analyst can easily prolong the period of transference idealization (Kohon, 2005).

I do not mean to say that love and idealization are synonymous, yet I agree with Green (2005) that although love is not a by-product of idealization, it can play a very important role in its formation. Although strongly criticized by some Kleinian colleagues, Rosenfeld (1987) argued that it is important not to interfere with a patient's idealization *just on principle*. After all, one of the main tasks of the analyst is to receive the patient's projective identifications, accept and contain them. This is not to say that the analyst should *never* interpret the idealized transference, only that this can wait (Kohon, 2005).

However, even within this perspective, idealization is defensive and must, sooner or later, be interpreted and the patient must give it up. Bollas (1989) argues that when a patient's affection for the analyst, inspiring a particularly glowing account of the analyst, is only interpreted as a defensive idealization leading to a pursuit of the split-off hate, affection and love are discarded not because hate is more important to spot, but from fear of gratifying the patient's wishes. He describes a patient who needed the analyst to find some way to talk about the patient's affection for him, an affection that was an outcome of their collaboration together, not just a transference expression of love of mother or father. In one session, after working fruitfully on a dream together, the patient was really almost ecstatic. Bollas decided to comment on the pleasures of their relationship and said, 'Not a bad team, are we!' and the patient replied, 'No, not half bad at all. In fact, terrific'. The patient could now talk freely about his gratitude and love of the analyst.

Bollas (1989) notes that we are often too willing to head for analysis of the negative transference, ostensibly because this is where the rough work is, but in fact because we often feel on surer ground analysing hate. Yet Bion (1962a) reminds us that "the part played by love may escape notice because envy, rivalry and hate obscure it, although *hate would not exist if love were not present*" (p. 10, italics added).

I think that our special attentiveness, the safety we provide our patients in the analytic setting, has the power to arouse strong feelings of love. This is perhaps similar to the feelings of love and gratitude spontaneously aroused in the infant in response to his mother's love and care (Klein, 1937).

Discussing this controversy further from a Kleinian perspective, Likierman (2001) cautions against the notion that only a moderate, good experience amounts to realistic, healthy love, whereas an intense experience indicates pathological, defensive, manic idealization. Since an ideal love is more primitive and thus earlier, one might conclude that according to Klein the infant does not love at first, only idealizes. However, primitive love, idealization, and mature love are in constant dialectic interplay. In fact, Klein (1944) too acknowledged the observation "…that love in some sense is discernible within earliest stages…", assuming that "… from the beginning the mother exists as a whole object in the child's mind, but in vague outlines as it were…" (pp. 756–757). Furthermore, Klein (1957) writes, "I would not assume that the breast is to [the infant] merely a physical object. The whole of his instinctual desires and his unconscious phantasies imbue the breast with qualities going far beyond the actual nourishment it affords" (p. 180). Likierman concludes that not only did Klein add early love to her theory, but she also gave it the central role in infantile mental life. Likierman (2001) concludes that

> …the primary good object cannot…embody the 'whole of [the infant's] instinctual desires and unconscious phantasies' and also form 'the foundation of hope, trust and belief in goodness' without being ideally experienced. But this kind of ideal cannot be due to a defensive exaggeration…for it represents the all-important core of the self.
>
> (p. 96)

It seems we are far better trained in surviving the patient's aggression than his love. The capacity to survive the patient's love, with all its intensity, the ecstasy of oneness, its demandingness, neediness, dependence, and intrusiveness, is no less difficult. In fact, it is often harder. Dave's regression derived, to the best of my understanding, from the intensity of feelings his love towards me aroused in him. *The aesthetic conflict emerges in the presence of the beautiful object and not in its absence.*

The patient's love is especially difficult to bear during a regressive state, for it is a primitive love. The rejection of the baby's infantile love is essentially an inability to accept his dependency needs, since in early infancy, there is an almost complete overlap between the expression of love and the expression of dependency. One of Winnicott's important contributions to psychoanalytic theory is his description of the ruthlessness inherent in primitive love. The normal child enjoys a ruthless relation to his mother, and he needs his mother because only she can be expected to tolerate his ruthless relation to her even in play, as this really hurts her and wears her out (Winnicott, 1945).

The patient's reaction to the experience of rejection: recoil and intrusion

I would like to emphasize not only the ruthless or greedy facet that is difficult to tolerate, but rather the open expressions of love. When the analyst interprets the patient's expressions of love as defensive idealization, or remains unresponsive and silent, or, as I myself thought at the beginning with Dave, that he is trying to comply, this may be experienced as a rejection of the love and as an inability to endure it. In the absence of an object receptive to his love and his sensuality, the patient may recoil from the aesthetic conflict into autistic and schizoid encapsulation and his love may become a frozen, imprisoned love.

The capacity to tolerate love in all its idiosyncratic manifestations, in its hidden, extinguished or extinguishing forms, enveloped by autistic and schizoid mechanisms, is often extremely difficult to bear and can cause the analyst to retreat and de-cathect the patient. However, I believe the patient's hope to realize the potential of his love may depend on the extent to which the analyst can preserve his libidinal investment in the patient, and hear the patient's need, and fear, of loving relations. In order for the patient to re-own his love, in order for him to be able to retrieve it out of its frozen state, it is imperative that the analyst recognize this hidden love and bring it out into the light incessantly. Rather than interpreting the attack, or the anxiety aroused in the *absence* of the object, it may be important for the analyst to interpret these powerful feelings, even if hidden, especially in his *presence*. Meltzer used to say you can't love the unlovable, so we need to seek out the tiny developing part which *is* lovable (Meg Harris-Williams, personal communication). Love may become the strongest of resistances before its hidden nature is recognized (Green, 2005).

When we come upon the primitive edge of experience, when the world is experienced in an autistic-contiguous mode (Ogden, 1989), experience is sensation-dominated, and emotions are experienced concretely. Primitive love is expressed through bodily adhesiveness, with no capacity to introjectively identify with the loved object. Love is degraded into sensuality. This is clearly visible in the intense possessiveness of the object prominent in children with autism. But as Meltzer (in Meltzer et al., 1975) suggests, what often appears as a ruthless cruelty to the mother's other babies is not dictated by sadism, but rather emerges in the service of an uncompromising and joyous possessiveness of the maternal object. This possessiveness constitutes a primitive form of love which is both tender and highly sensual.

When the mother cannot reciprocate the baby's adoration of the aesthetic object and rejects his passionate communications, the child must penetrate secretly, in phantasy, inside the mother, through intrusive identification, in an attempt to re-establish contact and deny rejection (Fano Cassese, 2002). Britton (1992) adds that if the patient feels he cannot 'get through', then an intensification may occur in his efforts to project and enforce feelings within the analyst. This often produces a vicious circle, since we are all apt to respond to such pressure from patients by 'hardening' inside. We may communicate this hardening in our choice of words or in our tone of voice. This, in turn, provokes more efforts to intrude forcibly.

At times, the patient's intrusiveness is very concrete, as in bringing gifts for the analyst and imploring they remain in the consulting room, or in bringing food. The refusal to accept these gifts may be experienced as a painful refusal of the patient's love and generosity. Freud (1913a) describes a patient who went through a period of severe depression following his request that she will not bring him any more flowers. Only later did he realize that his request was experienced as a rejection of the love and tenderness she offered him, thus reproducing the humiliating rejection of her love for her father.

Bion (1967c) noticed that there is great difference between a patient who is capable of love and admiration and a patient who has no particular capacity for affection but a great need to be its recipient (or perhaps this might be the same patient at different phases of the analysis or even of a single session). Bion describes his patient as one who felt an intense need for someone for whom he could entertain feelings of reverence and awe. Although Dave's love was often a primitive love, I think Dave was such a patient, and child, in search of an outlet for feelings of love and awe.

In the following vignette, I will present material from the analysis of Joe, where erotization was more prominent, and still not to exclude genuine feelings of love, distorted and intertwined in a perverse internal psychic world.

Joe

Joe was in his sixth year of analysis which had become very exhausting and persecutory for me, subsequently arousing guilt and feelings of impotence in me. His narcissistic, adhesive identification (Meltzer, 1974) was predominant, and soon there was no space between us, no mental space where something fruitful might be conceived. For many months, I had thought and interpreted his autistic, omnipotent defences against any awareness of twoness, but to no avail. I felt he was adhering to me as he began sounding and even dressing like me, whereas I was becoming emotionally distant, unable to think.[2] At times, I felt he was teasing me, provoking me, while all the time very attentive to my emotional reactions and to the effect he had on me. If he felt he had gone too far, and I might become irritated, he would immediately retreat and become the 'perfect' patient, apparently freely associating, 'dreaming', etc. I felt a perverse, sado-masochistic dance emerging between us.

Throughout the years, Joe used to bring me many gifts, which I felt were very intrusive. These consisted mostly of food from exotic countries he had visited, and I felt he was literally trying to get into my body. On one occasion, he had brought me a painting he wished me to hang on the wall of my consulting room. I accepted the painting, as I did with the other gifts, but was obliged to refuse hanging it up in my room. This left him feeling angry and disappointed and brought about an escalation of his intrusiveness.

On this particular session I would like to report, Joe was silent for about 40 minutes. He then said there is something he wants to say but cannot. Near the end of the session, he said he had wanted to tell me how much he loved me. I heard him but felt nothing in a way that was alarming for me. I was struck by my indifference to his words.

In the following session, he described a dream. In the dream, he is driving to see me. He can't see whether the traffic lights are red or green and assumes the lights are green and keeps on driving. When he arrives at our session, I am a juggler expertly throwing some balls in the air, but he senses that I am not focused. He thinks to himself that I am experienced enough to throw up a ball every once in a while and so keep the balls moving, yet I'm doing it quite automatically, and this seems to be enough. I felt the dream was a good and accurate description of his analysis with me. I interpreted that the previous session, when he said he loved me, I was like the traffic lights, and he could not sense a response from me: did I give him a green light to enter my mind, my heart? In the absence of an emotional echo from me, he decides to enter anyway. I said he felt I was like a juggler, experienced enough to throw up an interpretation once in a while, but that my heart was not in it.

I feel this is the essence of his analytic experience. He is trying to get inside me, but I'm inaccessible, protecting myself from his intrusiveness. At last, his dream touches me and brings *me* back to my senses. It seems that when I withdrew, it was he who reclaimed me with his dream and impressed upon me his need that I remain an alive object. However, the dream could only touch me after I was awakened by my painful awareness to my striking indifference.

The following day, Joe began by saying that he had looked me up on Google and found out my birth date which was coming up in a few days. He said he was thinking of getting me a gift but was unsure as to what my reaction would be. I interpreted the disappointment and despair he felt when I failed to hang up the painting he had brought me, and that perhaps he could not make sense of my reaction to gifts he had brought in the past. I added that his gifts may be his way of expressing his love and neediness for me, and a means by which to find a place in my mind. He remained silent for the rest of the session, and I felt he was moved. Over the next sessions, I communicated my thoughts that he was not sure whether he could actually find a place in my mind, and often felt he had to sneak in, which left him feeling in danger of sudden expulsion. It seemed that having recovered my capacity to think, and quite literally keep him in mind, the analysis was again set in motion and was released from its impasse. For the time being, at least.

One might caution not to confuse love and intrusiveness, and that the latter is not love. I disagree, for that is precisely the point I wish to emphasize. The patient's love may go through various transformations. Often, it is not pleasant but rather invasive, troublesome, violent – each individual according to his inner object relations, and the capacity required to tolerate it, is vast.

Joe seems to have been identified with a perverse, narcissistic internal object, incapable of conveying love in any other way but a distorted, intrusive manner. I, on the other hand, may have been identified with a detached aspect of his internal object. However, it was only after a long sojourn in my psyche that we could both begin to mentalize this primitive, unconscious internal world of his, and think as opposed to act it in the transference. The difficulty bearing Joe's love was probably due to the psychotic and perverse aspects of the transference and in many ways seemed to amount to defensive erotization.

Joe's love in the psychoanalytic setting lost its symbolic meaning, as may have occurred in his relations with his primary object, where there was no distinction between playing and reality, and forbidden fantasies were actualized.

*

We may ask, why call all this love? I think, along with Kristeva (1987), that the transferential discourse is one of love and that all the complaints and symptoms of the patient are expressions of love addressed to an impossible recipient. I think that when the analyst can hear the expressions of love, the patient feels, often for the first time, that there is an address for his love, that his ability to love can be actualized. Hence, the libidinal action of psychoanalysis may save love from its extinction.

Notes

1 According to Meltzer (1988), aesthetic reciprocity can be defined as "love-at-first-sight on the part of mother and baby alike" (p. 57). Just as the mother with her interior qualities produces an aesthetic impact on the baby, so does the baby, with its marvelous interior qualities, produce a similar impact on its parents. When this does not occur, the baby perceives his mother as unable to perceive its potentialities, and the primary relationship becomes emotionally disturbed (Fano-Cassese, 2002).

2 As described in Chapter 4, often, out of catastrophic anxieties of unintegration, the patient adheres to the analyst, through adhesive identification, for example by taking over some of the analyst's *external* characteristics, such as certain words, intonation, manner of dress, even the analyst's smell, and making it his own. Thus, there is no sense of twoness, and since it takes two to conceive something new, the analysis is rendered sterile. This sterility results in a sense of apathy and futility.

Chapter 7

Obsessionality

Modulating the encounter with emotional truth and the aesthetic object

"Obsessional neurosis", Freud (1926) writes, "is unquestionably the most interesting and repaying subject of analytic research. But as a problem it has not yet been mastered" (p. 113). Indeed, thanks to the contribution of psychoanalytic thinkers in the field of psychogenic autism and primitive mental states like Meltzer et al. (1975), Tustin (1992), and Alvarez (2010), classical psychoanalytic thinking has stepped out of the prevailing and saturated conception of the obsessional patient and has opened up to new horizons.

In what follows, I attempt to explore the implications of experiences with autistic and primitive mental states for our understanding of obsessional mechanisms and the suffering of some of our *so-called* 'neurotic patients'. I refer to obsessionality rather than obsessive neurosis, since I would like to highlight the role played by *primal psychotic and autistic* aspects of the personality in obsessional patients, hence reiterating the imperative of working with more primal, unmentalized layers of the mind. I wish to restate and illustrate the notion that at these primal levels of mental functioning, experience cannot be verbally communicated and dynamically interpreted but must first be lived, sometimes for the first time, in the here-and-now of the analysis. Interpretations focusing on conflicting desires, or linking repressed and displaced parts of the personality with the defences against them, or interpretations adding alternative symbolic meanings, do not reach these patients in a way that facilitates psychic change (Alvarez, 2010). The need to meet the patient at a more primal level of psychic functioning has been highlighted by several authors, yet the obsessional patient seems to present the analyst with a further difficulty. These patients, whose verbal capacity is often highly developed, stimulate in the analyst an overreliance on verbal content, distracting him from the nonverbal and *unverbalizable* elements of the total transference situation. As already stressed, the analyst may then be tempted to work at a more symbolic, insight-giving level, assuming higher psychic and mental integration.

Given the expansion of psychoanalysis and the encounter with patients whose thinking and dreaming capacities are defective, many authors feel that conceptualization of the unconscious in terms of the *repressed* unconscious is not sufficient (see, e.g., Matte-Blanco, 1988; Lombardi, 2009). This is notably evident in primitive and autistic mental states, where experience remains largely unmentalized. The *repressed* unconscious is the focus of psychoanalytic work when dealing with the non-psychotic parts of the personality. Whatever has become unconscious through repression is representable; it can appear in dreams, slips of the tongue, symptoms, and so on and can be brought into consciousness by interpretation. However when we speak of what is unconscious but *not repressed*,[1] we refer to impressions that are without representation, furnishing the psychotic parts of the personality. We are then faced with unrepresented and irrepresentable areas of psychic functioning.

A primitive mental state

Donald Meltzer's work with children with psychogenic autism, "surely the most primitive of all obsessional disorders" (1975, p. 209), has shed new light on the nature of obsessive defences and functioning. Meltzer (1975) views the fundamental mechanism called "obsessional" as consisting of "the separation and omnipotent control over objects, internal or external…as [a]…mode for mastering the evolving complexity of…object relations" (pp. 209–210). The segmentation and disintegration of the child with autism, encountered in a similar form in the obsessional individual, differ from the splitting processes that separate the good and the bad in the self and its drives. "The autistic mechanisms are attempts at a massive simplification of experience, dispersing the experience of objects into their sensory and motor modalities" (Meltzer, 1975, p. 211). This is a further display of Bion's depiction of the splitting enforced upon the individual who cannot bear the complexity of the emotional experience as elaborated in Chapter 1.

To recapitulate, Bion (1962a) stressed that the human mind is limited in its capacity to grasp the complexity of animate objects, especially when the object of investigation is the phenomenon of life itself. Thus, when the emotions aroused are too strong or intolerable for the infant, it may withdraw from the nourishing breast so as to avoid the complications inherent in the awareness of life and living objects. However, hunger and fear of death through starvation force the infant to resume feeding. The infant is compelled to split the material milk from the psychical breast. Hence, it can resume feeding with no need to acknowledge its emotions in the face of the animate, feeding object. The need for love, understanding, and mental development is now deflected into the search for material satisfaction. This search is reminiscent of the obsessive use the child with autism makes of autistic objects and his preference of these over contact with live persons. It is evident in the obsessional patient's split between the emotional and material aspects of the psychoanalytic experience, reducing the aesthetic impact of the analyst to a mere function and avoiding all contact with him as a human, feeling subject.

Intolerance of the live, unpredictable, and uncontrollable aspects of the object, and an incapacity to dream, lead the individual to deaden emotion, and to live in a delusional world of inanimate objects and causal thinking, in which there is allegedly an explanation for everything. Deadening of emotions induces "an over-prominence in the psychotic part of the personality of links which appear to be logical, almost mathematical, but never emotionally reasonable" (Bion, 1959, p. 109). The links are rendered sterile.

Obsessional mechanisms, being a particular instance of autistic mechanisms, serve to control emotional experience so as to avoid catastrophe. This is a way of evading emotional experience in a manner so primitive that it almost falls outside the mental realm (Meltzer, 1975). Meltzer employs the term *dismantling* to describe autistic segmentation, which emanates from the absence of mental "adhesion" capable of binding the parts of the personality in the face of intense emotional experience, and from the absence of a mind capable of holding and containing the overwhelming components of the experience. Dismantling is depicted as a passive process devoid of sadism, in which the self collapses and disperses, its fragments adhering to sensory stimuli in the environment, incapable of being gathered into a complex and meaningful emotional experience. The individual latches on to the most protrusive sensory stimulus at hand, which then colours the entire picture, isolating it from all the other components whose integration might lead to an unbearably complex experience. The sound of one's voice, for example, can become an all-encompassing experience of oneself or of the object. A single sensory stimulus seems to be dissociated from the complex emotional experience, hence emotionality is deadened. Experience then seems to be reduced to a level of simplicity that appears hardly mental.

The outcome of dismantling can often be seen in the analysis of an obsessional individual, when the unending verbosity becomes a cloud of meaningless syllables, devoid of symbolic representations, akin to a smokescreen or sandstorm. Thus, the obsessional patient's verbalizations and explanations are often more analogous to 'autistic objects' and 'autistic sensation shapes' (Tustin, 1992) serving an omnipotent self-holding survival function rather than the communication of symbolic thoughts. Trying to decipher the symbolic meaning of these words often misses the fact that the patient at times cannot think or dream, but rather evacuates the unbearable emotional experience through an outpouring of words.

Ogden (1989) views an autistic-contiguous mode of generating experience as an important dimension of all obsessive-compulsive defences. He believes

> that these defences always entail the construction of a tightly ordered sensory containment of experience that is never simply a symbolic, ideational ordering of experience designed to ward off, control and express conflicted unconscious anal-erotic wishes and fears. This form of defence regularly serves to plug sensorially experienced holes in the individual's sense of self through which the patient fears and *feels* (in the most concrete sensory way) that not only ideas, but actual bodily contents will leak.
>
> (p. 133)

Anal sadism and strong sadistic components of love have been widely understood as fundamental to obsessional phenomena.

However, Meltzer (1975) stresses that the need for omnipotent control is not necessarily motivated by sadistic tyranny or the wish to control sadistic impulses. In fact, he says, one can delineate a spectrum of sadism. At one end of this spectrum, we can place the extreme cruel and violent pleasure with which objects are taken to pieces, while at the other end would be the non-sadistic dismantling of the self encountered in autistic states, merely unhinging the capacity of objects to find one another for intimate contact, inflicting no pain. Between these poles, one can arrange the spectrum of obsessional disorders.

Without dismissing the significance of obsessional mechanisms as a defence against repressed instinctual conflicts, I would like to emphasize their use as a means of coping with the complexity of emotional experience and object relations. This complexity is illustrated in Meltzer's conceptualization of the mother as an evocative, aesthetic object– beautiful and ambiguous at the same time. I would thus like to suggest that obsessionality serves as a defence against encountering the overwhelming impact of the aesthetic object and the emotional truth of the psychoanalytic session, thereby avoiding the threat of change experienced as catastrophic.

Beck (2002) notes that "as finite beings, we can only tolerate so much excitation, so much aliveness" (p. 22). Objects and emotional experiences that arrive unexpectedly arouse and stimulate the mind. In this thinking, the death drive, usually thought of as designed to preserve a constant state by ridding the self of all excitement, serves to modulate the measure of emotional truth and aliveness that can be tolerated by the individual.

The obsessional personality is preoccupied ruminatively with an attempt to decipher how the elements in the world link to each other to generate the feeling of a predictable and intelligible world. This, Meltzer says, can be a foundation from which real scientific activity can emerge, and yet even though obsessional mechanisms can be employed in service of the search for truth and can contribute richly to the scientific spirit, they nonetheless operate on the basis of omnipotence. Often, this is the omnipotent phantasy of omniscience, and the illusion that all can be known and that one can evade any encounter with unbearable otherness and the enigma, mystery, and unknowability of human experience.

When omnipotence is hyperbolical, Meltzer writes poetically, although "the intention of creating a controlled situation in which [one's] love, and love-object, might blossom... [i]ts love object does not blossom but withers, the flowers being painted die, the experimental animal ceases, the frozen section desiccates" (1975, p. 221). This is a deeply tragic predicament, and children with autism, as Meltzer suggests, bring home to us this tragic element that arises from the lack of trust in good objects. This lack of trust, he presumes, stems from a disbelief in the object's capacity to modulate the painful revelation of psychic truth to the fragile and vulnerable self, and distrust that the object would agree to bear this encounter of truth along with the individual.

All this necessitates viewing obsessional mechanisms from a different vertex, redirecting our gaze to the pain intrinsic to the encounter with the intense emotional experience and with the enigmatic, stimulating, and overwhelming object which is separate and thus not under one's omnipotent control. Interpretation of repressed instinctual conflicts is therefore not enough to help the obsessional patient who has withdrawn from an intolerable emotional experience. One needs a fresh viewpoint facilitating development of the obsessional patient's capacity to bear the emotional experience and relinquish the need to segment, separate, and ward off in order to survive psychically.

Premature awareness of separateness and autistic states

A precocious awareness of separateness is at the core of the withdrawal to autistic protective manoeuvres. Tustin (1992) writes that when the child is left to bear the emotional experience on his own, he encounters a premature awareness of 'twoness' and separateness in an acute and abrupt way. He experiences "an agony of consciousness which is beyond [his] capacity to tolerate or to pattern. Various protective autistic manoeuvres are then used to deaden [his] awareness in order to avoid suffering" (Ibid, p. 107). Excessive awareness of emotional truth puts the individual in a state of extreme vulnerability, a root cause of the massive use of obsessional mechanisms, and it is only by helping the patient with this vulnerability that obsessionality can be mitigated.

The capacity to bear intense emotional experience is dependent on internalization of the mother's capacity to contain and tolerate it within herself. The absence of an object able to bear and contain the infant's intense and unbearable emotions is experienced as a sense of catastrophic separateness (Tustin, 1992; Mitrani, 2001) and leads to a severe disturbance of the impulse to be curious. This inhibition of curiosity is often encountered in the transference relationship with the obsessional patient, as well as in the analyses of children with autism, as an inhibition of emotional involvement with the analyst.

Drawing on her work with children with autism, Alvarez (2010) describes patients whose mother's withdrawal was chronic, resulting in states of mind in which the patient is not hiding, but lost. To that I would add cases where there was real and permanent loss of a primary object, where the infant was required not only to mourn her but to actually go on living and developing without her.

Meltzer (1984) suggests that the mind is "amazed" by emotional experience that has not yet been worked on by alpha-function. This is an emotional experience that has never been experienced before, and so does not immediately yield its meaning. To my mind, death or early loss of a primary object would be such an experience. It is a new, unfathomable, and unbearable experience, one the soul has never before encountered. "It has to be worked upon to discover its meaning, but first a container must be found to hold the experience" (Ibid, p. 69).

Tom

I would like to illustrate the fear-laden withdrawal to autistic and obsessional encapsulation in the transference relationship, echoing a past, unrepressed unconscious manner of coping with an overwhelming emotional experience of early loss that could not be mentally metabolized. I will argue that when the patient is approached at a more articulate, symbolic level of mental functioning, he often feels misunderstood, experiences the re-traumatization of a precocious awareness of separateness, and hence resorts to further entrenchment in obsessionality. I will illustrate how obsessional 'thinking', obsessive speech, and splitting between the emotional and functional aspects of self and object operate in modulating and coping with the emotional encounter and the aesthetic impact of the transference relationship.

The following material is from a phase in an analysis in which this experience was becoming more thinkable and thus could be more fully and openly explored.

I will describe a different phase in the analysis of Tom, whose analysis I referred to in Chapter 5. To recount, Tom, an intelligent and successful language editor at a major publishing house, sought treatment at the age of 40 as a result of feelings of emptiness and meaninglessness. From his early history, I will only restate the fact of his mother's abrupt death soon after his birth, after which he was sent to live with his unmarried aunt in a distant town; his father, unable to handle raising such a young infant.

Tom has now been in analysis for some years. I will focus on the patient's obsessional, circular, and repetitive mode of thinking and speaking and highlight the survival function of his omnipotence, a central characteristic of obsessional thinking and functioning. This often serves as a primitive self-holding, counteracting his catastrophic fear of disintegration and spilling out into space and never being found and held again (Symington, 1985).

Tom speaks incessantly, explaining and developing piles upon piles of theories about himself. His descriptions of himself often sound as if he is describing a well-oiled hydraulic system, with mechanisms and valves operated from a carefully planned control panel. Tom loves to talk and often seems to take delight from his words. However, his verbalizations are reminiscent of what Bion (1962a) refers to as a beta-screen, often evoking confusion, irritation, or boredom.[2] This is in effect the functioning of the psychotic part of the personality in which, as elaborated by Civitarese (2015),

> Instead of digesting the psychic tension—that is, the beta-elements—[patients portraying the psychotic parts of the personality] vomit it out. They use words as things and not as symbols. In this way one achieves a fictitious and omnipotent independence... One creates perfect illusory worlds set apart from all rivalry, envy, greed, threat, love and hate.
>
> (p. 1097)

Tom has always been an appeasing patient, with seemingly no needs and making no claim on me. He has the habit of saying the same thing over and over in several similar versions, and I often have the urge to shout "Okay! I understand! Enough!" Many times he talks about something he has mentioned in a previous session as if we both know what it is that he's talking about, even though I have no idea. It seems he does not take account of our separateness or the passage of time, and, by extension, of the notion of finiteness and death. Although it seems this is meant to induce an illusion of oneness between us, often it only amplifies my disconnectedness from him.

It took Tom almost five years in the analysis to begin talking of his feelings about the loss of his mother and to cry, and another two years until he could pluck up the courage to visit her grave for the first time. Even though his mother's death is always looming, he rarely makes emotional contact with this early loss. Lately, however, the increasing emotional contact he has in the transference relationship, and through it with his mother's loss, has begun to arouse feelings of longing in him. It now seems that he can begin to mourn her loss. This is expressed in greater curiosity about me in the transference, as well as increasing claims on me.

It was at this phase that Tom was exposed to the death of my own mother. He saw her obituary in the local newspaper, and I told him about it when I informed him I would cancel our meetings the following week. I assumed that this encounter with death would shatter him and fracture the rigid boundary he had kept between us. However, when we resumed our sessions, he said nothing more about it. No doubt I was more vulnerable myself in the following weeks, but I was also aware of my affinity with Tom, even though our circumstances were very different. I think Tom may have sensed this, if unconsciously, and that it must have confused him.

The sessions continued as before, but with time I began to notice that his speech had become more and more obsessive. For example, he might say, "I think there are things I'd like to say but it seems quite foolish to say them, but then there's this struggle with the wish to say things which are foolish, and then one can always adopt the criterion which says that although it's foolish to say them, it's still something I want to do. The question is which one overpowers the other. Ultimately, after all is said and done, the criterion by which to act should be not to say foolish things, but it's very hard not to say them. Much of the time there are many things I do say because they reflect thoughts or conclusions which I've constructed and determined as axioms, but reality is much stronger, and yet it's probably easier to ignore reality and adhere to axioms which have something magical about them, and there's a meta-rule that's easy to adhere to…".

And he will go on and on like this.

Some months after my absence following my mother's death, I took a week's break. I will present material from the session after my return, in as verbatim a manner as possible, in order to try and recreate its emotional tone as I remember it. At the risk of being tiresome and obsessive myself, I will try to bring the reader into close contact with the emotional experience of the analysis of this patient.

In response to a remark of mine after a 10-minute silence, Tom says, "I'm in a bubble. It's tricky to get out of the bubble, especially in situations where I feel like everything is under control".

I say, "You've closed yourself up in a bubble and you've achieved a sense of control which you're afraid to subvert".

He says, "I'm not afraid. There's nothing that succeeds in producing any need to get out of there". (His voice is very high-pitched and grating, and I realize he's very tense.) He continues, "It's not a rational decision whether to get out or not. I can easily criticize it, analyse it, understand it, succeed in getting myself out of there, but why bother? Why not accept this place I'm in? I can pull a thread but that would be very artificial. I can easily go into this thing which seems artificial and forget this feeling, but that too would be artificial. Conceptually, it's very difficult for me. I look at myself from the outside and it doesn't look good, so my instincts reject it".

He goes on in a gush: "Listening to what I say I realize I'm defending against something. I prefer not to see something. It's not an active preference or something that I stand on my hind legs and push away – I have to choose whether to skip over this little hurdle or not to skip, and I think, what's the point of skipping over it? I don't know what it is that accumulates so that at the end I feel I shouldn't skip. This struggle is always present – 'to do or not to do, to do or not to do.' And since I'm so used to it, it's not really a dilemma anymore because I act automatically in a way that creates the sense of harmony I need so as not to feel any dissonance".

I'm exhausted. I can't see where all this is leading. We are silent for a bit, and then he goes on: "Look, I don't ask you where you were this past week, and even if the question does bother me, it does so very slightly. It's almost negligible. I don't feel the need to ask you because I can live without knowing the answer. I don't need to know everything. But what I say sounds weird because I'm usually very curious, so when I say I can live without knowing, what is this? Pretence? Respecting your privacy? No doubt it's forced, unnatural, but I feel I'm so in control that I can't be persuaded to do otherwise. If I'd look at it from the side, I'd see many things that don't add up, many gaps, evasions, but somehow it's infinite and it's hard to take account of this infinity and gain a sense of control in this infinity. Flowing into this sense of infinity is very scary, and it's the opposite of control".

He goes on and on, and I feel paralyzed. I can think of nothing to say. No doubt this obsessive talk is also very violent. It immobilizes my mind and silences me. Yet more than this, I think Tom inflicts on me the experience of being veiled with words, which he must have felt, thus communicating his experience through primal communication. It seems to me that a primary function of the violence ingrained in his obsessive talk may be to control the possibility that my words might take him by surprise. If he does not let me speak, he will not be surprised; he will not meet my otherness and will not have to face an experience that might move him too much or precipitate catastrophic changes within him.

Later in the session, he tells of someone at work who infuriated him, "Some maniac I feel like ripping out his arteries!" He then goes on to explain: "It's an impulsive solution, but relative. And yet in the end everything is relative, so what criterion should I use?"

Realizing I might be the one whose arteries he would like to rip out, I break in and say, "So you need to control your wish to rip someone's arteries out".

He says, "Yes, but I realize how absurd this is, after all, my viewpoint is subjective and irrelevant".

He goes on with his obsessive speech and finally stops. We are both exhausted, lifeless.

Tom seems to be extremely anxious in this session, as expressed in his screeching voice. He cannot get emotionally in touch with this anxiety; overwhelmed, he needs to somehow evacuate this unmentalized turbulence raging within him. Yet by referring to his wish to rip out someone's arteries, I seem to have addressed his *secondary*, defensive instinctual wish and not his primary anxiety of being overwhelmed with unbearable curiosity and unmentalized emotions. This brings to mind Bion's description (1959) of the patient whose behaviour, isolated from the context of the analysis, might have appeared to be an expression of primary aggression, but Bion contends that this violence might be *a reaction* to what the patient felt was the analyst's defensiveness. Similarly, I think Tom's withdrawal into obsessionality might be a reaction to his experience of me as unable or unwilling to take in his communications. Feeling abandoned, he resorts to verbal self-holding.[3]

The session goes on, and I think of his grating voice, which almost literally scratches my ears. Ultimately, I manage to say, rather inarticulately, "It seems you feel some sort of painful, grating disharmony and perhaps you don't know how to deal with it".

He says, "The problem is that I don't know whether this disharmony is mine or inbuilt, and therefore cannot be overcome. So I'm entrapped".

"What is this disharmony?" I ask.

"I keep thinking that if only I could locate myself at some point where I could feel it's the exact point for me, a place which might reflect everything I need. It's a theoretical, absolutely subjective point. I'm looking for my point of equilibrium, and somehow I call this wish a disharmony. There's no such place".

I say, "The very fact of having a wish and curiosity – is in itself a disharmony. It seems you try to preserve some constant and invariant sound and all of a sudden there are these abrupt leaps, all sorts of wishes and desires that crop up and fracture this continuous sound".

He says, "I try not to get into these places. I invented a new voice for myself – an explanatory voice, but this voice is sterile. I'm tired of being the responsible adult".

He stops for a moment and then goes on: "I'm in a dispute with D [a friend]. I was on the phone with him last Tuesday and suddenly – pak! There was silence and I noticed I was talking to myself. I dialled again but got the voice mail. I tried again, and the same thing. So I called his home number, but there was no reply. I tried his mobile again, but again – a message. I realized he was screening me and I had no idea why. I said 'fine! Let *him* call *me* then!' Usually it's me who makes the calls. Today is the seventh day and he still hasn't called back. I can be the responsible adult and call him. If I could do that and ask why he hasn't called, then even if he didn't say the whole truth, in time it would be possible to say things which are uncomfortable. But I have no strength to get into it. However, I guess there's no other way but to get into it".

I think *I'm* the one who has disconnected from him for the last seven days (as well as in this specific session), and I am touched by his candid and unwitting way of disclosing how much he has missed me and could not find a way to get in touch with me. I realize he feels that it is his unbearable presence that has compelled me to take time off, to leave him.

I say, "I disappeared for a week and you can't understand why, what is it that is so intolerable about you?"

He seems caught off guard. He had not quite realized he was talking about his relationship with me. However, he quickly gets hold of himself and says, "Look, I keep thinking that one can air all sorts of things...". Here, he breaks off abruptly and says, "I've lost what I wanted to say. The thought slipped away."

I say, "Perhaps you tried to dismiss my words with an explanation, and yet something seems to have moved you".

He is silent for a minute or two until the end of the session.

The next day, Tom begins by asking me if I've ever had my tax returns audited. I am taken aback by his forward question, something that is very unusual for him. I think he must have felt shaken by his unexpected loss of control the day before, and that he would now like to regain his sense of control by intrusively entering my mind and body. This might be an expression of activity, counteracting a dreadful experience of passivity. It seems he now forces upon me the same unexpected intrusion he felt from me – an experience that must echo a deep inscription within him.

He is hurt by my not replying directly to his question and says that the fact that I don't reply shows just how much he must be cautious. He goes on explaining and then withdraws into silence and refuses to talk.

Suddenly, he slaps his forehead and says he recalls a dream he had the night before. "It's interesting", he says, "that before coming in,

I tried to remember if I had had any dream last night and came to the conclusion that I hadn't".

He says he dreamed about me. In the dream, he met me and my parents at a restaurant. He refuses to say anything more about the dream and claims he has no thought in relation to it.

I assume that as I did not answer his question, now he will not answer mine.

He then says, "One of the nuances I react to is when you as analyst respond professionally or else, when your personal emotions intervene and disrupt your professional judgement. I have a utopian fantasy that these can be dissociated, but I know that there is a small chance that this might really happen. Whenever I realize that a personal emotion of yours has crept in, I feel an element I can't deal with has intervened and I must break off contact. Otherwise, I might get into a turbulence that's impossible to get out of. I'm busy estimating the right distance to the danger zone. I usually build a protective buffer and take it into account, but in the case of the tax audit, I crossed over into the danger zone unwittingly, or out of enthusiasm, and so I had to stop and back off".

I think that having been caught off guard the day before, he must have felt he had crossed over into the danger zone of an emotional relationship with me.

He next goes into an obsessive discussion about the possibility of neutralizing emotions and the legitimacy of emotions between us. I relate to my being unpredictable when I respond emotionally, or when he encounters me as an emotional person, as he did after my mother's death. He then seems to enter an unbearably overwhelming turmoil that he feels he can't deal with.

Withdrawal into autistic and obsessional mechanisms often stems from the difficulty of bearing the emotional turbulence in the encounter with the loved object.

Tom's attempts to decipher what goes on in my mind have been with us to various extents throughout the analysis. His attempts at "decoding" relate mainly to the "rules" he feels he must obey in order not to infuriate me or drive me to abandon him. And yet at the same time, he makes a big effort to deaden all desire or curiosity about me. The contact with desire inevitably brings him in touch with the lack, as well as with all the terrifying things he might find out.

After references of mine to his dream about me and my parents, he begins one of the following sessions with a long and heavy silence. Then he says, "It's very hard for me to tell you the things I want to say, but I've decided to tell you anyway. I remember telling you that I had never looked you up on the internet, but after your mother died I thought it would be a good opportunity to do so. I saw all sorts of things and I left it there. All this got me into a very difficult situation and I felt I couldn't tell you about it. It might infuriate you, and rightly so. I carried it with me. I realize it's best to talk about these things as soon as they occur before they grow and lose proportion. But to do this, one needs courage, and I don't have any".

Moved by his confidence to tell me this, I say, "The curiosity you felt scared you and you were left alone and flooded by what you found out".

My own curiosity is aroused, and I wonder what he looked for and what he actually found out.

He says, "I'm very curious to know what you think, to interpret you. On the other hand, I avoid trying to find out. I've given up my curiosity or perhaps I prefer to leave it unsatisfied. I'd rather be alone with my ignorance. But your mother's death confronted me with aspects of yourself that I had preferred to ignore. And suddenly it came back to me from the rear door in a way I didn't expect".

I say, "Most of the time you manage to keep your curiosity locked up, but it suddenly broke out and you can't push it back in. It's overwhelming and threatening. You try hard to deaden your curiosity and your desire".

He says, "But why do I do it? I am curious and I do have desires. I manage to lock it up in a box and control it. I do it for some profit I think I might gain, but I can't see what that profit is. There's something very scary about giving these forces the freedom to dance around because they might implicate me in something I won't be able to get out of. It's very dangerous".

"It's very dangerous for you to be curious", I say.

"It's very dangerous to contain *the consequences* of that curiosity, the anger it might arouse in the people around me", he replies.

His fear of infuriating the people he depends on has been a focus of our work for a long time. This is something he is already well acquainted with and can speak of rationally. I sense that the danger he is in touch with may perhaps be different now. "Perhaps not just the anger", I suggest; "Perhaps the pain when your curiosity is left unanswered".

He recalls an incident where he was sitting with some friends, and after drinking some wine, he began asking one of them all kinds of questions about his personal life. At some point, the guy stopped and asked sharply, "What are all these questions?"

Tom says it was a moment when he felt he did things his way, but then, out of the blue, he was whacked.

"I don't always have the ability to understand what others feel", he says, "so I have to remain within the frame and not cross the boundaries. If I do – I receive a blow!"

I say, "When you don't get a reply from me, you're left alone and that also feels like a blow".

He is silent.

I add, "It seems you feel that my reply can help you bridge the desire".

He is silent a little longer and then says, "But how can one bridge this desire? How can one live with this desire in the reality of life? After all, *she's* gone".

Neither of us could have anticipated this sudden encounter with the lost, enigmatic mother, in the here-and-now of the analysis.

He cries quietly.

A few minutes later, he adds, "This is a very strange situation. I have an image that I live in a cartoon where I think I can really stretch pathways in the air on which I can walk, and suddenly it turns out that they are all in the air and I haven't moved an inch; they don't really lead anywhere. I've built all these paths in fantasy, trying to solve the rupture I've experienced. I probably realized that what was – will never be again, but apparently I denied everything, and I'm the outcome of all my denials".

We are silent for a few minutes until the end of the session.

Back to Freud

Many of the notions put forward here have their roots in Freud's elucidation of the obsessional individual. Already in his paper *The Neuro-Psychoses of Defence*, Freud (1984b) described the obsessional patient who in order to fend off an unbearable idea sets about separating it from its affect. He writes that in all the cases he had analysed, it was the subject's sexual life that had given rise to a distressing affect, yet theoretically, he adds, it is not impossible that this affect should sometimes arise in other fields. I suggest that clinical experience shows the significance of a precocious awareness of separateness in the genesis of autistic and obsessional states, experienced at its extreme in the 'dread-ful' confrontation with the actual death of the loved object.

In a letter to Ferenczi, Freud (1912b) writes of the significance of encountering death early in life and adds that in his case, it was a brother who died very young, when Freud was a little more than a year old (although he was, in fact, almost two when his brother Julius died). Freud (1913b) suggested that an outcome of precocious awareness of separateness is often premature ego development fostering an obsessional disposition.

The encounter with death confronts us with our absolute impotence in the face of reality that is not under our omnipotent control. Freud, invoking the loss of his own father, calls a father's death "the most important event, the most poignant loss, of a man's life" (1900, p. xxvi). It is interesting to note that many of the Rat Man's statements to Freud had to do with loss and death (Cripwell, 2011). Freud (1909), realizing the significance of death and the incapacity to mourn in his patient's psyche, writes that he pointed out to the Rat Man that "this attempt to deny the reality of his father's death is the whole basis of his [obsessive] neurosis" (p. 300). The encounter with actual death, especially in infancy when the child is unable to metabolize the occurrence, is an overwhelming emotional experience like no other. I think that the intensity of the emotional experience and the difficulty mourning his mother's death lie at the root of Tom's personality. I would emphasize, however, that despite the traumatic effect of such an event, I refer to the actual death of Tom's mother as an extreme case of premature awareness of twoness and an encounter with the experience of unbearable excess.

Lacan (1959) argues that Freud's first apperception of obsessional mechanisms was that "the object with relation to which the fundamental experience, the experience of pleasure, is organized, is an object which literally gives too much pleasure" (p. 64). Obsessionality thus seems to modulate the individual's experience in order to avoid excess.

Unbearable excess and the flight from the aesthetic conflict

Tom seems to have withdrawn from the aesthetic conflict (Meltzer, 1988) as was described in the previous chapter. This is the conflict that emerges between the aesthetic impact of the mother's external beauty on the infant and her enigmatic inside, her mood, tone, or expression, which can change mysteriously, arousing anxiety and uncertainty in the infant. As I have already mentioned, I believe that mental pain seems to overwhelm the infant as he is confronted by the fact that the loved object, arousing an ecstatic and sublime sense of oneness, is also ambiguous, separate, and beyond his omnipotent control. To my mind, this may be an experience encapsulated in the unrepressed unconscious and cannot be known; it can only be *lived* in the here-and-now of the transference situation.

When confronted with the aesthetic conflict, as when the patient cannot decipher what goes on in the analyst's mind, he may feel that "he has…come into a strange country where he knows neither the language nor the customary non-verbal cues and communications" (Ibid, p. 22). The patient is compelled to face the separateness and a primitive fear of imminent rejection. He may then react by recoil from the aesthetic conflict into autistic and primitive encapsulation on the one hand, or intrusive identification on the other (see Chapter 6). Tom was unable to bear the fact of my separateness and unknowability. He says, "There's no transparency here, and it drives me crazy! The fact that I don't know why you choose this or that drives me out of my mind! Why can't you explain your exact considerations? Is it the big secret of the Coca-Cola formula?"

Facing the unbearable uncertainty and overwhelming complexity of human relationships, Tom withdrew into verbal self-holding and obsessional encapsulation. Often, talking and the sound of one's own voice is a substitute for the absent mother's voice and for being touched by her (physically and psychically). The sound of one's voice and the obsessional use of thinking thus serve as a second skin in place of the mother. This omnipotent narcissistic retreat makes it possible for the patient to avoid the painful encounter with desire and need intrinsic to life. Tom articulated this aptly in one of our sessions when he said, "Life is anarchy. Only death brings order!"

As often happens when faced with autistic and primitive mechanisms, the analyst too may lose his vitality and feel useless, redundant, even mindless. With Tom, I became withdrawn and unempathic myself. We were caught up in a vicious circle of impermeability, withdrawal, and obsessionality. It seems this aroused even more anxiety in Tom, which in turn evoked an excess of unbearable dread, of which he was compelled to unburden himself. Not knowing what occurs inside me, Tom was driven to try entering my mind forcefully, in order to subvert my psychic equilibrium.

Further discussion of clinical material

Bion (1967c) stresses that a patient will accept an interpretation only if he feels that the analyst has passed through an emotional crisis himself as part of the act of giving the interpretation. This requires meeting the patient's dread of separateness and overwhelming emotionality, while avoiding the temptation to meet him on a more neurotic, symbolic, and articulate psychic level. At this phase in Tom's analysis, I seem to have been cast in the role of the despaired and impotent infant confronted by a torrent of words that veiled and concealed the emotional experience, leaving him feeling alone and abandoned.

As underscored by Oelsner (2013),

> it is essential that for the patient to be able to use the analyst as a supporting actor for his internal dramas he needs to rely on the analyst's capacity to play the roles, experience the pains he has been assigned, feel and contain the anxiety thus created, and be able to go on thinking.
>
> (p. 240)

However, it is only in retrospect, "after hours" (Ibid, p. 252) that we can reflect on our enactments and countertransference, which must be experienced before they can be used for getting in touch with the patient's unconscious inner world. Thinking back on moments when I felt despair, impatience, anger, and helplessness, I can speculatively imagine and perhaps reconstruct some of Tom's early experiences, which could be communicated only through (re)living them with me. It was now possible to imagine the despair Tom had felt as an infant, an experience which was unfathomable and which must have enwrapped him in a cloud of meaninglessness, as I often felt in the sessions with him.

Tom first encountered death at a time when his mind could not encompass its meaning or contain the enormity of the surprise, pain, helplessness, and absence of emotional meaning. In this situation, "either the feelings are so powerful that they fragment the personality of the child, or the child simply squeezes the life out of the emotion" (Bion, 1967a, p. 47).

> Obsessive-compulsive symptoms and defences have their origins in the infant's earliest efforts at ordering and creating a sense of boundedness for his sensory experience. Very early on, such efforts at organization and definition come to be utilized in the service of warding off anxiety related to the disruption of the sensory-dominated, rudimentary sense of self.
> (Ogden, 1989, p. 133)

Tom was left alone, without an object who could modulate the intensity of the emotional experience for him. He annihilated his desires and needs and found shelter in words and explanations, primarily as a psychic envelope and as sensory self-holding.

This is movingly described by Mauss-Hanke (2013) as the transformation of a catastrophic experience into an inner *terra cremata*, a "scorched earth" designed to eliminate all sensibilities that were injured in an overwhelming and dreadful experience, an absolute and decisive elimination of emotions and the knowledge they contain. However, as Mauss-Hanke notes,

> one condition of any 'scorched earth' is that it is impossible to erase the field itself. [Whether willing or unwilling] something will start growing again… In this frightening state of finding something uncontrollable developing within oneself, the mind is in a

paradoxical situation: it can never exist without movement, and it hinders any movement with all its power.

(p. 488)

This is the state in which we find the obsessional patient as we face his strong and stubborn resistance to encountering the emotional experience. Yet only by meeting this primordial dread, and surrendering to this inner deadness, can we paradoxically facilitate the revitalization of this inner *terra cremata* and the capacity to dare enter a *terra incognita*, an unknown and unexplored, potentially 'dread-ful' land.

The clinical material I have presented illustrates a moment of opening that sheds light, retrospectively, on Tom's predicament. It was only through living with me, and making me live-through this despair, numbness, and frustration, that Tom could communicate his inner scorched earth and the experiences encapsulated in the unrepressed unconscious.

*

Awareness of separateness is the first step to becoming aware of our mortality. Primitive autistic and obsessional mechanisms serve to modulate a precocious encounter with this unbearable truth. Becoming aware of separateness brings the recognition that we have a body, and hence of our eventual death and decay. This, as Freud (1916b) notes, arouses a revolt in the mind against mourning. Yet the excessive use of obsessional mechanisms tragically brings about psychic death and a persecuted and grief-ridden existence. For, as Freud suggests, only when mourning, however painful, has consumed itself and one can renounce what has been lost, is our libido once again free to replace the lost objects with fresh ones equally or even more precious.

Notes

1 I refer both to dissociated parts of the self that could not be elaborated psychically as in traumatic situations, and to emotional experiences where the ego is too immature to gather in, encompass, and integrate the experience (see Winnicott, 1974).
2 Nonetheless, Bion often stresses the operation of the non-psychotic part of the mind in the psychotic patient's personality – the communicative

aspect in that part of the personality that seemingly cannot think or communicate. Thus, although the patient's material may be confused and confusing, this might yet be what the patient is unconsciously trying to communicate through primitive, primal communication (see Chapter 5).
3 There are, of course, occasions when the aggressive conflict is a primary issue in the work with an obsessional patient, but this is often a more neurotic conflict that can be worked through effectively only once the psychotic, underlying parts of the personality are addressed. Otherwise, this can fall into the patient's masochistic need to wrap himself in guilt or his verbal pseudo-understanding.

Chapter 8

The ineffable

> Know that everything visible and perceivable to human contemplation is limited, and that everything that is limited is finite, and that everything that is finite is insignificant. Conversely, that which is not limited is called Eyn-Sof and is absolutely undifferentiated in a complete and changeless unity.
> (Rabbi Azriel of Gerona, 12th-century Jewish mystic, Explanations of the Ten Sefirot)

The silent, elusive movement of the emotional experience becomes a word when it crosses an invisible border, beyond which lay thoughts, words, and speech. However, this transition from experience to speech entails an essential loss. Experience is simplified and objectified, and the individual is drawn further away from the emotional truth of his being. Thought, right after providing a name, is fascinated by its own power and consequently forgets the reality which is represented by that name. This is the essential argument that Buber tries to articulate: objectification has replaced the encounter, and today one encounters thoughts and words, *not the reality that preceded them*. Buber's analysis seems to be an attack on the tendency of the mind to objectify and then relate to the abstract thought as if it were a real entity (Avnon, 1998). And the psychoanalyst too might become enthralled with the words and forget the inconceivable, elusive reality that preceded them.

Bion (1975) writes,

> ...All of us are intolerant of the unknown and strive instantaneously to feel it is explicable, familiar... The event itself is suspect

> *because* it is explicable in terms of physics, chemistry, psychoanalysis, and other *pre*-conceived experience. The "conception" is an event which has become 'conceivable', the 'conceivable' it has become is no longer the genetic experience.
>
> (p. 382)

How then can we maintain the essential perpetual movement between the prelinguistic relation to being and the verbal modes of communication; between the ineffable experience unmediated by thought and the possibility of communicating it to another, without objectifying it and denuding it of its essence?

"It is clear", Bion writes,

> that in psychoanalysis talking can be a method of communication of genuine thoughts. Unfortunately words can be used in such a way that they are a 'cosmetic' representation of thinking instead of being the outcome of the labour involved in thought.
>
> (Bion and Bion, 1981, p. 666)

Bion often addresses this paradoxical nature of the relationship between language and truth whereby linguistic expression is the path by which truth can be glimpsed at, while at the same time it hides and distorts it.

Healthy mental growth seems to depend on this truth as the living organism depends on food (Bion, 1965). This is the notion at the foundation of Bion's psychoanalytic thinking. This is not necessarily an empirical truth, but rather a *sense of truth* at a certain moment. Psychoanalysis strives towards this truth. This is its essence. However, this truth cannot be known and is often not amenable to verbal communication. This is the paradox which creates the tension generating the infinite psychic movement. This is the paradoxical movement of language as veiling and unveiling. It is neither one nor the other, but rather a constant movement between the two modes. The mere use of words is often insufficient in the attempt to understand the live, ever-changing, ever-moving individual. Without this movement, we collapse to stagnation, to an inanimate, static portrayal that cannot capture the psyche's aliveness.

Bion (1970) maintains that any truth that can be thought is no longer truth but its *evolution*[1] into material reality, that which can be known through the familiar senses. Thus, any truth that penetrates into the realm of verbal language is a falsity.[2]

This thinking is essentially similar to that of philosophers like Plato, Hume, Kant, Berkeley, and others who postulated a gap between the phenomenon as it is realized in the world and the thing-in-itself, i.e. between the sensuous manifestation and the pure form which is beyond sensuous perception. David Hume (1748) put it deftly when he wrote that the most lively thought is still inferior to the dullest experience.

The limited human nature, which does not permit knowing anything beyond the phenomena amenable to sensuous perception, cannot bridge this gap. All we can do is *deduce* that which exists beyond our sensuous perception. Every form of expression, be it verbal communication, painting, music, etc., is only a transformation of the thing-in-itself, and it is only its transformation that can be known.

The invariant psychic reality of the session, O, can be described as a space with an infinite number of dimensions (Neuman, 2010), and thus cannot be grasped in its totality, due to the fact that the human mind is limited to only three dimensions. Our perceptual capacity, as Kant might say, is discursive and not intuitive. We learn circuitously, one thing from another, through deductions, judgements, and general concepts and do not perceive directly, or all at once, the object's entirety. However, "ultimate reality must be a whole even if the human animal cannot grasp it" (Bion, 1977e, p. 229).

*

As elaborated in Chapter 5, the urge to communicate, alongside the painful recognition of the difficulty to communicate, seems to be the Ariadne's thread running throughout Bion's work. He often seems to go out of his way to describe the frustration and suffering he feels in the face of the inability to represent and communicate the emotional experience. He writes,

> The experience of the patient's communication and psychoanalyst's interpretation is ineffable and essential...What has to

be communicated is real enough; yet every psycho-analyst knows the frustration of trying to make clear, even to another psychoanalyst, an experience which sounds unconvincing as soon as it is formulated. We may have to reconcile ourselves to the idea that such communication is impossible at the present stage of psycho-analysis.

(Bion, 1967a, p. 122)

Every testimony, be it as reliable as it may, is in effect only an interpretation, dressed in familiar categories and symbols.

Towards the end of his life, Bion writes,

The nearest that a psychoanalytic couple comes to a 'fact' is when one or the other has a feeling. Communicating that fact to some other person is a task which has baffled scientists, saints, poets and philosophers as long as the race has existed.

(1979, p. 536)

In fact, Bion (1970) cites Isaac Luria, the 16th-century Jewish mystic who left no writings and when asked by a disciple about his reasons for not setting out his teaching in book form, replied: 'It is impossible because all things are interrelated. I can hardly open my mouth to speak without feeling as though the sea burst its dams and overflowed. How then shall I express what my soul has received, and how can I put it down in a book?'

Moreover, Bion seems to identify with Milton's yearning in *Paradise Lost*: "that I may see and tell of things invisible to mortal sight" (Bion, 1977e, p. 225). He is always reiterating that the analyst must develop his capacity to intuit a psychic reality that has no 'senseable' foundation. The analyst, he says, must 'blind himself' to the evidence of engaging in a conversation seemingly between two adults and loosen the grip on familiar anchors of mature thought, so as to get in touch with "the *un*observed, *in*comprehensible, *in*audible, *in*effable... from which will come the future interpretation" (Bion, 1974, p. 127, italics added).

We are thus thrust into the realm of *the negative*, a core notion in both psychoanalytic thinking and the mystical traditions.

The negative in psychoanalytic thinking

In describing the notion of the negative in psychoanalytic thinking, I would like to begin with an illustration from a Hasidic[3] tale depicted by Buber.[4] A great Hasidic leader said that

> ...the Torah [The Jewish Law or Bible] received by Moses on Mount Sinai...cannot be changed and we are forbidden to touch its letters. But, in fact, not only the black letters but also the white gaps between them are letters of the Torah. However, we cannot read the white gaps. In the future, God will reveal the white hiddenness of the Torah.
>
> (In Avnon, 1998, p. 122)

We read in this tale an allusion to a hidden reality indicated by white gaps between the black letters. Its absence is only apparent, an effect of the reader's focus on the foreground of the text at the expense of noting its interwoven background. We can see and read the black letters and usually do not pay attention to the gaps between them. To render the white gaps relevant to our understanding, we first have to see them as signs necessitating a release of the attention that is ordinarily focused on the black, dominant script. Perceiving the black letters differently, in a manner that would bring the *white* gaps to the fore as 'letters', implies experiencing the text in a new, revitalized, mystical way (Ibid).

Likewise, Bion stresses that psychoanalytic listening includes the silences, or rests as the musicians might say. The totality of the musical composition includes these silences which play a very big part in the composition. No doubt they cannot be neglected. Bion adds that every now and then, you get some sort of curious event, like a person who for some obscure reason, doesn't, or won't, listen to the music but listens to something else. Freud, who Bion sees as a mystic, did not listen to the words uttered but to something else, and "the next thing you know, you have this vast realm of psychoanalysis" (in Aguayo, 2013, p. 64).

Mystical thinking maintains that truth is hidden from the senses, from language and from thought. It is concerned with the unknown, concealed, and zero-ness; in effect – with the negative. But "...how does one discover a negative?" (Bion, 1975, p. 268).

The intuition of the negative appears throughout Freud's writings beginning with the very fact that the free associations are connected to each other with apparently invisible, unconscious threads which are sensuously non-existent. It is realized pre-eminently in the creation of an analytic setting negativizing perception as an indispensable means of approaching the psyche (Botella and Botella, 2005). And what appears in the space that is generated, is not that which was repressed or the return of something that was once represented in the mind, but rather an encounter with the *irrepresentable*.

Freud described two forms of the same existence of reality – material reality and psychic reality. Bion (1970) elaborated the notion of these two aspects of reality and wrote of 'reality sensuous *and* psychic'. Whereas sensuous reality is perceived through the five basic senses, psychic reality is *intuited*. Intuition is an unmediated knowledge or understanding of truth, not supported by any information derived from a familiar sensual source. Since it cannot be communicated to another and cannot be corroborated by a rational method of scientific knowledge, it is often seen as close to mystical revelation (de Bianchedi, 1991). Hence, the analyst 'sees' an internal world and has no doubt of its existence, even though he has no sensuous evidence for it.

Winnicott (1969b) writes of the 'non-event'. He 'hears' the scream which the patient is always not experiencing. The great non-event of the session is the screaming that the patient does not scream. This seems to be an illustration of Winnicott's intuition of the negative as described by Green (1997), who himself wrote widely of the negative, emphasizing that he does not use the word absence, because in the word absence, there is the hope of a return of the presence. It is also not a loss because this would mean that the loss could be mourned. The reference to the negative is to the non-existence, the void. Winnicott's contribution, according to Green, is to show how this negative, the non-existence, will become at some point, the only thing that is real.

Bion (1974) illustrates this further by describing the observation of a game of tennis, looking at it with increasing darkness, while dimming the intellectual illumination and light. First, we lose sight of the players, and then we gradually increase the darkness until only the net itself is visible. If we can do this, it is possible to see that the only important thing visible to us is a lot of holes which are collected together in a net.

Botella and Botella (2005) speak of the negative of the trauma which has its origin not in a quantifiable positive, but in the absence of what, for the child's ego, should have occurred as a matter of course. Something fundamentally evident for the subject that should have happened did not happen, even though he is not aware of it, let alone form an idea of what this negative is. These authors too argue that the negative of the infantile trauma is not a product of the abolition of a representation but the consequence of a lack at the outset, a missing inscription, at any rate in the form of a representation.

All these lead up to Sandler's (2011) conceptualization of the realm of Minus, "a non-concrete, immaterial realm that complements the positive 'senseable' realm of the material reality" (p. 13). Again,

> the realm of Minus cannot be equated to denial; It contemplates the possibilities of impossibility and its propositional content cannot be seen on the same level…as the 'Plus realm', what is affirmative; in other words, what occupies a position in space-time. Therefore, since it indicates 'what is not'…it cannot have the properties assigned to what would be the opposite of 'what is'. It is ineffable.
>
> (Ibid, p. 14)

The clinical implication of this is that we are required to listen not only to the words, or to their semantic meaning, but rather to their *effect* on us, to the emotional experience generated by them. The very fact that the analysand lies on the couch liberates the analyst to be immersed in a trance-like state so as to promote the encounter with irrepresentable areas of the analysand's internal world. "Phantasies sometimes burst through into articulate words when the individual is 'off his guard'" (Bion, 1979, p. 485). Accordingly, Bion advocates the analyst's *negative capability*, i.e. being in uncertainties, mysteries, doubts, without any irritable reaching after fact and reason, thus capacitating the analyst's formal regression of thought, a quasi-hallucinatory mode of being as described by the Botellas, or in Civitarese's (2015) elaboration of Bion's transformations in hallucinosis as a feature of the analyst's receptivity.

In fact, Bion (1967a) says that "the proper state for intuiting psycho-analytical realizations...can be compared with the states supposed to provide conditions for hallucinations. The hallucinated individual is apparently having sensuous experiences without any background of sensuous reality". So the analyst too must be able to identify something that cannot be perceived by any of the familiar senses, but rather through primordial, *mystical* intuition. Some authors question whether mystical intuition is to do with encountering emotional truth or to do with psychosis (see O'Shaughnessy, 2005). However, admitting the caesura (i.e. a break *and* a continuity) between the psychotic and the non-psychotic parts of the personality, entailing some overlap between them, the intuitive, mystical state of mind differs fundamentally from the psychotic one. The incapacity to tolerate the negative, the no-breast, is a fundamental characteristic of the psychotic personality, whereas toleration of the negative and the frustration this entails, is a defining characteristic of a psycho analytically trained intuitive or mystical state of mind. In his mystical diary, Rabbi Isaac of Acre, the 13th-century Spanish Kabbalist, warns the mystic against quenching his soul's thirst lest he be utterly consumed by fire [or might I add, insanity?]. He draws on Moses as an example of a person who controlled himself and did not stare into the burning bush nor satisfy his soul's hunger and thirst.

The psychoanalytic attitude, much like the mystical one, is a deliberate, conscious act of discipline which depends on an *active* suspension of memory and desire. Bion (1970) proposes a discipline for the analyst that increases his ability to exercise 'acts of faith'; however, he stressed that this must be distinguished from the religious meaning with which it is invested in conversational usage. This is *faith that truth exists* and is calculated to meet that irrepresentable part of the personality and an ineffable emotional truth *while retaining an attitude as an observer* by virtue of training, experience, and personal analysis.[5]

No doubt suspension of memory, desire, understanding, and all that binds us to external reality brings the analyst, as well as the mystic, closer to an animistic world; however, the *collapse* to animistic thinking, characteristic of the primitive religious world or psychotic-hallucinatory states, is precisely the result of an individual's *inability* to maintain a psychoanalytic, or mystical, state of mind. Bion (Ibid) comments that it may well be that analysts who attempt this approach will find that the test of sensuous deprivation involved in eschewing memory and desire will cause them to feel the need for further analysis that would not have occurred had the analyst remained content with the atmosphere of deprivation as it has been understood in classical psychoanalytic thinking.

Bion emphasizes that the purpose of the analyst's partial severance with external reality differs from the purpose of the psychotic manoeuvre. The psychotic wishes to destroy contact with psychic reality, whereas the analyst wishes to establish it. And this psychic reality is ineffable, not because it is experienced *beyond or outside* reality, but precisely because this *is* what real experience feels like when infinite dimensions are perceived simultaneously, paradoxically, with no boundaries of time and space; this is why linear, narrative language cannot grasp it.

And so, we are again in the realm of what is sensuously invisible but intuitively visible, the juxtaposition between psychoanalytic thinking and mysticism.

Emotional truth and ultimate reality: Bion and Jewish mysticism

The fact that different disciplines, at different times and from different vertices, describe the same experience gives this experience greater validity and enables a 'multi-ocular' view of truth. And this encounter between the different disciplines is an emotional experience in itself, an emotional experience of discovering coherence. It is a mode of being in which different facets of the emotional experience can be 'observed' from different vertices, integrated in a way that feels truthful, affording *a sense of truth*.[6]

Bion drew a parallel between psychoanalytical and mystical states of mind. Since Bion's reference and affinity to Christian mystics have been widely explored (e.g. Reiner, 2012), I will focus predominantly on Jewish mysticism. The only Jewish mystic Bion mentions is Isaac Luria, and yet he also mentions the Jewish philosopher Martin

Buber, as well as Gershom Scholem, a scholar of Kabbalah and Jewish mysticism who seems to have made a big impact on his thinking.[7]

Indeed, both Jewish philosophy and Jewish mysticism try to address the problem of ineffability through the issue of God. Inasmuch as one cannot describe in words the ultimate reality of the emotional experience, Jewish philosophy asserts that any attempt to describe God undermines its very essence. In contrast to Jewish philosophers, Jewish mystics cannot say enough about God and describe him inexhaustibly. Yet, the name of God is merely *a symbolic representation* of an ultimate reality which is forever unformed and amorphous (Scholem, 1960). There is no word that can encompass the entire meaning of God, hence a superfluousness of words is needed.

It seems to me that these are two complementary modes of dealing with the ineffability of the deity in its entirety: the former asserting the absence of words in relation to God, thus espousing silence, whereas the latter advocates contriving genres of discourse about the Naught, transforming it into the Infinite.

Similarly, Bion (1965) designates the sign 'O' to denote unknowable ultimate reality, the Godhead,[8] the infinite. In a striking parallel, he specifies its definitory qualities through repeated *negations*: "It is not good or evil; it cannot be known, loved or hated… The most, and the least that the individual person can do is to be it" (pp. 139–140). Bion, like the mystics, writes of the countless, and yet insufficient number of words required to describe the emotional experience. He writes,

> I do not feel able to communicate to the reader an account that would be likely to satisfy me as correct. I am more confident that I could make the reader understand what I had to put up with if I could extract from him a promise that he would faithfully read every word I wrote; I would then set about writing several hundred thousand words… In short, I cannot have as much confidence in my ability to tell the reader what happened as I have in my ability *to do something to the reader that I have had done to me*. I have had an emotional experience; I feel confident in my ability to recreate that emotional experience, but not to represent it.
> (Bion, 1992, p. 219, italics added)

In an attempt to describe the ultimate reality symbolized by O, Bion writes,

> It is perhaps too mathematical to call it infinity, too mystical to call it the infinite, too religious to call it the Godhead... Verbal expressions intended to represent the ultimate object often appear to be contradictory within themselves, but there is a surprising degree of agreement, despite differences of background, time and space, in the descriptions offered by mystics who feel they have experienced the ultimate reality.
>
> (1965, pp. 150–151)

Mysticism

Science and mysticism are seemingly opposites. Science deals with knowledge, with what is revealed, with 'what is'. Mysticism deals with the unknowable, the hidden, the Naught. However, over the years, this dichotomy has lost its meaning. Truth, as noted by Civitarese (2013), is neither scientific/philosophical nor mystical/aesthetic. The former is lacking in emotions/feelings, the latter in concepts. One has only to think of the immaterial nature of the negative or imaginary numbers in mathematics in order to illustrate the overlap and dialectic interplay between science and the mystical tradition. Referring to Bion's later writings, Sandler (2015) notes that the scientific vertex is always put into constant conjunction with at least two other vertices, the mystical and the artistic traditions. Nevertheless, the word mysticism is saturated with connotations, often in the service of religious, esoteric, or new-age dogmas that its depth is lost and often denigrated in psychoanalytic thinking. One must, therefore, go back to its original definition to allow the affinity between the two disciplines to become apparent, as well as to capacitate the mutual inspiration inherent within such an affinity.

The word 'mysticism', derived from the Greek μυω, and meaning "to conceal", was defined by Celsus, a 2nd-century Greek philosopher and opponent of Early Christianity. It was defined as the closing of the senses to all worldly matters, sensations, passions, and desires, so as to enable the soul to be open to the spiritual matters of the sublime. It is from this definition that the two characteristics of most mystical traditions derive: first, most mystical methods require detachment from mundane desires as a precondition for spiritual wholeness, and view abstinence as a way to achieve this goal. Second, the mystical way leads to an experience in the realms of an ineffable reality. It is caught in the dire straits of the intense desire for expression on the one hand, and the inability to express itself on the other. The mystical literature stresses that any talk or speech is only an allegory. Mystical literature is therefore inclined to puns and paradoxical expressions. Interestingly, referring to Bion's semi-autobiographical psychoanalytic novel *A Memoir of the Future*, Meltzer and Harris-Williams (1985) remark that the way of playing fast and loose with language, with wit, obscenity, endless punning, splitting, and recombining words, is part of the method that the characters in the book use to try to 'get through' to one another.

Another trait of the mystical experience is its unitive essence. The mystic feels that he 'unites' with a sublime, divine, or cosmic reality. However, most Jewish mystics have referred to 'adherence' or 'closeness' to God (Devekut) and avoided talking about a complete, actual, and substantial union. In fact, as Scholem (1971) argues, the avoidance of a complete union with God (unio-mystica) differentiates Jewish mysticism from all other mystical traditions. It is in the nature of Jewish mysticism that one should at most aspire to communion with God, but never to union. Whereas in Catholic mysticism, 'communion' was not the last step on the mystical way, in Kabbalism, it is the last grade of ascent to God. It is not union, because union with God is denied to man according to Kabbalistic theology, even in that mystical upsurge of the soul. I suspect this reverberated Bion's notion of the endless striving for unreachable, unknowable truth. In a similar vein, Bion hyphenated the word atonement, making it into at-one-ment, which may, in the spirit of the Jewish mystical tradition, denote that there is never a complete union in this experience of being at-one with ultimate reality.

These mystical notions are incredibly similar to Bion's notion of eschewing memory, desire and understanding, and closing the familiar senses so as to facilitate an intuitive state of mind, hence becoming at-one with the emotional truth of the moment. Mysticism is thus a way of delving into one's inner world, shutting one's eyes to sensuous reality enabling the individual to see with one's "inner eye" (Bion, 1977e, p. 225), much like the way dreams are created.

Mysticism, not religious dogma

> P. A. It appears to me that unquestioning belief in God is demanded by the Church or its representatives. Perhaps I am misled by the Institutions of Religion which have obscured for me the chance of going beyond the institutions' dogmata to a reality beyond.
>
> PAUL There are certainly plenty of religious teachers who have developed that and warned against it. St. John of the Cross even said that reading his own works would be a stumbling block if they were revered to the detriment of direct experience. Teachings, dogma, hymns, congregational worship, are supposed to be preludes to religion proper – not final ends in themselves.
>
> P. A. This sounds not unlike a difficulty which we experience when psycho-analytic jargon...[is] substituted for looking into the patient's mind itself to intuit that to which the psycho-analyst is striving to point; like a dog that looks at its master's pointing hand rather than at the object the hand is trying to point out.
>
> (Bion, 1975, p. 267)

It is true that both established religion and mystical traditions share the same Scriptures, yet they differ from each other in the most drastic manner. A religious person believes in the word of God incorporated in Scriptures and is certain that he understands it, or at least that its core, its most important meaning, has been absorbed by him. His 'truth' is therefore often static and finite, and so does not pertain to psychoanalytic truth. God then becomes an idol. The mystic, on the other hand, knows that various levels of communicative interpretation, including allegory, analogy, and the like, cannot reveal the hidden divine truth, which can be approached in non-linguistic ways alone. His truth is therefore dynamic, transient, and infinite. The mystical meaning and message of the Scriptures is beyond communication. It is hidden within the text, but the mystic, by his meta-sensual and meta-intellectual perceptions or experiences, can achieve a glimpse of the hidden truth. A sensuous-intellectual approach to the text of the Scriptures is either meaningless or false (Dan, 2002).

Bion refers to the question of religious dogma as opposed to the mystical tradition throughout *A Memoir of the Future* with the aid of sundry characters who voice Bion's various thoughts. The rejection of any dogmatic authority is echoed by the character BION who says, "...We do not know the cost in suffering associated with the belief in a Christian God, or the God of Abraham's Ur, or Hitler's Germany, or peyotism – or God of any kind" (Bion, 1975, p. 172). And further on, in another debate, ROLAND remarks that "Religion has been aptly described as a drug", to which PAUL replies, "Because it is used for that purpose by some people I do not see why religion should be held responsible, any more than why wine should be blamed for alcoholism..." (Ibid, pp. 271–272). Further still, religious feelings, or a "religious impulse", are distinguished from religious institutions. Perhaps the most defining differentiation is voiced by P.A. as to whether it "is capable of development rather than decay" (Ibid, p. 287).

Elsewhere Bion (1977f) writes, "Religious dogmata are...vulgarizations of that which the religious mystic can achieve directly" (p. 32).

To my mind, Bion's psychoanalytic writings testify to the fact that there is no necessary connection between a deep devotion to a certain religion and the specific characteristics of a mystical view. As a matter of fact, Bion seems to present us with non-religious mysticism.

Bion began to be interested in mystics in 1965 when he realized that many of them had found it very difficult to put their revelatory experiences into words and manage to communicate them to others who had not had this unique experience themselves (de Bianchedi, 2005). This is a similar difficulty Bion experienced when trying to communicate the intuitively perceived psychoanalytic experience to a person who had not been present and who had not had the same experience. Moreover, Bion (1967a) wanted to bring the notion of the mystic, which he regarded as interchangeable with the word 'scientist' or the word 'artist', into the psychoanalytic discourse. He was aware that 'mystic' has a much more religious connotation, and he had indeed referred in his late writings to religious and theological terms such as 'Godhead', 'faith', and 'at-one-ment'. However, these terms were used in an attempt to borrow concepts from different disciplines in order to avoid the collapse to psychoanalytic terms that have become jargon.

Bion did not try to describe the psychoanalytic experience as religious, but he did see the advantages of religious metaphors and thought that at times, these are superior to psychoanalytic models in addressing that quintessential mystery known as man (Grotstein, 2007). Moreover, the use of words such as God and Godhead, were borrowed to try and depict an emotional truth, or ultimate reality, which like God, is transcendental, existing beyond the possibility of human knowledge and consciousness. As Bion states,

> I use these formulations to express, in exaggerated form, the pain which is involved in achieving the state of naivety... The relevance of this to psychological phenomena springs from the fact that they are not amenable to apprehension by the senses.
>
> (1965, p. 159)

Bion makes use of mystical writings to interpret psychoanalytic problems, as he does with other cultural myths which have a universal or a large social value (see Bion, 1992). He suggests that the scientist must know enough mathematics to have an idea when he is confronting a problem to which a particular mathematical procedure would apply. The psychoanalyst likewise might use myths or mystical writings as a tool comparable to that of the mathematical formulation, for investigating emotional problems. Associating on a chosen myth, and selection of the myths on which to associate, plays an important part in the promotion of psychoanalytic intuition and in the reinvigoration of the analyst's alpha-function (Ibid). Hence, Bion's attitude to myths is similar to the use Buber makes of Hasidic legends and Biblical tales as conveying philosophical insight. Buber's hope was that these would help readers gain access to the truth conveyed by such myths, which would otherwise require complicated philosophical reasoning. Bion's turn to mystical exegeses too is derived from his belief that these could facilitate the communication of emotional truth that is beyond verbal communication. He writes, "...I was compelled to seek asylum in fiction. Disguised as fiction, the truth occasionally slipped through" (Bion, 1975, p. 302).

The mystic and the psychoanalyst

I would like to address the mystical state of mind of analyst and analysand, whose mutual work of analysis facilitates the development of their intuitive capacity. Thus, I suggest that *mystical qualities are not reserved for a privileged, 'illuminated' few, but are part of what psychoanalysis strives to attain and develop.*

Mystics are individuals who by their own inner experience and their speculation concerning this experience discover new layers of meaning *in their tradition.* A mystic is a person who has been favoured with an immediate, and to him real, experience of the divine, of ultimate reality, or who at least strives to attain such an experience. His experience may come to him through sudden illumination, or it may be the result of long and often elaborate preparations (Scholem, 1960).

The moment a mystic tries to clarify his experience by reflection, to formulate it, and especially when he attempts to communicate it to others, he cannot help imposing a framework of conventional symbols and ideas upon it. Yet, there is always some part of it that he cannot adequately and fully express. But if he does try to communicate his experience – and it is only by doing so that he makes himself known to us – he is bound to interpret his experience in a language, images and concepts that were created before him.

The mystic's attitude to religion is one of deep doubt that verbal communication can reveal divine truth. The mystic is someone who knows that real truth, meaningful truth, can never be expressed in words. And it is not only language that the mystic distrusts. The whole range of means by which people acquire knowledge, especially the senses, logic and thought, are suspected as a cause for error and meaninglessness (Dan, 2002).

The mystic discovers a new dimension, a new depth in his own tradition. In employing symbols to describe his own experience and to formulate his interpretations of it, he transforms and *reinterprets* established religion, and his symbolism is the instrument of this transformation. He uses old symbols and lends them new meaning; he may even use new symbols and give them an old meaning. In either case, we find a dialectical interrelationship between the conservative aspects and the novel, productive aspects of mysticism (Scholem, 1960). The mystic, Bion (1970) writes, is both creative and destructive. These two extremes coexist in the same person.

The analyst's state of mind, defined *negatively* as being with no memory, no desire and no understanding, strives, like that of the mystic, to blur the familiar and conventional interpretation, so as to allow openness to a new impression, a fresh interpretation. Mental growth, analytic transformation, and the encounter with emotional truth are made possible through a 'break-up' of the familiar meaning and a 'breakthrough' of the new discovery.

This is illustrated in Bion's paper *Evidence* (1976a). The patient associated: 'I remember my parents being at the top of a Y-shaped stair and I was at the bottom and...'. That was all. There were no further associations. Bion was struck by the statement being so brief, stopping short at that point, and he thought it must have a lot of meaning that was not visible to him. It then occurred to him that the statement would be more comprehensible if it was spelled 'why-shaped stare'. However, Bion could not see how he could say this to the patient in a way which would have any meaning, nor could he produce any evidence for it. Bion said nothing, fearing it was just a pun, a fanciful free association of his or an interpretation that would be incomprehensible to the patient. The analyst had plenty of associations and possible interpretations while playing with this image. However, it was only in the next session, after "killing time" with conventionally acceptable interpretations, that he dared to say to the patient: 'I suggest that in addition to the ordinary meaning of what you have told me – and I am perfectly sure that what you said means exactly what you meant – it is also a kind of visual pun'. And then he gave him the interpretation. The patient replied: 'Yes, that's right. But you've been a very long time about it...'.

The deconstruction of the familiar meaning, and awarding a new meaning, grants the text a mystical tenor. In this sense, a mystical interpretation is akin to an intuitive interpretation, which is often uncanny and even terrifying.

Scholem (1960) writes,

> The genius of mystical exegeses resides in the uncanny precision with which they derive their transformation of Scripture into a *corpus symbolicum* from the exact words of the text. The literal meaning is preserved but merely as the gate through which the mystic passes, a gate, however, which he opens up to himself over and over again. The *Zohar*,[9] the foundational book of Jewish mystical thought, expresses this attitude of the mystic very succinctly in a memorable exegesis of Genesis 12:1. God's words to Abram, 'Lekh lekha' [Go thee out of thy country, and from thy kindred, and from thy father's house], are taken not only in their

literal meaning, 'Go thee out'. That is, they are not interpreted as referring only to God's command to Abram to go out into the world, but are also read with mystical literalness as 'Go to thee', that is, to thine own self, away from the habits to which you are accustomed.

(p. 15)

In fact, the *Zohar* interprets every place Abram travelled to, as a psychic state of mind, and his journeys throughout the land as the inner journey of the psyche. The divine world which was concealed from Abram opens up before him. The verse "And Abram journeyed, going on still toward the south" (Genesis 12:9) describes Abram ascending further and further towards encountering his own truth (Hellner-Eshed, 2009). Mystical interpretations are thus often predisposed towards the inner world.

London and Edinburgh

An intuitive and, to my mind, essentially mystical interpretation, reinterpreting the patient's text and directing the meaning further inwards, into the internal world, can be found in Bion's (1967a) Los Angeles seminars. The patient was apparently talking quite obviously about a particular group known to him, in external terms. As the session evolved, the analyst began to feel this wasn't simply an external group that he was talking about, even though it was *also* that. The patient had been talking about people, about London and Edinburgh, and Bion drew his attention to the fact that these were not simply London and Edinburgh. They were names of places where it was once a mother and a father. It was simply a way of describing not the father and mother, but the place where the father and mother were until something or other happened to them, which had turned them simply into a place. And then, that these other objects which he'd been mentioning were really felt to be the children of this pair (these two objects which had now turned into places). From that, Bion gave the interpretation that it was, in fact, the patient himself, only he himself was now split up. The parents had been attacked so that they were only places where parents used to be, and he himself had been destroyed in the process, split up into a whole lot of particles which can be described in terms of these people, with names, and so forth.

Following this interpretation, the patient started on a series of hypochondriac complaints.

This may obviously be a controversial interpretation, but Bion contends a process by which *the external objects had been gathered inwards into the internal world and transformed into internal objects* like his spleen, his hernia, and so on. (These words are mentioned as bodily objects whereas they also have a psychic meaning, spleen meaning hate, anger, depression, and hernia meaning a fracture or a rupture.) Bergson asserts that the intellect has a tendency which impels us to think on all occasions of *things* rather than movements (Torres, 2013). Bion's interpretation of London and Edinburgh transforms the places, the things, back into internal psychic movement, the inanimate back to the animate. This may seem very similar to our ordinary work of deciphering the symbolic meaning of the patient's repressed or displaced material. However, we may have here, as suggested by Meltzer (2000), a distinction between allegory and symbol. Allegory is taken by Meltzer to consist of the rather ingenious substitution of known elements for what is mysterious and unknown; it is a kind of cheat because it pretends to bring the unknown within the sphere of the already-known. Symbol, on the other hand, is full of mystery, and inexhaustible, however much one digs into it. Its many levels are not just an ingenious emblem. A symbol, Meltzer writes, carries with it the gift of humility; *you know perfectly well you will never understand it completely.*

In a lucid passage which I can imagine might have inspired Bion, Scholem (1961) writes,

> If allegory can be defined as the representation of an expressible something by another expressible something, the mystical symbol is an expressible representation of something which lies beyond the sphere of expression and communication, something which comes from a sphere whose face is, as it were, turned inward and away from us. A hidden and inexpressible reality finds its expression in the symbol... Where deeper insight into the structure of the allegory uncovers fresh layers of meaning, the symbol is intuitively understood all at once – or not at all.
>
> (pp. 26–27, italics added)

'London and Edinburgh', the symbol in the above description, much like the symbol in Jewish mysticism, is paradoxically utilized since no words can encompass the infinite meanings of the ineffable, *emotional experience* or the ultimate reality concealed in the patient's 'dream'. There is no realization which approximates the verbal description of the emotional experience which is concealed in the words 'London and Edinburgh'. These words do not symbolize the persons of the parental couple *per se*, but rather evoke a caesural experience, a complex *link* which is ineffable due to its infinite dimensions. It is a constant conjunction encompassing a myriad of elements comprising the experience of the emotional link.

One might conjecture the patient as a sensitive infant overwhelmed by an emotional atmosphere, perhaps too depressed or pressured, which was too intense for his fragile, immature self and was thus felt as violently attacking him. Overstimulated, and lacking the capacity to deal with the emotional experience, this infant might have been compelled to attack his contact with himself or his primary objects, since such contact threatened him with an emotional turbulence beyond his capacity to mentally metabolize. When the infant is thus compelled to deaden his contact with animate objects for fear of excessive emotionality, we often hear of inanimate objects, or even of places, when we would normally expect to hear of people (Bion, 1962a).

However, the patient's experience (which I have now, for the sake of exposition, described as a linear, sequential chain of events, far from the original emotional experience) has never been mentalized and therefore has never been repressed. The patient could never have uttered his experience because it was never mentally registered. Nevertheless it is burnt and encapsulated in the *unrepressed unconscious*, awaiting an intuitive, mystical moment when it can emerge as a symbol. The Kabbalistic symbol paradoxically expresses in language what the mouth cannot utter and the ear cannot hear (Scholem, 1975), thus steering us towards the unknowable navel of the dream, the noumena beyond the phenomena. This, to my mind, may be a major contribution of Jewish mysticism to psychoanalysis. It illuminates the reality of a hidden life. It sharpens our listening to the *unrepressed unconscious* and enhances our capacity to attend to the words uttered in a fresh, intuitive, and mystical way.

As already stressed in Chapter 2, the value of intuitive interpretations like these is therefore not in uncovering historical truth or repressed unconscious material. Nor are they evaluated for the 'correctness' of their *content*. Rather, their merit lies in their capacity for *generating psychic movement*, transforming psychic barriers into caesuras, affording a multidimensional view, and enabling the patient to move from a preoccupation with external reality to an observation of his internal reality. The patient may thus get in touch with remote, encapsulated parts of the psyche. *Preoccupation with external reality is finite, whereas internal reality and the unconscious are infinite.* Any interpretation is only a partial representation, retaining an irrepresentable navel which will forever remain unknown and evoking a feeling of mystery and unknowability.

This lengthy discussion, in the attempt to give meaning to the above vignette, is brought about in retrospect, after several readings of Bion's seminar. However, my first impression of reading it was of being immensely moved, without being able to comprehend or describe in words why it was so moving. I am inclined to think that this is due to the awe generated when, as Bion says, "one meaning turned out to have, like a many faceted diamond, a fresh, fiery brilliance of truth" (1975, p. 234). Furthermore, it seems that by evoking an experience analogous to a mystical union, these interpretations revive our intrinsic tendency to experience the numinous. In these rare and privileged moments, the intuition becomes at-one with a conception, akin to mystical at-one-ment. Since such interpretations *evoke an experience* rather than being subject to discursive understanding, it is often difficult for anyone, other than the patient himself, to sense or to comprehend the experience implicit in the interpretation.

As already mentioned, "we have thus approached a mental life unmapped by the theories elaborated for the understanding of neurosis" (Bion, 1962a, p. 37), and this mental life, I suggest, is the realm of the ineffable, unrepressed unconscious.

Concluding remarks

Bion (1970) reminds us that it is often forgotten that the gift of speech, so centrally employed, has been elaborated as much for the purpose of concealing thought as for the purpose of elucidating or communicating thought.

However, I would not like to collapse to abolishing the power of language. As Bion (1967a) says, "If the psycho-analytical situation is accurately intuited...the psycho-analyst finds that ordinary conversational English is surprisingly adequate for the formulation of his interpretation" (p. 134). The continuous struggle, striving to find words for the ineffable reality is at the heart of the psychoanalytic quest. The analyst attempts to interpret that part of experience which has penetrated the sensuous world and language. Any new formulation, from an additional vertex, allows us to expand our psychic world ad infinitum. And yet, we must remember that any utterance is just a reminder, a pale shadow of the thing-in-itself.

The analyst is thus left to hover in the dialectic interplay, in the caesura, between intuition and conception. Intuition is essential due to the immaterial nature of psychoanalysis, and yet it must not be dissociated from a scientific outlook lest it leads to careless, wild interpretations.

Bion says,

> ...infants...know all about what it *feels* like, but they have no concepts, they cannot write any of these great books – their concepts are blind. Later on they have forgotten what it is like to feel terrified; they pick up these words but the words are empty – "I'm terrified"... it is an empty phrase, it is a concept; it is only verbal; the intuition is missing.
>
> (1977g, p. 40)

We are thus faced with the problem of marrying the *concept* of terror with the corresponding *feeling*.

So again one must ask how can we move in the caesura between the infinite unknowable and the finite sensuous, verbalizable experience that is derived from it?

In an imaginary dialogue between the characters of BION and MYSELF in the *Memoir*, Bion writes,

> BION: ...You must often have heard, as I have, people say they don't know what you are talking about and that you are being deliberately obscure.
> MYSELF: They are flattering me. I am suggesting an aim, an ambition, which, if I could achieve, would enable me to be deliberately and *precisely* obscure; in which I could use certain words

which would activate precisely and instantaneously, in the mind of the listener, a thought or train of thought that came between him and the thoughts and ideas already accessible and available to him.

(1975, p. 191)

Similarly, it is said that when God was revealed on Mount Sinai when the Torah was handed down to the people of Israel, all illnesses and handicaps were cured. Moses, who had been stammering since he was an infant, refused to be cured. When asked why, he replied that his stammer is the way he communicates with God…

Postscript

The Memoir of the Future *and the* Zohar

The *Zohar*, as maintained by Scholem (1961), has stood out for centuries as the expression of all that was profoundest and most deeply hidden in the innermost recesses of the Jewish soul. I do not know whether Bion had ever read the 2,400 densely written pages of the *Zohar*, although I assume he did not. However, there is no doubt that he was acquainted with parts of it through the writings of Gershom Scholem which he refers to. Be it as it may, the similarity between the *Zohar* and Bion's *Memoir* is striking, and it seems to me that the *Memoir*, albeit not being a mystical text, can be read as one might read the *Zohar*.

In its manifest appearance, the *Zohar* is a scriptural exegesis, i.e. a mystical interpretation of the Torah. But the *Zohar*, much like the *Memoir*, is also an epic fiction. It portrays the epic story of Rabbi Shimon and his companions, who are fictitious or legendary embellishment of real historical persons. Its dramatis personae include other wondrous characters such as an old man, young child, and donkey driver, who reveal ancient secrets to the companions or describe the primordial world before emanation. Much like the *Memoir*, the author tries to capture the multidimensional transient truth through the multitude of characters. Hellner-Eshed (2009) compares the *Zohar* narrative to a jazz jam session, where a common melodic theme performed by the ensemble branches into solo improvisations that build to greater surprise, complexity, and crescendo – the more virtuosity, the more wonderful and surprising the innovations. One could perhaps say the same of the *Memoir*.

I dare to think that the *Memoir*, like the *Zohar*, was written in a dreamlike, at times quasi-hallucinatory state, with Bion delving into his inner world, awakening primordial sights and visions. It is an attempt to *be in* the dream rather than *talk about* it. Both texts are thus often obscure and perplexing, inclined to puns and paradoxical expressions, and should be read together in a circle of colleagues. Reading both is an emotional experience of capturing glimpses of an ineffable, hidden reality, arousing an emotional turbulence, at times bordering on ecstasy, in response to its aesthetic capacity of awakening the realm of noumena. Moreover, they both seem to be an attempt at bearing the pain inherent in the ineffability of the emotional experience.

The unknown author(s) of the *Zohar* makes use of numerous literary sources from classical Jewish writings. These sources are usually not mentioned. Instead, the author contents himself and discontents the reader, with vague references to ancient writings or mystical tracts dealing with the same topics. Thus, the discovery of the real sources, which he is so careful to obscure, is one of the main pre-requisites for an appreciation of the historical and doctrinal significance of the *Zohar* (Scholem, 1961). The mystics related to the Scriptures which populated their literary world as reference points to their revelatory experiences. Similarly, by abundantly quoting classical poets such as Virgil, Milton, Shakespeare, Goethe, Wordsworth, Shelley, and Keats, it seems that Bion is making a similar reference in the *Memoir* to the literary and cultural climate of *his* world, as a way of conveying his ineffable emotional experience.

The author of the *Zohar*, as Scholem tells us, employs the pointed language of the ancient sages, although he is usually less successful than them in making himself understood. The author, much like Bion, is not worried by chronology and lets his imagination roam freely between the different generations. He frequently loses himself in mystical allegorizations, and not infrequently he becomes abstruse, but again and again a hidden and sometimes awe-ful depth opens before our eyes, and we find ourselves confronted with real and profound insight.

Notes

1 The concept of *evolution*, or *hishtalshelut*, as used in Jewish mysticism, refers to the metaphysical process, the chain of events, whereby the complex and finite reality of the universe unfolds out of God's absolute oneness. This evolution proceeds by ten degrees, the attributes through which God reveals Himself, called the ten Sefirot. Yet, the Sefirot themselves are only varying degrees of expression of the unchanging, all-encompassing 'Eyn-Sof' (infinite). It seems this might have reverberated for Bion the notion of transformation in O, and it is perhaps from here that he drew the concept of *evolution*. Like the 'Eyn-Sof', ultimate reality is unknowable. The analyst must wait for the reality of the session *to evolve*, and it is only the events that are *evolutions* of O which he is able to know.

2 Bion uses the word *falsity* to denote the transformation of the emotional experience into a word. A word is thus always false compared to the original emotional experience. However, falsities are distinguished from *lies*, which are conscious attacks on truth.

3 Ḥasidism is a Jewish spiritual movement founded in the Ukraine in the 18th century. It is characterized by mysticism and opposition to secular studies and Jewish rationalism. One of its aims was to popularize Jewish mysticism and to allow ordinary people access to the Kabbalah. It was opposed by the orthodox rabbinical establishment.

4 Buber's *Light of the Hidden* (1976) is a collection of Hasidic tales in which he uses biblical interpretations, inserted into Hasidic legends. Buber stripped the legends of their magical and ecstatic elements, at the same time emphasizing a new way of seeing and experiencing reality.

5 In a striking resemblance to the role of the training and supervising analyst, Scholem (1960) stresses "the widespread belief that a mystic requires a spiritual guide... He prevents the student who sets out to explore the world of mysticism from straying off into dangerous situations. For confusion or even madness lurk in wait; the path of the mystic is beset by perils. It borders on abysses of consciousness and demands a sure and measured step...The guide should be capable of preserving the proper balance in the mystic's mind. He is familiar with the practical applications of the various doctrines, which cannot be learned from books. And he has an additional function... he represents traditional religious authority. He provides at the outset the traditional coloration which the mystical experience, however amorphous, will assume in the consciousness of the novice...to be safeguarded against uncontrollable emotional excesses" (pp. 18–19).

6 See Chapter 5, note 2.

7 Bion cites only seven authors apart from himself, in his book *Attention and Interpretation*, Scholem being one of them. Moreover, I am greatly indebted to Joe Aguayo for sharing the following significant anecdote

with me: When Bion went to lecture and supervise in Buenos Aires in 1968, he let his dinner host, Leon Grinberg, know of his interest in Jewish mysticism in a most amusing way. Grinberg had received a copy of *The Maggid of Caro*, a book by the famous 16th-century Kabbalist, Yosef Caro, who lived in the time of the Spanish Inquisition. The book was given to Grinberg as a gift by the Israeli ambassador to the United States. As Bion looked at the book titles in Grinberg's library, his attention was immediately drawn to this volume. Grinberg was instantaneously torn: he saw Bion's interest in the book from the way he was leafing through it and from his remarks about the Kabbala, and it would have made a splendid gift to commemorate Bion's visit to Buenos Aires. But Grinberg also could not bear to part with the book. At that point, Bion tore himself away from the book and said to Grinberg: 'Don't worry Grinberg; I won't ask you to give it to me. I would be grateful though if you would let me borrow it over the weekend, so that I could read it in the hotel'. Grinberg was surprised, and at that point, both men broke out in laughter.
8 The Godhead is a concept borrowed from the German theologian, mystic and philosopher Meister Eckhart (1260–1328). Godhead, which is infinite, is often contrasted with God, which is finite (Bion, 1975, p. 180).
9 The *Zohar* (Book of Radiance) is the classic text of Kabbalah and consists of homilies on the Torah. Yet it is not only a collection of Kabbalistic teachings but also sophisticated literary work. It tells of a circle of rabbinical sages and their adventures as they wandered the Galilee. The Kabbalistic teachings emerge as the rabbis analyze biblical verses spontaneously, in a trance like state. Most people believe the Zohar was largely composed in 13th-century Spain.

References

Aguayo J (2013). Wilfred Bion's 'Caesura'. In HB Levine & LJ Brown (eds.), *Growth and Turbulence in the Container/Contained: Bion's Continuing Legacy*. London: Routledge, pp. 55–74.

Aharoni H (2010). Placental economy: Thoughts on the movement between linkage and separateness and their paradoxical coexistence. *Maarag: The Israel Annual of Psychoanalysis* 1:39–64.

Alvarez A (1992). *Live Company*. London & New York: Routledge.

Alvarez A (1999a). Addressing the deficit: Developmentally informed psychotherapy with passive, 'undrawn' children. In A Alvarez & S Reid (eds.), *Autism and Personality*. London & New York: Routledge, pp. 49–61.

Alvarez A (1999b). Disorder, deviance and personality: Factors in the persistence and modifiability of autism. In A Alvarez & S Reid (eds.), *Autism and Personality*. London & New York: Routledge, pp. 62–78.

Alvarez A (2002). Failures to link: Attacks or defects, disintegration or unintegration? In A Briggs (ed.), *Surviving Space: Papers on Infant Observation*. London: Karnac, pp. 240–255.

Alvarez A (2010). Levels of analytic work and levels of pathology: The work of calibration. *International Journal of Psychoanalysis* 91:859–878.

Anzieu D (1989). *The Skin Ego*. New Haven, CT & London: Yale University Press.

Avnon D (1998). *Martin Buber: The Hidden Dialogue*. Maryland: Rowman & Littlefield Publishers, Inc.

Balint M (1959). Regression in the analytic situation. In *Thrills and Regressions*. London: Karnac, pp. 91–100.

Beck J (2002). Lost in thought: The receptive unconscious. In J Scalia (ed.), *The Vitality of Objects: Exploring the Work of Christopher Bollas*. New York: Continuum, pp. 9–36.

References

Bégoin J (2000). Love and destructivity: From the aesthetic conflict to a revision of the concept of destructivity in the psyche. In M Cohen & A Hahn (eds.), *Exploring the Work of Donald Meltzer*. London: Karnac, pp. 119–135.

Bick E (1962). Symposium on child analysis. *International Journal of Psychoanalysis* 43:328–332.

Bick E (1968). The experience of the skin in early object relations. *International Journal of Psychoanalysis* 49:484–486.

Bion F (1997). Introduction to Diary. In F Bion (ed.), *War Memoirs, 1917–19*. London: Karnac.

Bion WR (1955). Language and the schizophrenic. In M Klein, P Heimann & RE Money-Kyrle (eds.), *New Directions in Psycho-Analysis: The Significance of Infant Conflict in the Pattern of Adult Behaviour*. London: Tavistock, pp. 220–239.

Bion WR (1957). On arrogance. In *Second Thoughts: Selected Papers on Psycho-Analysis*. London: Karnac, 1967, pp. 86–92.

Bion WR (1959). Attacks on linking. In *Second Thoughts: Selected Papers on Psycho-Analysis*. London: Karnac, 1967, pp. 93–109.

Bion WR (1962a). *Learning from Experience*. London: Karnac, 1984.

Bion WR (1962b). A theory of thinking. In *Second Thoughts: Selected Papers on Psycho-Analysis*. London: Karnac, 1967, pp. 110–119.

Bion WR (1965). *Transformations*. London: Karnac, 1984.

Bion WR (1967a). *Wilfred Bion: Los Angeles Seminars and Supervision*. J Aguayo & B Malin (eds.). London: Karnac, 2013.

Bion WR (1967b). *Second Thoughts: Selected Papers on Psycho-Analysis*. London: Karnac, 1987.

Bion WR (1967c). Reverence and awe. In *Cogitations*. London: Karnac, 1992, pp. 284–292.

Bion WR (1970). *Attention and Interpretation*. London: Karnac, 1984.

Bion WR (1974). *Brazilian Lectures*. London: Karnac, 2008.

Bion WR (1975). The dream. In *A Memoir of the Future*. London: Karnac, 1991, pp. 1–217.

Bion WR (1976a). Evidence. In *Clinical Seminars and Other Works*. London: Karnac, 1994, pp. 312–320.

Bion WR (1976b). Emotional turbulence. In *Clinical Seminars and Other Works*. London: Karnac, 1994, pp. 295–305.

Bion WR (1976c). On a quotation from Freud. In *Clinical Seminars and Other Works*. London: Karnac, 1994, pp. 305–311.

Bion WR (1976d). Four discussions. In *Clinical Seminars and Other Works*. London: Karnac, 1994, pp., 241–292.

Bion WR (1977a). Caesura. In *Two Papers: The Grid and Caesura*. London: Karnac, 1989, pp. 35–56.

Bion WR (1977b). New York – five. In F Bion (ed.), *Bion in New York and São Paulo*. Perthshire: Clunie Press, 1980, pp. 58–74.

Bion WR (1977c). Untitled. In *Taming Wild Thoughts*. London: Karnac, 1997, pp. 27–51.

Bion WR (1977d). *The Italian Seminars*. London: Karnac, 2005.

Bion WR (1977e). The past presented. In *A Memoir of the Future*. London: Karnac, 1991, pp. 219–426.

Bion WR (1977f). The grid. In *Two Papers: The Grid and Caesura*. London: Karnac, 1989, pp. 1–33.

Bion WR (1977g). New York – three. In F Bion (ed.), *Bion in New York and São Paulo*. Strathclyde: Clunie Press, 1980, pp. 32–45.

Bion WR (1979). Making the best of a bad job. In *Clinical Seminars and Other Works*. London: Karnac, 1994, pp. 321–331.

Bion WR (1982). *The Long Week-End 1897–1919: Part of a Life*. Abingdon: Fleetwood Press.

Bion WR (1992). *Cogitations*. London: Karnac.

Bion WR (1997). *War Memoirs 1917–19*. London: Karnac.

Bion WR, Bion F (1981) A key. In *A Memoir of the Future*. London: Karnac, 1991, pp. 579–678.

Bléandonu G (1990). *Wilfred Bion: His Life and Works 1897–1979*, C Pajaczkowska (trans.). London: Free Association Books, 1994.

Bollas C (1987a). The transformational object. In *The Shadow of the Object: Psychoanalysis of the Unthought Known*. London: Free Association Books, pp. 1–29.

Bollas C (1987b). Loving hate. In *The Shadow of the Object: Psychoanalysis of the Unthought Known*. London: Free Association Books, pp. 117–134.

Bollas C (1989). The psychoanalyst's celebration of the analysand. In *Forces of Destiny*. London: Free Association Books, pp. 77–92.

Bollas C (2002). *Free Association*. Cambridge: Icon Books.

Bollas C (2013). C Bollas interviewed about new book 'Catch them before they fall'. www.routledgementalhealth.com/psychoanalysis/articles/christopher_bollas_interviewed_about_new_book_catch_them_before_they_fall/.

Boris HN (1986). Bion re-visited. *Contemporary Psychoanalysis* 22:159–184.

Botella C, Botella S (2005). *The Work of Psychic Figurability*. New York: Brunner-Routledge.

Britton R (1992). Keeping things in mind. In R Anderson (ed.), *Clinical Lectures on Klein and Bion*. London: Routledge, pp. 102–113.

Britton R (2013). Commentary on three papers by Wilfred R. Bion. *Psychoanalytic Quarterly* 82:311–321.

Britton R, Steiner J (1994). Interpretation: Selected fact or overvalued idea? *International Journal of Psychoanalysis* 75:1069–1078.

Buber M (1976). *Or Haganooz* (in Hebrew: The light of the hidden: Hasidic tales). Tel Aviv: Schocken.

Carpy DV (1989). Tolerating the countertransference: A mutative process. *International Journal of Psychoanalysis* 70:287–294.

Cartwright D (2010). The analyst's containing mind. In *Containing States of Mind: Exploring Bion's 'Container Model' in Psychoanalytic Psychotherapy*. New York: Routledge, pp. 46–62.

Cecchi V (1990). Analysis of a little girl with an autistic syndrome. *International Journal of Psychoanalysis* 71:403–410.

Chuster A (2013). Transference – or caesura? In R Oelsner (ed.), *Transference and Countertransference Today*. London and New York: Routledge, pp. 215–235.

Chuster A (2014). *A Lonesome Road: Essays on the Complexity of W.R. Bion's Work*. Rio de Janeiro: Imago.

Civitarese G (2008). 'Caesura' as Bion's discourse on method. *International Journal of Psychoanalysis* 89:1123–1143.

Civitarese G (2013). Bion's *Evidence* and his theoretical style. *Psychoanalytic Quarterly* 82:615–633.

Civitarese G (2015). Transformations in hallucinosis and the receptivity of the analyst. *International Journal of Psychoanalysis* 96:1091–1116.

Cripwell C (2011). Finding the depressed object in the obsessional: A clinical study. *International Journal of Psychoanalysis* 92:117–133.

Dan J (2002). *The Heart and the Fountain: An Anthology of Jewish Mystical Experiences*. Oxford and New York: Oxford University Press.

Davison S (2002). Bion's perspectives on psychoanalytic method [Panel report]. *International Journal of Psychoanalysis* 83:913–917.

de Bianchedi ET (1991). Psychic change: The 'becoming' of an inquiry. *International Journal of Psychoanalysis* 72:6–15.

de Bianchedi ET (2005). Whose Bion? Who is Bion? *International Journal of Psychoanalysis* 86:1529–1534.

de M'Uzan M (2000). Dream and identity. *Canadian Journal Psychoanalysis* 8:131–146.

de M'Uzan M (2003). Slaves of quantity. *Psychoanalytic Quarterly* 72:711–725.

Dictionary.com "reverie," in Dictionary.com Unabridged. Source location: Random House, Inc. www.dictionary.com/browse/reverie. Available: www.dictionary.com/. Accessed: October 20, 2017.

Eaton JL (2005). The obstructive object. *Psychoanalytic Review* 92:355–372.

Eigen M (1999). *Toxic Nourishment*. London: Karnac.

Eliot TS (1952). *The Complete Poems and Plays, 1909–1950*. New York: Harcourt.

Faimberg H (2012). José Bleger's dialectical thinking. *International Journal of Psychoanalysis* 93:981–992.

Fano Cassese S (2002). *Introduction to the Work of Donald Meltzer*. London: Karnac.

Ferro A (1993). The impasse within a theory of the analytic field: Possible vertices of observation. *International Journal of Psychoanalysis* 74:917–929.

Ferro A (2005). Bion: Theoretical and clinical observations. *International Journal of Psychoanalysis* 86:1535–1542.

Flax J (1990). *Thinking Fragments: Psychoanalysis, Feminism, and Postmodernism in the Contemporary West*. Berkley: University of California Press.

Freud S (1894a). Draft E. How anxiety originates. From extracts from the Fliess papers. *SE*, 1, 189–195.

Freud S (1894b). The neuro-psychoses of defence. *SE* 3:45–61.

Freud S (1895[1894]). On the grounds for detaching a particular syndrome from neurasthenia under the description 'anxiety neurosis'. *SE*, 3:85–117.

Freud S (1900). The interpretation of dreams. *SE* 4/5.

Freud S (1905). Fragment of an analysis of a case of hysteria. *SE*, 7.

Freud S (1909). Notes upon a case of obsessional neurosis. *SE*, 10:155–318.

Freud S (1911). Formulations on the two principles of mental functioning. *SE*, 12:219–226.

Freud S (1912a). Recommendations to physicians practising psycho-analysis. *SE* 12, 109–120.

Freud S (1912b). Letter from Sigmund Freud to Sándor Ferenczi, December 9, 1912. In E Brabant, E Falzeder & P Giampieri-Deutsch (eds.), *The Correspondence of Sigmund Freud and Sándor Ferenczi: Volume 1, 1908–1914*. Cambridge: Harvard University Press, 1993, pp. 440–441.

Freud S (1913a). Two lies told by children. *SE* 12:303–310.

Freud S (1913b). The disposition to obsessional neurosis: A contribution to the problem of choice of neurosis. *SE* 12:317–326.

Freud S (1915a). The unconscious. *SE* 14:166–215.

Freud S (1915b). Observations on transference love. *SE* 12:157–171.

Freud S (1916a). Letter to Andreas-Salomé, May 25, 1916. In E Pfeiffer (ed.), *Sigmund Freud and Lou Andreas-Salomé Letters*. New York: Harcourt, Brace, Jovanovich, 1966, p. 45.

Freud S (1916b). On transience. *SE* 14:305–307.

Freud S (1917). A metapsychological supplement to the theory of dreams. *SE* 14:217–235.

Freud S (1920). Beyond the pleasure principle. *SE* 18:3–64.

Freud S (1921). Group psychology and the analysis of the ego. *SE* 18:65–144.

Freud S (1923a). Two encyclopaedia articles. *SE* 18:235–259.

Freud S (1923b). The ego and the id. *SE* 19:1–66.

Freud S (1926). Inhibitions, symptoms and anxiety. *SE* 20:75–176.

Freud S (1930). Civilization and its discontents. *SE* 21:57–146.

Freud S (1933). Revision of the theory of dreams. *SE* 22:7–30.
Green A (1975). The analyst, symbolization and absence in the analytic setting. In *On Private Madness*. Madison: International University Press, pp. 30–59.
Green A (1997). The intuition of the negative in *Playing and Reality*. *International Journal of Psychoanalysis* 78:1071–1084.
Green A (2005). To love or not to love: Eros and Eris. In A Green & G Kohon (eds.), *Love and its Vicissitudes*. London: Routledge, pp. 1–39.
Grimalt A (2017). Book review of R. Lombardi, *Formless infinity: Clinical explorations of Matte-Blanco and Bion*. European Psychoanalytic Federation online, June 29.
Grinberg L, Sor D, Tabak de Bianchedi E (1975). *New Introduction to the Work of Bion*. Oxford: Rolland Harris Trust.
Grotstein JS (2004). The seventh servant: The implications of a truth drive in Bion's theory of 'O'. *International Journal of Psychoanalysis* 85:1081–1101.
Grotstein JS (2007). *A Beam of Intense Darkness*. London: Karnac.
Grotstein JS (2009). Dreaming as a 'curtain of illusion': Revisiting the 'royal road' with Bion as our guide. *International Journal of Psychoanalysis* 90:733–752.
Guntrip H (1968). *Schizoid Phenomena, Object Relations and the Self*. London: Hogarth.
Hellner-Eshed M (2009). *A River Flows from Eden: The Language of Mystical Experience in the Zohar*. Stanford: Stanford University Press.
Horovitz M (2007). Transfert et vérité. In F Guignard & T Bokanowski (eds.), *Actualité de la Pensée de Bion*. Paris: Editions in Press, pp. 45–51.
Hosseini K (2003). *The Kite Runner*. New York: Riverhead Books.
Hume D (1748). *An Enquiry Concerning Human Understanding*. New York: Dover.
Irigaray L (1990/1993). *Je, Tu, Nous: Towards a Culture of Difference*. New York: Routledge.
Jones E (1953). *The Life and Work of Sigmund Freud. Vol. 1*. London: Hogarth Press.
Joseph B (1982). Addiction to near-death. *International Journal of Psychoanalysis* 63:449–456.
Joseph B (1985). Transference: The total situation. *International Journal of Psychoanalysis* 66:447–454.
Khan MMR (1986). Introduction. In Winnicott DW, *Holding and Interpretation*. London: Hogarth, pp. 1–18.
Kinston W, Cohen J (1986). Primal repression: Clinical and theoretical aspects. *International Journal of Psychoanalysis* 67:337–353.
Klein M (1937). Love, guilt and reparation. In *Love, Guilt and Reparation and Other Works*. London: Hogarth Press, 1975, pp. 306–343.

Klein M (1944). The emotional life and ego-development of the infant with special reference to the depressive position. In P King & R Steiner (eds.), *The Freud-Klein Controversies 1941–1945*. London: Tavistock/Routledge, 1991, pp. 752–796.

Klein M (1946). Notes on some schizoid mechanisms. *International Journal of Psychoanalysis* 27:99–110.

Klein M (1952) The origins of transference. In *Envy and Gratitude and Other Works, 1946–1963*. London: Hogarth Press, 1975, pp. 48–56.

Klein M (1957). Envy and gratitude. In *Envy and Gratitude and Other Works, 1946–1963*. London: Hogarth Press, 1975, pp. 176–235.

Kohon G. (2005). Love in a time of madness. In A Green & G Kohon (eds.), *Love and its Vicissitudes*. London: Routledge, pp. 41–100.

Kristeva J (1987). *In the Beginning was Love: Psychoanalysis and Faith*. New York: Columbia Universities Press.

Lacan J (1959). Das Ding. In *The Ethics of Psychoanalysis, 1959–1960*, D. Porter (trans.). New York: Routledge, 2008, pp. 51–68.

Laplanche J, Pontalis JB (1967). *The Language of Psycho-analysis*, T. Nicholson-Smith (trans.). London: The Hogarth Press, 1973.

Laub D (1992). An event without a witness: Truth, testimony and survival. In S Felman & D Laub (eds.), *Testimony: Crises of Witnessing in Literature, Psychoanalysis and History*. New York: Routledge, pp. 75–92.

Likierman M (2001). And who would doubt this? Early object love, psychical defenses and dissociation processes. In *Melanie Klein: Her Work in Context*. New York: Continuum, pp. 85–99.

Lombardi R (2009). Symmetric frenzy and catastrophic change: A consideration of primitive mental states in the wake of Bion and Matte-Blanco. *International Journal of Psychoanalysis* 90:529–549.

Maiello S (2008). On the nature of the autistic core: An adult patient's survival code. Paper presented at *The Fourth Frances Tustin International Conference*, Tel Aviv, Israel.

Maimonides M (1191). Introduction. *The Guide of the Perplexed*, C. Rabin (trans.). Indianapolis: Hackett Publishing, 1995.

Mason A (2000). Bion and binocular vision. *International Journal of Psychoanalysis* 81:983–988.

Matte-Blanco I (1981). Reflecting with Bion. In JS Grotstein (ed.), *Do I Dare Disturb the Universe?* London: Karnac. pp. 489–528.

Matte-Blanco I (1988). *Thinking, Feeling and Being: Clinical Reflections on the Fundamental Antinomy of Human Beings and World*. New York: Routledge.

Mauss-Hanke A (2013). Psychoanalytic considerations about the *antioedipal condition* in Heinrich von Kleist's *Penthesilea* and in the analysis of Miss M. *International Journal of Psychoanalysis* 94:477–499.

McDougall J (1989). *Theatres of the body*. London: Free Association Books.

Meltzer D (1974). Adhesive identification. In A Hahn (ed.), *Sincerity and Other Works*. London: Karnac, pp. 335–350.

Meltzer D (1978). *The Kleinian Development*. London: Karnac, 2008.

Meltzer D (1984). Dreaming as unconscious thinking. In *Dream life: A Re-examination of the Psychoanalytic Theory and Technique*. London: Karnac, pp. 51–70.

Meltzer D (1986). *Studies in Extended Metapsychology: Clinical Applications of Bion's Ideas*. London: Karnac, 2009.

Meltzer D (1988). *The Apprehension of Beauty: The Role of Aesthetic Conflict in Development, Art, and Violence*. London: Karnac, 2008.

Meltzer D (2000). Signs, symbols and allegory. In M Harris-Williams (ed.), *A Meltzer Reader*. London: Karnac, 2010, pp. 121–130.

Meltzer D (2005). Creativity and the countertransference. In: M Harris-Williams (ed.), *The Vale of Soulmaking: The Post-Kleinien Model of the Mind*. London: Karnac, pp. 175–182.

Meltzer D, Bremner J, Hoxter S, Weddell D & Wittenberg I (1975). *Explorations in Autism*. London: Karnac, 2008.

Meltzer D, Harris-Williams M (1985). Three lectures on WR Bion's *A Memoir of the Future*. In A Hahn (ed.), *Sincerity and Other Works*. London: Karnac, 1994, pp. 520–550.

Meltzer D, Mack Smith C, Psychoanalytic Group of Barcelona (2002a). Jordi: From bi to tridimensionality. In *Psychoanalytic Work with Children and Adults*. London: Karnac, pp. 45–60.

Meltzer D, Mack Smith C, Psychoanalytic Group of Barcelona (2002b). Yolanda: Vicissitudes and failures of symbolism. In *Psychoanalytic Work with Children and Adults*. London: Karnac, pp. 61–74.

Mitrani JL (1995). Toward an understanding of unmentalized experience. *Psychoanalytic Quarterly* 64:68–112.

Mitrani JL (2001). *Ordinary People and Extra-Ordinary Protections*. Philadelphia: Brunner Routledge.

Neuman Y (2010). Penultimate interpretation. *International Journal of Psychoanalysis* 91:1043–1054.

Oelsner R (2013). Transference minute to minute: Analysis of an analysis. In: R Oelsner (ed.), *Transference and Countertransference Today*. London and New York: Routledge, pp. 236–255.

Ogden, TH (1989). On the concept of an autistic-contiguous position. *International Journal of Psychoanalysis* 70:127–140.

Ogden TH (1995). Analysing forms of aliveness and deadness of the transference-countertransference. *International Journal of Psychoanalysis* 76:695–709.

Ogden TH (2004). This art of psychoanalysis: Dreaming undreamt dreams and interrupted cries. *International Journal of Psychoanalysis* 85:857–877.

O'Shaughnessy E (2005). Whose Bion? *International Journal of Psychoanalysis* 86:1523–1528.

Parsons M (2005). Introduction. In C Botella, S Botella. *The Work of Psychic Figurability*. London: Karnac, pp. xvii–xxiii.

Pascal B (1669). *Pensées and Other Writings*, H Levi (trans.). New York: Oxford University Press, Inc., 1999.

Paz O (1975). *A Tree Within*. E Weinberger (ed.). New York: New Directions Books, 1988.

Phillips A (1993). On being bored. In *On kissing, Tickling and Being Bored*. London: Faber and Faber, pp. 71–82.

Piontelli A (1992). *From Fetus to Child: An Observational and Psychoanalytic Study*. London: Routledge.

Press J (2016). Metapsychological and clinical issues in psychosomatics research. *International Journal of Psychoanalysis* 97:89–113.

Reiner A (2012). *Bion and Being: Passion and the Creative Mind*. London: Karnac.

Rose JS (2007). *Symbolization: Representation and Communication*. London: Karnac.

Rosenfeld H. (1987). *Impasse and Interpretation*. London: Tavistock Publications.

Roussillon R (2013). The function of the object in binding and unbinding of the drives. *International Journal of Psychoanalysis* 94:257–276.

Sandler PC (2005). *The Language of Bion*. London: Karnac.

Sandler PC (2011). The realm of Minus and the negative. In: *Analytic Function and the Function of the Analyst*. London: Karnac, pp. 13–34.

Sandler PC (2015). *An Introduction to WR Bion's A Memoir of the Future, Vol. 2: Facts of Matter or a Matter of Fact?* London: Karnac.

Sapisochin G (2013). Second thoughts on Agieren: Listening to the enacted. *International Journal of Psychoanalysis* 94:967–991.

Schneider JA (2005). Experiences in K and –K. *International Journal of Psychoanalysis* 86:825–839.

Scholem G (1960). *On the Kabbalah and Its Symbolism*, R Manheim (trans.). New York: Schocken Books, 1969.

Scholem G (1961). *Major Trends in Jewish Mysticism*. New York: Schocken Books.

Scholem G (1971). *The Messianic Idea in Judaism and Other Essays on Jewish Spirituality*. New York: Schocken Books.

Scholem G (1975). *Explications and Implications: Writings on Jewish Heritage and Renaissance* [Devarim BeGo]. Tel Aviv: Am Oved.

Spector-Person E (1993). Introduction. In E Spector-Person, A Hagelin & P Fonagy (eds.), *On Freud's "Observations on Transference Love"*. New Haven: Yale Universities Press, pp 1–14.

Steiner J (2000). Containment, enactment and communication. *International Journal of Psychoanalysis* 81:245–255.

Symington J (1985). The survival function of primitive omnipotence. *International Journal of Psychoanalysis* 66:481–487.

Szykierski D (2010). The traumatic roots of containment: The evolution of Bion's metapsychology. *Psychoanalytic Quarterly* 79:935–968.

Tamir Y (2003). Idealization in the analytic process as a curative emotional experience. *Sihot-Dialogues: Israel Journal of Psychotherapy* 17:123–130.

Torres N (2013). Intuition and ultimate reality in psychoanalysis: Bion's implicit use of Bergson and Whitehead's notions. In N Torres & RD Hinshelwood (eds.), *Bion's Sources: The Shaping of His Paradigms*. London and New York: Routledge, pp. 20–34.

Tuckett D, Levinson NA (2010). Prenatal states of mind. *PEP Consolidated Psychoanalytic Glossary*, 1.

Tustin F (1990). Psychotherapy with children who cannot play. In *The Protective Shell in Children and Adults*. London: Karnac, pp. 97–121.

Tustin F (1992). *Autistic States in Children* (Revised edition). London and New York: Tavistock/Routledge.

Waddell M (2005). Forward. In A Green & G Kohon (eds.), *Love and Its Vicissitudes*. London: Routledge, pp. ix–xviii.

Winnicott DW (1945). Primitive emotional development. In *Through Paediatrics to Psychoanalysis*. London: Karnac, 1958, pp. 145–156.

Winnicott DW (1947). Hate in the countertransference. In *Through Paediatrics to Psychoanalysis*. London: Karnac, 1984, pp. 194–203.

Winnicott DW (1949). Mind and its relation to the psyche-soma. In *Through Paediatrics to Psychoanalysis*. London: Karnac, pp. 243–254.

Winnicott DW (1952). Anxiety associated with insecurity. In *Through Paediatrics to Psychoanalysis*. London: Karnac, 1984, pp. 97–100.

Winnicott DW (1969a). The use of an object and relating through identifications. In *Playing and Reality*. London and New York: Routledge, pp. 86–94.

Winnicott DW (1969b). Additional note on psycho-somatic disorder. In: C Winnicott, R Shepherd & M Davis (eds.), *Psycho-Analytic Explorations*. London: Karnac, 1989, pp. 115–118.

Winnicott DW (1974). Fear of breakdown. *International Review of Psychoanalysis* 1:103–107.

Winnicott DW (1988). Chaos. In *Human Nature*. London: Free Association Books, pp. 135–138.

Yeret A (2004). On the hunger for certainty. Unpublished manuscript.

Young EB (2004). Presentation of *The Analyst's Capacity to Bear Love*. Seattle Society of Psychoanalysis.

Index

absence 72–3, 78, 80, 110–11, 113, 119, 131–2, 134, 139, 143, 146, 163, 165, 168
absolute truth 66
addictions 14
adhesion 88, 139
act of faith 71
adhesive identification 78, 80, 133
adolescents 81
adults 38, 126, 162
aesthetic conflict 118–20, 125, 127–8, 131, 154
aesthetic impact 119, 139, 143, 154
aggression 23, 106
agitation 19, 67, 73
agonies 74, 142
Aguayo, J. 40, 49, 71, 102, 163
Aharoni, H. 33
algebra/algebraic 4–5, 10
Alice's Adventures in Wonderland (Carroll) 5, 13
alimentary model of thinking 31
aliveness 58, 86, 96, 141
allegory 170–1, 177
alpha-elements 14, 19, 60
alpha-function 14, 26, 39, 43, 47, 81–2, 143
Alvarez, A. 12, 14, 26, 43, 79, 81, 137, 143
amniotic fluid 30, 38

analyst 6–9, 19–26, 33–37, 39–44, 76–8, 80–2, 85–9, 94–7, 106–8, 111–13, 115, 129
analytic session 35, 40, 50, 108
anger 2, 23, 151, 156, 177
anxiety 42, 51, 56, 65, 67–8, 70, 72, 80–1, 86, 147, 155–6
anxiety attacks 65, 70, 72
anxiety disorder 72–3
anxiety neurosis 70, 73
Anzieu, D. 82
apprehension 3, 5–6, 127, 173
approximations 4, 8–9
archaic 31, 61, 127
arrogance 102
Asperger syndrome 77
Atonement, at-one-ment 23, 66, 170, 172, 179
attack 12, 14, 20, 44, 51, 56, 95, 101–3, 106–7, 110–12, 114, 178
attacking 95, 102, 112, 178
attention 3, 8, 20, 49, 60, 76, 87, 113, 163, 176
attention deficit disorder 46
Avnon, D. 163
autism 20, 79, 81–3, 85–6, 88, 132, 138–9, 142–3
autistic-contiguous mode 132, 140
awake 36, 58, 61–2, 65, 124
awareness 5, 12, 14–15, 38, 89, 133, 139, 142

Index

baby 18, 30–1, 44, 64, 93, 126, 128, 132
balanced outlook 44
Balint, M. 125
beauty 119, 127
Beck, J. 141
becoming, becoming O 65, 71
Bégoin, J. 120
behaviour 2, 16, 23, 59, 64, 81, 83, 99, 106, 120, 122, 148
belief 24, 44, 129–30, 172–3
Berkeley, G 161
beta-elements 14, 17, 19, 24, 47, 73, 144
Bible 163
Bick, E. 43, 78–9
bidimensionality 78
Bion, W. R: on arrogance 102; *Attacks on Linking* 44, 102; *Attention and Interpretation* 49; on beta-screen 144; Caesura, notion of 2, 29, 31; on communication method 160; conception of K 101–2, 112; on cultural myth 173; on deficient part of personality 12–15; *Diary* 99; *Evidence* 50, 175; on hallucinations 166; ice/cream as I/scream (vignette) 49; on inaccessible part of personality 11–12; on infant's receptiveness 18; Jewish mysticism and 167–70; *Language and the Schizophrenic* 13; *Learning from Experience* 21, 32 *Long Week-End* The 99; *Memoir of the Future, A* 170–1, 180–1; on non-psychotic transformations 6, 101; notion of thought 72; patient description 2, 106–16, 133, 148, 155–6; on projective transformations 7; psychoanalytic endeavours 2–3; reference to Freud 49, 69; reference to Klein's theories 3; reference to Isaac Luria 162; reference to Valéry 5; religious metaphors 171–3; on reverie and dreaming 33–8; *Second Thoughts* 41, 102, 105; on speculative imagination 74; on state of mind (conscious and unconscious) 38–44; *Theory of Thinking, A* 102; on thinking process 34; on trained intuition 37; transformations in hallucinosis 9; use of mathematics 4; on verbal communication 55; *War Memoirs* 98
birth 28–30, 63, 66, 71, 108, 120, 144
Bléandonu, G. xiii, xiv
blind 17, 37–8, 180
Bollas, C. 65, 95, 103–4, 129
boredom 21, 76–97, 144
Boris, H. N. 37
Botella, C. 40–2, 70, 164–5
Botella, S. 40–2, 70, 164–5
boundaries 26, 57, 145, 152, 167
breakdown 60, 64–65, 74, 102
breast 103, 107, 119, 126, 130
breastfeeding 83, 88
Britton, R. 74, 105, 132
Buber, M. 159, 163, 168, 173

caesura 28–53, 64–5, 71, 74, 88, 106, 112, 166, 178–80
Carpy, D. V. 66
catastrophe 32, 34, 59, 62, 70–1, 77, 139
catastrophic anxieties 80
catastrophic change 32, 49–52, 55, 69, 71, 74
Cecchi, V. 87–8
chaos 5, 59, 115
chaotic 9, 115
children 43, 79, 81–2, 86, 105, 120, 132, 138, 142–3, 176
Chuster, A. 3, 18–19, 26
Civitarese, G. 9, 23, 144, 169
communication 31–2, 37, 42, 44, 100–1, 103, 106–7, 112, 148, 160, 162, 171, 173, 177
complexity 10, 13, 45, 138–9, 141, 182

complexity theory 27
conception 9, 79, 101, 160, 179–80
conceptualization 12, 138, 165
confusion 8, 21, 34, 73, 86, 115, 144
consciousness 35, 38, 43, 138, 142, 173 *see also* unconsciousness
constant conjunction 169, 178
contact barrier 32, 44, 60
container 9, 48, 52, 78, 79, 84, 102, 104, 107, 143
container-contained 98
corpus symbolicum 175
countertransference 66, 86, 129, 155
counterdreaming 33, 52
Cripwell, C. 153
curiosity, inhibition of 143, 145, 148, 150–52

Dan, J. 171, 174
Davison, S. 48
deadening 57–8, 66
deadness 18, 58, 61, 65–6, 85, 88, 91, 96, 124
death 41, 56, 58, 63, 69, 71, 88, 91, 93–4, 122, 143–5, 153, 155, 157
de Bianchedi, E. T. 30, 33, 164, 172
defences 3, 18, 23, 26, 65, 96, 140–1, 152, 156
deficit 12, 97
de M'Uzan, M. 40, 57
dependence 43, 50–1, 66, 131
depression 88, 99, 125, 132, 177
destruction 49, 128
detachment 23, 65, 115, 170
differentiation 12, 73
disciplines 4, 166–7, 169, 172
discovery 36, 48–9, 104, 182
disintegration 44, 65, 138, 144
dismantling 139–40
displacement 27, 58
disruption 74, 156
dissociation 77, 115, 150
distortion 27, 32
distractions 33, 49, 98

distress 1, 13, 21, 50–2, 60, 76, 86, 115, 119, 153
disturbances 5, 115, 143
divine 170, 174
divine truth 174
dread 12, 19, 31, 41, 61, 70, 89, 91
dream 14, 16–17, 19, 21, 23, 27, 31, 33, 35–6, 39–40, 42, 47–8, 52, 56, 58–60, 62–3, 66, 73–4, 101, 129, 134, 139–40, 149–51, 178, 182
dreaming 12, 14–15, 21, 24, 27, 31, 33–6, 38, 40, 42–3, 48, 50–2, 74, 111, 125, 133, 138
dreamwork 54
drugs 56, 121, 172

Eaton, J. L. 102
ecstasy 9, 86, 125–7, 131, 182
ecstatic 119, 129, 154
ego 69–70, 81, 153, 165
Eigen, M. 9, 65
Eliot, T. S. 92
emotional experience 139–43, 146, 153, 155–6, 159, 161, 165, 167–8, 178, 182
emotionality 23, 140, 155, 178
emotional life 4, 15
emotional response 21, 110
emotional truth 4, 23, 34, 37, 44, 49, 52, 65, 70, 74, 104, 106, 141–2, 159, 166–7, 170, 173–4
emotional turbulence 18, 27, 32–3, 49, 51–2, 150, 178, 182
emotions 15, 20, 23, 29, 33, 81, 86, 102, 106, 112, 119, 132, 139, 143, 148, 150, 156, 169
emptiness 76, 78, 80, 86, 88–9, 91, 93, 95–7, 108, 144
enactment 155
encapsulation, encapsulate 14, 18, 21, 131, 143, 154
enforced splitting 15, 138
enliven 89, 91, 97, 122, 125–6
environment 12, 18, 77–8, 102–3, 114, 128, 140

envy 30, 101, 102, 106, 130, 144
Eternal Sunshine of the Spotless Mind (Movie) 46
Euclidean geometry 4
evolution 2, 37, 45, 66, 71, 161
excitation 57, 72–3, 141
excitement 84–5, 120, 122, 128, 141
experience, learning from 21, 32

Faimberg, H. 111
faith 44, 88, 100, 166, 168, 172 *see also* act of faith
False Self 69
falsity 161, 183
Fano Cassese S 132
fantasy 128, 150, 152
fatigue 58, 124
fear 9, 15–16, 28, 31, 41, 44, 49–52, 56, 60, 63, 66–7, 69–71, 74, 77, 82, 88–9, 94–5, 99, 102–3, 121–2, 124, 129, 131, 139–40, 143–4, 151, 154, 175, 178
Ferro, A. 34, 65
foetus 30, 33, 38, 74
formless infinite 11, 42, 48
fracture 19, 145, 148, 177
fragmentation 5, 7, 19, 101, 115
franticness 14, 73, 128
free associations 16, 38, 43, 104, 164, 175
free floating attention 8, 36–7, 39–40
Freud, S.: 126; on anxiety disorder 72; Bion's reference 2, 49, 69, 163; caesuras, notion of 28–9, 32, 38; on dream 39; on free floating attention 36; *Formulations on the Two Principles of Mental Functioning* 3; *Fragment of an Analysis of a Case of Hysteria* 98; 11; *Language and the Schizophrenic* 6, 13; *Neuro-Psychoses of Defence* 152; on obsessionality 137, 152–3, 157; patient's emotional experience 8–9; psychotic part of personality 13, 73; *Revision of the Theory of Dreams* 33; on symptomatic act: 98; transference, definition 6; on transference-love 118–19; 9–10; on two forms of reality 164; on unrepressed unconscious. 69–70
frustration 13, 35, 37, 51, 100, 119, 157, 161–62, 166

gap 28–9, 31–3, 37–8, 40, 45, 50, 57, 88, 90, 115, 147, 161, 163
Genesis 175–76
God 163, 168, 170–3, 175–6, 181
Godhead 168–9, 172
Goethe, J. W. 182
gratitude 22, 129–30
Green, A. 95, 127, 129, 132, 164
Grimalt, A. 16
Grinberg, L. 33
Grotstein, J. S. 19, 36, 103–4, 172

hallucination 16, 40–1, 166
hallucinosis 9–10, 23, 166
hate 61–2, 106, 126, 129–30, 144, 177
Hellner-Eshed, M. 176
helplessness 21, 73, 115, 156
Holocaust 105, 108
Horovitz, M. 104
Hosseini, K. 55
hostility 30, 57
human mind 3–4, 30, 139, 161
Hume, D. 161
hunger 15, 29, 31, 121, 139, 166

idealization 22, 122, 127, 129–31
identification 3, 8, 14, 22, 26, 31–2, 38–9, 78, 80, 102–3, 105–7, 132–3, 154
illusion 19, 29, 141, 145
imagination 5, 29–30, 43, 74, 81–2, 182
imaginative conjecture 29
impasse 1, 3, 25, 72, 135
impotence 21, 133, 153
incarnations 37, 45, 128

incisions 29, 31, 49
ineffability, ineffable 9, 159–84
infancy 28, 107, 131, 153
infant 15, 18, 31, 35, 38, 41–2, 44, 78–9, 85–6, 88, 95, 101–3, 105, 107, 112, 119, 126, 130–1, 139, 143–4, 154–6, 165, 178, 180–1
infinite 4, 9, 11, 12, 22, 25, 26, 42, 48, 61, 147, 160, 161, 167–9, 171, 178–80
inhibitions 2, 50, 143
inner object 66, 78, 89, 139
inner world 58, 65, 86, 89, 94, 156, 170, 176, 182 *see also* psychic world
insanity 29, 31, 166
internalization 78, 102, 143
internal objects 101, 107, 126, 135, 177
internal world 31, 42–3, 46, 48, 77, 97, 108, 114, 135, 164–5, 176–7
interpretations 1, 3, 8, 13, 16, 20–1, 23–4, 26, 29, 35, 38, 42, 44, 48–9, 50–2, 70–1, 77, 80–1, 95–6, 100, 104, 106, 122, 134, 137–8, 142, 155, 161–2, 171, 174–81
intonation 80, 84
intrusion 95, 124, 131, 149
intrusiveness 131, 134–5
intuiting 4, 41, 166
invariant 2, 8, 25, 148, 161
invariance 5
Irigaray, L. 161
irritation 21, 144

Jewish mysticism 167–8, 170, 177–8 *see also* Zohar
Jones, E. 118
Joseph, B. 8, 97

K (knowledge) 53, 101
K link 31, 53
-K link 101, 102, 112
Kabbalah 168, 170, 183, 184

Kant, I. 37, 161
Keats, J. 37, 182
Khan, M. M. R. 76–7
Klein, M.: Bion's reference 2, 5, 12; on internalization of object 78; *Notes on Some Schizoid Mechanisms 3*; on love 130; projective identification theories 3; on psychotic functioning 7–8, 12
Kohon, G. 119, 127, 129
Kristeva, J. 135

Lacan, J. 153
language 5, 24–5, 37, 39, 79, 108–9, 112, 126, 144, 154, 160–1, 163, 170, 174, 178–80, 182
Language of Achievement 37, 39
Language of substitution 39
learning disability 46
lifeless 76–7, 81, 85, 87, 91–2, 96, 147
Likierman, M. 130
Lombardi, R. 138
loneliness 31, 90, 100
longing 94, 123–4, 145
Los Angeles Psychoanalytic Society 29
loss 1, 16, 37, 42, 49, 65, 72, 88, 95, 99, 108, 143, 145, 149, 153, 159, 164
love 12, 15, 30, 35, 46, 48, 56, 69, 94, 96, 114, 140, 142, 144; patient's 118–35
love object 119, 142
Luria, Isaac 162, 167

MacDougall, J. 86
madness 5, 68, 70, 126, 127
Maiello, S. 108
Maimonides, M. 34
Mason, A. 11
masturbation 57, 98
mathematics 4, 6, 45, 139, 169, 173
Matte-Blanco, I. 26, 138

Mauss-Hanke, A. 156
meaninglessness 16, 156, 174
Meltzer, D.: on autism affected children 79, 81–2, 142; on Bion's use of mathematics 4; on boredom 78; on counterdreaming 33, 52; on distinction between allegory and symbol. 177; on love 132; on pains of aesthetic conflict 119–20, 128; on psychogenic autism and primitive mental states 137–9; reference to Klein 8; on sadistic impulses 141; on sense impressions and consciousness 38; on withdrawn mental state 43
memory and desire 17, 26, 29, 38, 48, 72, 79, 89, 91, 92, 94, 98, 103, 105, 113, 115, 130, 137, 148, 150, 151, 155, 156, 166, 167, 169, 170, 171, 174
mental activity 40–1, 77–8, 95
mental capacities 13, 35, 55, 73
mental functioning, two principles of 78–9, 82, 102, 137, 143
mental life 11, 26, 39, 43, 55, 81, 96, 130, 179
mental pain 15, 65, 119–20, 154
mental processes 6, 14, 128
mental space 9, 25, 48, 77, 79, 133
mental states 11–12, 29, 31–2, 38–9, 43, 80, 137–8
mentalization 30, 97, 114
metabolize 17–18, 31, 153, 178
metaphors 5, 25, 71–2, 129, 172
Milton, J. 182
mindlessness 17, 39, 48, 78, 99, 155
Minus, realm of 165
Mitrani, J. L. 35
mother 30–1, 35, 38, 41, 44, 48, 56, 58–9, 62–4, 69, 74, 78–79, 81, 83, 85–8, 94, 101–3, 105, 107–8, 119–120, 123–6, 128–32, 141, 143–6, 150–4; motherhood feelings 86

motion 6, 21, 29, 32–3, 111, 135
mourn 143, 145, 153
multidimensionality 5, 8, 179, 181
music 28, 90, 161, 163
musicians 87, 163
mysteries 37, 141, 165, 172, 177, 179
mystical 30, 162–4, 166–7, 169–73, 175–9, 181–2
mysticism 167–72, 174, 177–8
myths 173
nameless dread 9

neediness 120, 131, 134
negative 48, 129, 163–7, 169, 174
negative capability 37, 165
Neuman, Y. 161
neurosis 11, 70, 73, 137, 153, 179
neurotic 55, 69, 73–4, 96, 137, 155
nightmare 1, 13, 17, 23–5, 40, 42, 99
non-existence 60, 94, 164
non-psychotic parts 3, 12, 24, 34, 41, 69, 102, 138, 166
non-sensuous 3 *see also* sensuous
nonverbal 40, 78, 138
nothingness 21, 61, 78, 113
noumena 178, 182
numbness 62, 90–1, 95–6, 157

O 66, 71, 168, 169
object relations 12, 78–9, 94, 97, 113, 135, 138, 141
observation 17, 52, 98, 130, 164, 179
observer 50, 166
obsessionality 19, 77, 137–44, 148, 150, 152–5, 157
Oelsner, R. 155
Ogden, T. H. 34, 80, 96, 132, 140, 156
omnipotence 70, 73, 142, 144
omnipotent control 81, 85, 119, 125, 138, 141–2, 153–4
omnipotent independence 144
omniscience 21, 141
oneness 85, 119, 126, 131, 145, 154
otherness 34, 119, 141, 147

pain 9–10, 13–16, 19, 27, 37, 50–1, 65, 71, 79, 86, 90, 93, 102, 119–20, 123–5, 128, 141–2, 152, 154, 156, 173, 182
panic 56, 59–60, 64–5, 67–9, 87
Parsons, M. 39–40
Pascal, B. 1
passion 95, 128
patience 52, 121, 156
Paz, O. 61
perception 5, 17–18, 40, 49, 55, 119, 153, 161, 164, 171
personality 1–4, 6, 8–9, 11–15, 17–21, 23–6, 30, 33–4, 41–3, 59, 66, 69–70, 73–4, 78, 96, 101–4, 106, 137–9, 141, 144, 153, 156, 166
perspectives 8, 97, 129, 130
perverse 133, 135
phantasies 12, 106, 130
phenomenon, phenomena 3, 9, 10, 24, 40, 70, 118, 126, 139, 140, 161, 173, 178
Phillips, A. 89, 96
philosophers 5, 34, 161–2, 167–9
Piontelli, A. 29
Plato 161
possessiveness 132
prenatal 28–30
preverbal
Press, J. 24
primal communication 103, 107 *see also* primitive communication
primary object 86, 88, 97, 102–3, 113, 135, 143, 178
primitive communication 31–2, 66
primordial 14, 31, 38–9, 69, 74, 157, 166
projective identification 3, 8, 14, 22, 26, 31, 32, 35, 36, 39, 78, 102, 103, 105–7, 129
proto-mental 40
psyche 11, 26, 28–9, 31, 33–4, 36, 39–42, 66, 71, 73–4, 78, 89, 96–7, 103, 107, 135, 153

psychic equilibrium 25, 34, 49, 71, 155
psychic reality 45, 161–2, 164, 167
psychic world 18, 27, 40, 133, 180 *see also* inner world
psychoanalysis 2–3, 30, 49, 72–3, 86, 103, 118, 135, 138, 160, 163, 178, 180
psycho-analyst 6, 41, 100, 162, 171, 181
psychoanalytic theory 131
psychoanalytic thinking 137, 160, 162–3, 167, 169
psychopathology 97, 120
psychosis 9, 166
psychotic 2–14, 17–18, 20–1, 23–5, 33–4, 41, 43–4, 49, 55, 59, 66, 69–70, 73–4, 96, 101–3, 112, 135, 138–9, 144, 166–7; personality 9, 166

quantities 57, 72–3
quasi-hallucinatory 19, 40, 165, 182

rage 9, 22, 23, 80, 109
reality principle 13, 104
realization 25, 27, 41, 86, 93, 96, 108, 112, 178
receptiveness 18, 26, 41, 44
receptivity 66, 103, 166
regression 42, 126–7, 131, 165
Reiner, A. 167
religion 4, 171–2, 174
reliving 74, 78, 97, 112–13
repetition 84, 111
representation 40, 104, 138, 160, 165, 168, 177, 179
resistance 3, 49, 65, 71, 119, 157
reverie 21, 33–6, 38, 42, 44, 48, 52, 79
rivalry 22, 130, 144
Rose, J. S. 113
Rosenfeld, H. 129
Roussillon, R. 58, 107

sadism 12, 132, 139–41
sadness 90, 92, 113
Sandler, P. C. 37, 106, 112, 169
sanity 11, 29, 31, 166
Sapisochin, G. 72
Schneider, J. A. 101–2
Scholem, G. 168, 170, 174–5, 177–8, 181–2
scream 16, 27, 44, 49, 50, 59, 108
Scriptures 171, 182
second skin 79, 154
selected fact 26, 36
sense impressions 9, 14, 31, 33, 35, 38, 47
sensuality 131, 132
sensuous 3, 8, 18, 35, 41–2, 47, 72, 108, 161, 164, 166–7, 170–1, 180
separateness 80, 82, 115, 126, 128, 142–3, 145, 153–5, 157
separation 28, 32, 121, 123, 138
Shakespeare, W. 182
shame 1, 50, 84, 93
Shelley, P. B. 182
silence 1, 23, 57, 76, 90–1, 94, 109, 114, 123–4, 146–9, 151, 163, 168
skin 18, 31, 56, 57, 59, 78, 79, 85, 90–1, 93, 100, 149, 152, 154
sleep 1, 17, 19, 22, 27, 29, 33, 36, 40, 52, 57, 58, 61–2, 65, 90, 93–4, 108–109, 124–5
smell 35, 41, 80
Sor, D. 33
soul 92, 127, 143, 102, 166, 169, 170, 181
Spector-Person, E. 118
spectrum 55, 72, 141
speculative imagination 30, 174
stammers 64, 68, 181
starvation 15, 104, 139
Steiner, J. 74, 115
stimuli 13, 16, 18–20, 33, 101, 140
sublime 85, 119, 126, 154, 169, 170
subvert 5, 25, 34, 49, 62, 71, 146, 155

surprise 5, 23, 48, 50, 58, 93, 147, 156, 182
survival 13, 15, 30, 93, 105, 128, 140, 144
survivors 105, 108
symbols 12, 59, 81, 109, 144, 162, 174, 177–8
synapse 31, 32, 38, 44, 48
synaptic model 31, 32
Szykierski, D. 99

temptation 40, 45, 50, 155
testimony 162
thing-in-itself (things-in-themselves) 17, 96, 161, 180
thinker 2, 14, 20, 48, 72, 74, 111, 134
thinking 29, 31, 34, 36, 77, 102, 114, 143, 144
thought without a thinker 72
Through the Looking-Glass (Carrol) 5
tolerance/tolerating 8–9, 11, 19, 37, 52, 66, 106, 129
Torah 163, 181
Torres, N. 177
traditions 50, 162, 169, 170, 171, 174
trained intuition: Bion, W. R. 37; intuition 8, 21, 25, 30, 36–7, 41, 73, 104, 164, 166, 173, 179–80
transference 3, 6, 8, 12, 20, 25–6, 29, 58, 66, 71, 73, 77–8, 85, 86, 94, 97, 104, 107, 108, 111, 113, 115, 118–19, 123, 127, 129, 135, 138, 143, 145, 154–5
transformations 4–10, 13, 26–7, 31–3, 44–5, 48, 49, 51, 71–3, 97, 104, 106, 161, 174–5: emotional experience of 33; 'Freudian' transformations 9; in hallucinosis 10, 166; 'Kleinian transformations' 9; projective transformations 7, 26; rigid motion transformations 6, 27; transformations in O 71, 183

Index 203

transience 5, 8, 10
transition 19, 32, 159
trauma 70, 73, 74, 87–8, 98, 143, 153, 165
tridimensionality 78–9
truth 16, 29, 30, 48, 102–5, 141, 149, 157, 160, 161, 163, 164, 167, 169, 170, 173, 179, 181
truth drive 103, 104
turbulence 18, 27, 32–3, 49, 51–2, 62, 123, 147, 150, 178, 182
Tustin, F. 12, 18, 81, 86, 126, 137, 140, 142–3
twoness 80, 126, 133, 142, 153

ultimate reality 72, 161, 167–70, 173–4, 178 *see also* O
unconscious 8–9, 11–12, 14, 23–7, 29, 31–4, 38–41, 43, 47–8, 52, 58, 61, 98, 103–4, 112, 114, 123, 128, 130, 135, 138, 140, 143, 145, 156–8, 164, 178–9; unrepressed 69–74
unintegration 69, 80, 136
unknowability 33–4, 39, 141, 154, 179
unmentalized experience 38–44, 47, 59, 72, 109

verbal communication 66, 78, 106–7, 160–1, 173–4
verbal formulation 45, 59, 109
verbalizations 37, 140, 144
vertex 26, 31, 50, 65, 112, 142, 169, 180
violence 5, 16, 23, 106–7, 147–8
Virgil 182
vitality 86, 91, 155

Winnicott, D. W.: on amorphous experience 60; on analyst's mistakes and failures 66; on boredom 77; on catastrophic anxieties 69; fear of breakdown 69–71; *Holding and Interpretation* 76; on intuition of negative 164; on primitive love 131; on primitive agonies 65; on psychotic parts of personality 25, 73; reference to Freud 69
withdrawal 94, 142–3, 148, 150, 155
Wordsworth, W. 182
World War I 98–9

Yeret, A. 29
Young, E. B. 125

Zohar 175–6, 181–2

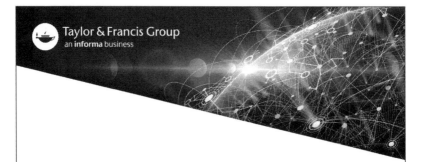